LITERARY CRITICISM AND CULTURAL THEORY

Edited by

William E. Cain
Professor of English
Wellesley College

LITERARY CRITICISM AND CULTURAL THEORY

WILLIAM E. CAIN, *General Editor*

REVISITING VIETNAM

Memoirs, Memorials, Museums

Julia Bleakney

Routledge

New York & London

Routledge
Taylor & Francis Group
711 Third Avenue
New York, NY 10017

Routledge
Taylor & Francis Group
2 Park Square
Milton Park, Abingdon
Oxfordshire OX14 4RN

First issued in paperback 2014
Routledge is an imprint of the Taylor & Francis Group, an informa business

© 2006 by Taylor & Francis Group, LLC

Library of Congress Cataloging-in-Publication Data

Bleakney, Julia.
  Revisiting Vietnam : memoirs, memorials, museums / by Julia Bleakney.
    p. cm. -- (Literary criticism and cultural theory)
  Includes bibliographical references and index.
  ISBN 978-0-415-97840-8 (hbk)
  ISBN 978-1-138-01178-6 (pbk)

  1. Vietnamese Conflict, 1961-1975--Monuments--United States. 2. Vietnamese Conflict, 1961-1975--Monuments--Vietnam. 3. Vietnamese Conflict, 1961-1975--Veterans--United States. 4. Vietnamese Conflict, 1961-1975--Psychological aspects. 5. Vietnam--Description and travel. I. Title. II. Series.

DS559.825.B44 2006
959.704'36--dc22   2006005510

Visit the Taylor & Francis Web site at
http://www.taylorandfrancis.com

and the Routledge Web site at
http://www.routledge-ny.com

Contents

List of Figures

Acknowledgments

Without the initial encouragement of William T.M. Riches and Kathleen McCracken, my undergraduate professors at the University of Ulster at Jordanstown, I never would have pursued graduate school let alone this project or believed that I could complete either. Now, there are many to thank for helping me understand the Vietnam War and the memory practices of its veterans. My colleagues at the University of Minnesota—Ilene Alexander, Beverly Atkinson, Matt Basso, Melanie Brown, David Gray, Mary Rizzo, Rebecca Scherr, Angela Smith, Christina Schmid, Marie Sulit, Dorthe Troeften, Allison Wee, and Dave Wehner—read rough chapters and provided helpful feedback and scholarly and personal support over the years. In addition to their ongoing engagement and encouragement, my dissertation committee members Thomas Augst, Paula Rabinowitz, and Karen Till proposed new ways to frame ideas and helped me understand particular theoretical or literary concepts. (Any failure to integrate or apply these concepts is of course my own responsibility.) Jacqueline Bailey, Tim Edensor, and Naomi Scheman offered specific comments at conferences or in graduate seminars that enabled me to see parts of my project in more complex ways. A special thank you to my committee member Elaine Tyler May, who has been continually supportive, helpful, and thoughtful in comments and conversations. Finally, my advisor Ellen Messer-Davidow read and re-read endless versions of drafts, commenting thoroughly and usefully every time and offering substantive suggestions that shaped the project in important ways.

During the initial writing process, several individuals provided me with crucial information: thank you to Mary Cheville, Assistant Librarian, Waverly Public Library; Col. Dick Leighninger, Minnesota Wing Commemorative Air Force; and Richard Kaspari, Minneapolis-based amateur gun expert. Grateful acknowledgments to Scott Laderman and Edwin Martini for giving me access to unpublished material.

As I worked on revisions to the manuscript in 2005, many people helped me with additional information and gave me permission to use text or images. Thank you Jess DeVaney, President, Tours of Peace; Art Dockter; Jane Ann Cable Fulkerson, Sgt. U.S. Army, 1965–68; Valeska Hilbig, Smithsonian's National Museum of American History; Larry James, Vietnam Veterans Memorial Wall page; Judy Keyserling, Vietnam Veterans Memorial Fund; Jennifer Komorowski, National Vietnam Veterans Art Museum; Jerry Sax, Gridley High School; Ted Sampley, *U.S. Veteran Dispatch*; and the volunteers at The Virtual Wall (TM), www.VirtualWall.org. I also wish to thank the anonymous veterans and family members and friends of the deceased who gave me permission to use their online postings.

The revision process was ably assisted by Liz Hutter, who provided much needed feedback on one chapter, and Elizabeth Oliver, who proofread the chapters. Also making the process easier has been the support and encouragement of my colleague at Saddleback College, Amy Ahearn. Thank you to William E. Cain, the Literary Criticism and Cultural Theory series general editor, for the opportunity to publish the manuscript, to Max Novick, the patient and tolerant-of-many-questions editor, and to Carey Nershi, who with good grace and humor helped me through the final stages of the book's proofs.

And finally, on a more personal note, I wish to thank my husband Matt Bryant who has never known me at a time when I was not working on this project but who has put up with the long conversations and the visits to museums, memorials, and veterans' ceremonies with good humor and genuine interest borne from love and respect. Despite their distance from my home in Southern California, my family in Northern Ireland—my parents Roy and Norma and my sister Sheena—has always been supportive and understanding of this project, so many years in the making. The book is dedicated to the memory of my grandmother, Ellen Lavinia Bleakney, who—in working her way through the entire book collection at the local library in the basement of my elementary school in East Belfast—inspired in me a, somewhat belated, love of reading.

Introduction

Revis(it)ing Vietnam

On 16 February 2004, *The New York Times* published an article about recent restoration work going on in Hue, Vietnam's imperial city.[1] Asia correspondent Jane Perlez commences her article not with a discussion of contemporary Hue but with a literary reference from an earlier period:

> In *Dispatches*,[2] the book that captured the Vietnam War like few others, Michael Herr describes the "damp gloom," and the "cold and dark" that hung over this city as American troops fought house-to-house after the surprise 1968 Tet offensive by the North Vietnamese.
>
> Dead bodies bobbed in the moat of the old imperial city and littered all its approaches, Mr. Herr wrote. When the battle for Hue, in what was then [s]outh Vietnam, was over, "70 percent of Vietnam's one lovely city was destroyed, and if the landscape seemed desolate, imagine how the figures in that landscape looked."

Perlez locates contemporary western knowledge of Hue firmly within Herr's representation of the Vietnam War. By using this frame, she assumes that her American readers will be more familiar with the Hue Massacre than with the city of Hue.[3] In addition, by using the war to introduce the city, she conflates the two: in Perlez's prose, the term "Hue" becomes a metonym for the Hue Massacre in the same way, as Brian Balogh has suggested in "From Metaphor to Quagmire," that the term "Vietnam" functions in popular discourse as a metonym for the Vietnam War.

Published in 1985, Richard Nixon's *No More Vietnams* declares, contrary to fact, that the United States won the war in Vietnam. At the same time Nixon admits that "no event in American history is more misunderstood than the Vietnam War. It was misreported then, and it is misremembered now" (9). Nixon's declaration and admission are ironic in the extreme:

in *No More Vietnams*, Nixon seeks to undo all of the misunderstanding, mis-reporting, and misremembering and to tell (his version of) the truth about the war; however, by also declaring that the United States won the war, he supports the very falsehoods he seeks to redress.

Together, Perlez's opening and Nixon's words suggest the significance of my project, which examines how the Vietnam War is remembered by American veterans of the war. Both authors call attention to the layers of myth and misinformation that since the end of the war have constructed the popular and official discourses of "Vietnam."[4] The way Perlez intro-duces Hue parallels how the war is often described in popular discourse: cities in Vietnam—Saigon, Hanoi, Danang, Hue—signal "war," and "Viet-nam" signals a quagmire that the United States stumbled into as early as 1954 and then took approximately twenty years to get out of. Nixon's dec-laration that there will be "no more Vietnams" extends this metonymic use but also illustrates how that use has changed. When Nixon declared "no more Vietnams" in 1985, he was implying that conflicts like the one in Vietnam were no longer necessary because the United States had finally won the Cold War. Today, when political or media commentators evoke "no more Vietnams," they warn of the U.S. becoming entrenched in a war, such as that going on currently in Iraq, from which it might not be able to extricate itself. Perlez's use of "Hue" and the shifting meanings of "no more Vietnams" illustrate how the war's terminology is adapted to fit cur-rent issues and ideologies.

The U.S. government's exaggeration of the Hue Massacre and Nixon's fanciful mis-imagining of the outcome of the war remind us that many facts of the war are not in dispute. Much popular writing and scholarship, for instance, is concerned with constructing as accurate and complete a history of the war as possible. Believing, rightly, that great danger lies in misun-derstanding, misreporting, and misremembering, these writings constantly search for the facts in order to record and teach the history and legacies of the war. That said, this book is not concerned with the facts of the war, not because they are not important, but because they do not tell us why and how murders committed by U.S. allies in south Vietnam were both exaggerated and reattributed to the communist government of the north, nor do they tell us why and how the war was misreported, misunderstood, and now misre-membered, as Nixon suggests.

Thus I examine not the facts of the war but the processes that create new meanings of it. Rather than speaking in terms of misremembering or misunderstanding, I use the prefix "re"—re-remembering or re-understand-ing—to call attention to the ways the war is continually reconstructed and reimagined in the present. Because these processes evolve over time, under-standing how, where, and why they occur is as important as the meanings produced. Various groups narrate different stories of the war for their own purposes; for example, the Prisoner of War/ Missing in Action movement, which lobbies the government to find those it believes are still missing in Southeast Asia, will construct a different narrative of the war than former or current members of Vietnam Veterans Against the War, which cam-paigned for an immediate end to the conflict from the mid-1960s on. My project highlights how these different narratives are produced without sug-gesting one is more truthful than another—hence re-remembering rather than misremembering. In this way, my project aligns with but also extends the claim in postmodern studies that one feature of contemporary society is its refusal of a metanarrative of the war that would provide a political or ideological explanation for it. Thus, rather than agreeing that an imperial-ist agenda brought the United States into Vietnam in the first instance, many veterans believe instead that no metanarrative of the war exists; this denial in turn allows thousands of individual and group narratives about the war to circulate. And yet, this refusal of a master narrative has become in fact a new master narrative of the war with the result that many veterans produce meanings of the war by rejecting its larger political or historical causes and explanations.

In this work, I examine the new meanings of the war produced through American veterans' memorializing practices at various sites of memory in the United States and Vietnam. I argue these practices, like cultural memory more generally, have become more conservative, individualized, privatized, commodified, and materialized since the end of the war in 1975. I also work from the premise that cultural memory shapes social understandings of the war as much if not more than published history, noting how memory increasingly is validated as the authentic representation of the war. Because memories shape ways of knowing the war, they function as both alterna-tive forms of history as well as alternatives to it. Veterans' memorializing practices attempt to make sense of the war by negotiating the connections between individual and cultural memory and between memory and history, and these junctions continually illuminate the processes of remembering and forgetting. While seeking to problematize the notion of authenticity and the ingenuous acceptance of memory as valid representation, I also note how this trend is a feature of contemporary cultural practice.

The myth of the lack of a metanarrative of the war allows a proliferation of individual and cultural narratives to circulate. How the war is remembered has shifted from national soul searching toward personal identity and recovery, and because of this the narratives become detached from the specific history of the war and its political controversies. Since the 1980s, the war has been reimagined around two central themes: one of "nostalgia, healing, and forgiveness," as Marita Sturken points out (45); the other around the war as a noble cause and its veterans as heroes. During the war, the most prominent veterans were those who spoke out against the war as they challenged official narratives about the United States' purpose in Vietnam. But in the postwar shift from national to individual identity and memory, the most pervasive veteran voices, often emerging from self-professed marginalized positions, present views on the war that are conservative and reactionary.

This conservative turn started after World War II, Jonathan Schoenwald argues in his book on the rise of modern conservatism, when "anticommunism sparked the birth of the postwar conservative movement" (33). Before the war, no such movement existed. The nascent coherence of the conservative movement in the 1960s, solidified for example in the formation and popularity of the John Birch Society and Republican presidential candidate Barry Goldwater, suggests disillusionment with liberalism among some camps as well as an increasing support for conservative extremism. But the 1960s is generally understood as a decade shaped by political and judicial liberalism, from the dominance of the New Deal Coalition until Lyndon Johnson's election in 1964, to Johnson's Great Society policies through 1968, as well as the passing of the Civil Rights Act in 1964 and Voting Rights Act in 1965. In addition, the decade also is defined, in part, by protest and rebellion: the mass organized protests against the war, drawing participants from all sectors of society including students, church goers, and labor union members; the rise of black power and women's liberation struggles; and the counterculture movement that prompted connection to notions of sexual freedom and drug culture. Indeed, popular support for the war declined dramatically as the decade progressed: in an American Institute of Public Opinion (Gallup) Poll, Americans were asked: "In view of the developments since we entered the fighting in Vietnam, do you think the U.S. made a mistake sending troops to fight in Vietnam?" From August 1965 to May 1971, the percentage of those asked this question who supported the war dropped from 61% to 28%. Only two times during these six years did the percentage increase: in December 1967, at the time of the Tet Offensive, the percentage increased to 46% from 44% two months prior; and in October 1968, when Nixon was elected, the percentage increased to 37% from 35% in August (Mueller 54).

While support for the war was decreasing, the American Conservative Union was suggesting the majority of Americans favored conservatism. The Union, one of four leading conservative organizations at the time, found in a 1968 poll it conducted that "most voters took conservative stances on major issues affecting the country," and that, "with the exception of medical care, Americans wanted to move away from Great Society programs" (Schoenwald 218). In his famous "Silent Majority" speech to the nation on 3 December 1969, President Nixon contrasted the vocal opposition to the war—"the minority"—to the silent majority, whom he assumed, or at least wished, would support him in his policy of Vietnamization. The belief that people were basically conservative in politics and values—opposed to liberal domestic policies, supportive of continued involvement in Vietnam, and shocked by the perceived decline of morality among youth as evident in the counterculture—was most effectively utilized by the then governor of California and the conservative movement's greatest hope for its future: Ronald Reagan. By the time Reagan became president in 1980, conservatism had been able to shake off its dependence on ideology as well as its extremism (see Schoenwald 190–220), and the war had been reshaped in Americans' minds—especially those with short memories—as a noble cause. In a speech to a Vietnam Veterans Memorial Day ceremony in 1984, Reagan describes how "the veterans of Vietnam who were never welcomed home with speeches and bands, but who were never defeated in battle and were heroes as surely as any who have ever fought in a noble cause, staged their own parade on Constitution Avenue. As America watched them—some in wheelchairs, all of them proud—there was a feeling that this nation—that as a nation we were coming together again and that we had, at long last, welcomed the boys home."[5]

The general trend toward conservatism inevitably is reflected in veteran activity. If veteran activism in the 1960s generally opposed the war, since the 1980s, dominant veteran activism—particularly around the Prisoner of War issue as well as the various attempts to patriotically commemorate the war—has instead focused on reclaiming both support for the war and its veterans as heroes. Yet during the war many antiwar protestors saw their actions as patriotic as they exercised their constitutional rights to free speech and opposition (Kammen 645; Hunt 5–32). Now, as Bruce Franklin suggests, to be considered a patriot or a hero today means not to have opposed the war in the 1960s and 1970s. He writes: "The antiwar movement has been so thoroughly discredited that many of the people who were the movement now feel embarrassed or ashamed of their participation even such prudent and peripheral participants as William Jefferson Clinton [and, of course, also John Kerry]. . . . It's no wonder that many people are reluctant to be identified as active opponents of the war" (1993: 48). Giving the examples of the films *Gardens of Stone* and *Forrest Gump*, Franklin continues: "At the height of the deliberate reimaging in the 1980s and 1990s, Hollywood presented antiwar activists as so contemptible that they should be beaten up" (48). The demonization of the antiwar movement coincides with the emergence of neo-conservatism and the Christian Right in the United States. As Schoenwald suggests, even as early as the 1970s, conservatism was "located comfortably in the center of the American political conversation" (257); this conservative shift contributes to the changes in memory practices and affects how the war is perceived individually and culturally, as I examine throughout the book.

Of course, any generalization of how veterans' attitudes toward the war were affected by their political leanings during the era or since has its limita-tions: many veterans during the war continued to support both the U.S.'s reasons for being in Vietnam and/ or the methods used there by the mili-tary, in numbers higher than the general public even as public opposition continued to rise; today, national organizations such as Veterans for Peace campaign for alternative, peaceful solutions to war. However, in many of the veterans' practices examined in this book, the process of remembering the war has entailed simplifying and sometimes even ignoring the history of dis-sent in order to present a narrative that celebrates veterans' heroism and the war as honorable. Reimagining the war as a noble cause erases complicat-ing perspectives, such as those that questioned the reasons for U.S. involve-ment or those that exposed the shameful atrocities committed in Vietnam. In addition, the homogenization of the image of the soldier and the veteran during the war and after is troubling, as it ignores how those images evolved and changed over time.

Pervasive images of the Vietnam veteran helped shape and also are shaped by public perceptions of the war, and these images can be simply traced. Before the Tet Offensive of January 1968, American veterans generally received a warm welcome on their return to the United States with attitudes toward them chilling as the public became increasingly disillusioned with the war. As atrocities such as the My Lai Massacre and the use of napalm on vil-lages came to public attention in the late 1960s, returning veterans increas-ingly became scapegoats for public opposition to governmental policies. As the Nixon administration negotiated withdrawal in the early 1970s, Ameri-can distaste for the mistreatment of Vietnamese civilians, which resulted in the presentation of the soldier as victimizer, began to shift, in part, due to the increased awareness of Prisoners of War mistreatment in Vietnam. At the same time, the antiwar GI rose to prominence, testifying in public against war crimes, speaking against the war at protests on college campuses, and marching in Vietnam Veterans Against the War demonstrations. Negative reactions from political figures as well as veteran and nonveteran activists to prominent images of the veteran as mentally disturbed or drug crazed and psychological studies in the late 1970s leading to the recognition of post-traumatic stress disorder both contributed to a new image of the veteran as victim. Today, a different image has replaced those that circulated during and after the war. If the stereotypical image of the late war-era veteran depicted a long haired, headband wearing, sometimes wheelchair using hippie protesting the war, one of today's most prominent stereotypes portrays a veteran on a Harley-Davidson motorcycle, wearing a leather jacket adorned with POW/MIA and anti-Jane Fonda patches.

But just as the term "Vietnam" cannot be used as shorthand for the complexities of U.S. involvement in that country, so "veteran" no longer simply signifies the American male combat veteran. Rather we now accept (though not without a history of contention) that veterans include women who were stationed in Vietnam as nurses, intelligence officers and those working in other support-service roles, and people who served in a variety of noncombatant military positions. Additionally, many Americans are now willing to extend veteran status to south Vietnamese allies from the Army of the Republic of Vietnam and even to former members of the National Liberation Front and North Vietnamese Army, America's "enemies" during the war. And, of course, the veteran label has been used for noncombatant activists on the home front who spoke out against the war. The veterans examined in this project are, for the most part, those who have constructed a postwar identity wholly or primarily contingent on their veteran status. Unlike many thousands of veterans who have willfully or nonwillfully forgotten their time in Vietnam or who have allowed it to fade into their personal history, the veterans I focus on build their lives around actively remembering the war and around encouraging others to remember also.

In this book, I also argue that in the move from the national soul searching to individual recovery, memorializing has become increasingly material and commodified. From objects left at the Wall to those purchased at it, the grunt's tour of duty to the veteran's return trip to Vietnam, and the therapeutic talking cure to the mass-produced memoir—the material objects and experiences of memory can now be bought and sold. The war's commodification is not always aligned with a particular political agenda, although the most visible Vietnam veterans on the streets today are those who purchase and wear the accoutrements of the right wing—stars and stripes or "Proud to be a Vietnam veteran" patches, "God Bless America" or "POW/MIA" tattoos, and so on. But veterans' attitudes toward the commodification of the war's memory are complex: the example of the memoir shows that the war experience can be reproduced and packaged into a highly desirable commodity at the same time as the memoir's content challenges this fetishization. There may be a general shift toward a war memory industry, but individuals and groups often resist the trend.

As the book progresses, it maps a development of war memorializing that is physical as well as material. It charts the progress of commemoration away from the National Mall, starting in 1982 with the National Vietnam Veterans Memorial and the practice of leaving objects at it. This practice can be understood in at least three ways. First, it illustrates how people have embraced the Wall's perceived lack of political commentary and produced their own heterogeneous narratives of the war at it. As the practice has become more popular, it also indicates that people's behaviors at the Wall have become more routinized and less reflective over time. Finally, it may also bespeak an anxiety, particularly among veterans, about the lack of patriotic celebration of the war hero and about the blank walls of the memorial that some feel need to be made meaningful with additional monuments and objects. I examine these various responses and chart veterans' searches for a perceived authentic memorializing that moves them away from the Wall, around the country, and ultimately back to Vietnam. Veterans groups, dissatisfied with the Wall, create alternatives to it in replica walls and museums that make memorializing more accessible to people in towns and cities across the United States. Memoirs create an opportunity to memorialize the war in more sustained and personal ways, and they bring the writers back to Vietnam emotionally. But for many veterans, returning to Vietnam is the final and most important step toward recovery from their traumas of the war. Thus, the progression of memorializing and this work's examination of it are both physical and chronological, as the practices move away from Washington, to the metonymic town square, to cyberspace, and on to Vietnam. But despite how practices have evolved away from the Wall, the Wall's importance to the cultural memory of the war continues to affect veterans' memory practices as it also reverberates through all chapters of this book. To a certain extent, all veterans' practices—the making of alternative memorials most obviously, but even the creation of museums or memoirs, as well as the return trip to Vietnam—are created in dialogue with the Wall, with the notion that the Wall shapes new ways of memorializing and is central to "the process of healing, of confronting difficult past experiences" (Sturken 45).

Veterans' memory practices not only evolve spatially and temporally, as they move away from but in dialogue with the Wall, they also evolve formally, as different memorializing forms produce different narratives of the war. Veterans produce these narratives by negotiating a path through the memorial, museum, memoir, and return trip to Vietnam. The most significant revisiting of the war takes places at these particular sites of memory, which can be at once material, functional, and symbolic, to use Pierre Nora terms (19). By constructing alternatives to the Wall, veterans embrace the master narrative of patriotism that circulates at the National Mall but detach it from historic specificity and political dissent.[6] In the veteran-led museum, veterans challenge the relative sterility of war exhibits in traditional museums, but in recreating the war as an aesthetic experience they are in danger of ignoring the specifics of history. By returning to Vietnam, veterans often reinforce the paternalistic beliefs that sent them to Vietnam in the first place, but they quickly learn that contemporary Vietnam does not support their preconceived ideas of the country. At these venues, the narratives of the war produced are more homogenous and depoliticized, even as the range of practices has become more democratic and varied. Memoirs function somewhat differently in that their sustained investigation of traumatic experiences or feelings of guilt intrinsically challenge uncritical patriotic or homogeneous war narratives. While memoirs are not always opposed to the war, those that critically examine the writers' participation in the war unavoidably reject its simplification and question the homogeneous and depoliticized turn in contemporary memorializing. If, as Andreas Huyssen argues, "a society's memory is negotiated in the social body's beliefs and values, rituals and institutions, and in the case of modern societies in particular, it is shaped by such public sites of memory as the museum, the memorial, the monument" (1993: 249), the memoir adds a complicating layer to this analysis, as it presents a form of memory that is simultaneously public and private, social and personal. In addition, the memoir has become the prominent expressive mode of individual memory and history in a culture, as James Berger describes it, obsessed with the trauma of others and, as Dominick LaCapra has suggested, in which scholars see the trauma in everything."[7]

The work's title, "Revisiting Vietnam," calls attention to the processes that construct intellectual knowledge and visceral understanding of the war. Revisiting might be literal, such as when veterans return to Vietnam, or it might be psychological, when they reconstruct ideas and memories of the war. Revisiting, then, can be physical or psychological, literal or symbolic, real or imagined. As a concept, revisiting illustrates how knowledge of the war is produced through individual, cultural, and institutional memory and memorializing. Following Maurice Halbwachs, Pierre Nora, and others, I argue that memories are actively and collectively constructed in the present through communication and interaction with others. Personal memories are made meaningful through acts of memorializing and, at the same time, memorializing shapes individual and cultural memory. When a veteran visits the Wall, he or she brings memories shaped during and after the war, performs a memorializing act cued by the Wall and its cultural resonance, and through this interaction builds new memories. This process is cyclical and reflects the symbiotic nature of individual and cultural memorializing. However, often it is the case that scholars of cultural memory, in their attempts to examine the intersections of individual and cultural memory, underplay the increasing individualization of memory in contemporary memorializing practices. Theories of cultural memory must therefore account for the forms of memorializing that have become increasingly private, pedestrian, and individual—enacted in people's homes or offices, through material artifacts such as photographs or scrapbooks, or online at memorial websites.

The role of the individual in cultural memory practices and the cyclical aspects of memorializing first sparked my interest in this project. When I started, I wanted to trouble what seemed to me an irresolvable tension between scholarship that attends to the meanings of individual texts and practices and scholarship that investigates how social structures, discourses, and institutions shape them. As Gillian Rose describes this difference, one approach focuses more on the meanings in texts and images while the other framework focuses on "issues of power" and "regimes of truth" in the practices of institutions (140). Yet, memorializing practices create a bridge between these two approaches because they are, as James Young suggests after Bakhtin, dialogical: meanings are constructed and practices are shaped by the interactions between institutions and individuals. In Chapter Four, for example, I examine how artworks and curatorial practice work together to represent the war as quagmire in visceral ways for visitors to experience. While recognizing the power differential at play in the relationship between institutions and individuals, I agree with Young that their relationship is dialogical. Indeed, because memories shape and are shaped through the interactions of individuals, communities, and institutions, a reading that combines both approaches is better able to account for how individuals and society remember and memorialize.

Initially, I set out to examine performances of trauma in memoirs by Vietnam veterans. But as I was reading veterans' memoirs as expressions or enactments of individual traumas, I realized that the memoir itself is a cultural product, imbued with cultural meaning. I quickly came to see that writing and reading memoirs are memorializing practices like designing and visiting statuary war monuments are, and that the personal and cultural aspects of these practices are mutually dependent. To position memoirs in the larger cultural context of public war memorializing, I observed visitors at museums and replica walls in the United States and Vietnam; read postings at online memorial sites and publications from memorials, museums, and tourist agencies in both countries; talked to museum staff; and took photographs. By using empirical methods, I allow veterans' texts and practices to direct and complicate my uses of analytical and theoretical approaches to memory and memorializing from sociology, ethnography, and geography as well as cultural and literary studies. As part of the ethnographic spirit of my research, I place myself "at the scene," so to speak, drawing on James Young's positioning, which he describes in relation to his study of Holocaust memorials: "detached reflection on these memorials is no more possible than it is desirable: there is no way around the author's eye. Insofar as I stand within the perimeter of these memorial spaces, I become part of their performance, whether I like it or not" (1993: xii). By examining and foregrounding my own response to memorials, museums, and memoirs—my part in their performance—I can hope to understand the visitor's essential role in the memorial space.

But I must also recognize the limitations of understandings and analyses that emerge from ethnography. Common to the constructions of memoirs, museums, and memorials are the veterans' attempts to evoke visceral experiences in their readers or visitors, to "tell it like it was" or to create "the real Vietnam." As I visit veteran-led sites of memory, I do not experience the real Vietnam, but rather I appreciate how veterans construct an approximation of it. To note this limitation is not to suggest a cynical reading of the simulacra of experience but simply to recognize the difficulties of thinking intellectually about viscerality. In addition, visiting these sites of memory makes me sharply aware of my outsider status. I am not there to help celebrate Vietnam War heroes or commemorate the war necessarily; rather, I am there to study the events and practices of the commemoration. But I am also an outsider because of my non-American status, because I grew up within, and am a child and product of, the political and social conflict in Northern Ireland known colloquially as "the troubles." Thus, my own visceral experience at these sites will always be mediated by my own, very different, visceral experience of violence and conflict and also by my intellectual knowledge of the Vietnam War.

Just as the limitations of ethnography, of the researcher's experience, must be noted, so also must the limitations of privileging veterans' experiences. The problem of uncritically accepting experience as evidence is central to the tension between intellectual knowledge and viscerality. Joan Scott has carefully traced the inadequacies of what she calls the evidence of experience in her eponymous article, arguing that if experience is "taken as the origin of knowledge . . . questions about the constructed nature of experience . . .

are left aside" (777). While "histories of difference" crucially have recorded or presented marginalized voices, the "project of making experience visible precludes critical examination of the workings of the ideological system itself" (778). What results, then, is the reinforcement of orthodox epistemologies that "reproduces rather than contests given ideological systems" (778). By examining how veterans, and others, use war experiences to claim authentic knowledge, my book not only problematizes the too easy acceptance of experience as evidence but also positions the privileging of personal experience within the context of the increasing individualization of memory, in which individual memory is increasingly and uncritically perceived as trustworthy and authentic.

Ultimately, by combining analyses of texts and practices with observation, my goal is not to find the truth in veterans' narratives of the war but rather to describe how memory-narratives are produced at and through various sites of memory. In Chapter One, "A Brief History of Memory," I chart developments in the theoretical concepts of trauma and memory in parallel with the history of war memorializing in the United States, mapping the features of contemporary memorializing as memory scholars have identified them and examining the centrality of the Wall to discussions of contemporary memory. Chapter Two, "Trauma, Metaphors, and the Body," examines how veteran writers use metaphor and experimental narrative structure to perform the effect of trauma and to bring their "body memories" into language. In this chapter, I argue that memoirs, like traumatized bodies, are physical manifestations of memory and that to write the body into memoir is itself a memorializing act. Memoirs, in these terms, do more than present individual memories of war; they help both writers and readers to understand and "work through" traumas as LaCapra, after Freud, would put it, and as cultural products they shape cultural memory of the war. The next two chapters are case studies of specific sites of memory to the Vietnam War. Chapter Three, "Moving Walls," examines the relationship between memory and place by focusing on traveling and virtual replicas of the Wall. Here I point out that veterans' memorializing practices have become increasingly decentralized and democratized and, yet, as they physically move away from the Wall, the narratives of the war they produce are increasingly homogeneous and dehistoricized. Chapter Four, "Objects of War and Remembrance," examines memory and materiality by focusing on the display of objects in two museum spaces related to the war: "Personal Legacy: The Healing of a Nation" at the Smithsonian Institute's Museum of American History and the National Vietnam Veterans Art Museum in Chicago. The chapter compares display techniques at the traditional museum in Washington for how they erase details of the war with those of the contemporary veteran-led museum in Chicago for how they cast the war as an aesthetic and visceral experience. The final chapter, "Returning to Vietnam," examines the impact of revisiting the sites of their war experience on veterans' memories of it. Here I propose that because Vietnam has rewritten its own narratives of the war, erasing details of the American experience in order to celebrate its resistance and endurance, Vietnamese memorializing practices alter the way American veterans remember the war.

I could have selected many other memorials, museums, and memoirs to address, but the ones I have chosen represent general patterns in memorializing among American veterans of the Vietnam War. This trend, with memoirs as somewhat of a counterpoint, generally supports a conservative agenda that minimizes the history of political dissent and reconceives the war patriotically; all practices move toward forms of memorializing that are increasingly materialized, commodified, and individualized. Because my focus is on this trend, the book does not discuss, for example, antiwar veterans' organizations, nor does it consider the experiences of Vietnamese veterans who have immigrated to the United States and now memorialize the war here. Certainly, these groups' narratives create very different memories of the war as they circulate in the United States. The absence of their voices in this book is no attempt to silence or deny them or the important ways their narratives contribute to a more complex memory of the war. However, in this project, my interest is in mapping the set of heterogeneous memory practices that build increasingly homogeneous and personal narratives of the war in ways that re-imagine the war and simultaneously reflect the contemporaneous political and social climate. In short, I seek to examine the meanings of the war that emerge from an American Vietnam War veteran memory that attempts to re-imagine the war as a worthy cause and its veterans as heroes.

Finally, in this study I draw a distinction between political and traumatic forgetting. Military and political discourses erase details of the war in order to cover up embarrassing or even questionably legal acts or to further particular political agendas. This erasure also occurs in popular discourse such as *No More Vietnams*, or in the Prisoner of War/ Missing in Action movement I examine in Chapter Three. Some veterans' organizations also forget specific aspects of the war in order to craft a more homogeneous and patriotic narrative of it. But individual veterans may erase details for different reasons. For example, in veterans' memoirs, omission of details can capture what veterans believe to be the truth of their war experiences and memories. Elisions in their stories may occur because an event is too painful to hold in active memory, thus revealing the repressive drive after traumatic experience. Veterans' trauma narratives force readers to see the difference between deliberate omission for political ends and unbidden forgetting that reveals traumatic experience. This distinction is particularly significant in a milieu in which trauma has almost become meaningless because it is everywhere, as previously noted.[8]

As Marita Sturken reminds us, memories are not recollected, they are reenacted. Reenactments take the form of visiting museums, writing memoirs, leaving gifts at memorials, posting messages on websites, and traveling to Vietnam, among others. These reenactments do not imply that an original authentic act exists from which the practice of revisiting draws on. Rather, the act of revisiting is a pastiche of memory, calling attention to how earlier memories are hopelessly distorted by trauma or erased by political forgetting. If, as I suggested earlier, commentators stress the need to constantly search for the facts and teach the legacies of the war, I would argue that knowing how others remember is equally important. Today, when media continues to be saturated with thousands of representations of the war and yet the war's history is fading from public discourse, knowing the war intellectually—knowing its facts—is not enough to forestall forgetting. Thus, veterans remember.

Chapter One
A Brief History of Memory

Within hours of the attacks on the World Trade Center in New York on 11 September 2001, websites related and unrelated to the WTC added condolences to their front pages, thousands of New York citizens flocked to lower Manhattan to offer help and support, and "webloggers" speculated about every aspect of the attacks in their online diaries.[1] According to the Pew Internet and American Life Project, after "9/11," as it has become known, the web provided an important "public commons," creating "a virtual space where grief, fear, anger, patriotism and even hatred could be shared."[2] Government sites, for example, "retooled quickly to allow individuals to provide tips in the terrorism investigations and to help people find means to provide assistance to victims and their families." At the same time "[r]eligious, educational, and personal sites expanded their capabilities" to "help . . . people both provide and obtain assistance" (17). Beyond the internet, candlelit vigils were held across New York from September 12 on, with similar ceremonies occurring in other cities in the United States and around the world. Impromptu memorials were erected in Washington and New York, and across the country every available Stars and Stripes flag sold out within days as citizens rushed to display their patriotism.

Twenty-four hour satellite news broadcasts, constantly updated websites, and streaming online documents brought the 9/11 attacks into people's workplaces and homes across the country, and indeed the world, in such a way that the distance between space and time appeared to collapse: television viewers and internet users in California, Idaho, and Texas and everywhere in between saw the same images as residents of lower Manhattan; everyone online or watching television saw in real time the second plane hit the tower. Because information about the attacks was accessible right away, because "the highly compressed space-time of today's electronic media gives distant events a compelling immediacy" (Geoffrey White 295), people's responses were also instantaneous, in everything from weblogs to vigils and religious services, to food drives, fundraising, and flag waving. While family members and friends desperately searched for the missing, posting "Have you seen . . . ?" flyers everywhere and refusing to accept that their loved one might not be alive, others had already started the process of memorializing the event and those who died.

On 27 August 2001, two weeks before American homes were saturated with images of the World Trade Center's collapse, a team of contractors quietly started preparing the area around the Rainbow Pool on the National Mall for the foundations of the National World War II Memorial. The construction marked the beginning of the end of the long drawn-out battle over the location and design of the memorial. As Nicolaus Mills examines in *Their Last Battle: The Fight for the World War II Memorial*, this debate started in 1987 when World War II veteran Roger Durbin, who campaigned for the memorial until his death in 2000, asked Ohio Congresswoman Marcy Kaptur, "how come there's no memorial to World War II in Washington?" (1). The memorial, which some would argue was fifty years in the making, was delayed for over ten years because of bureaucratic opposition to its construction and position

Figure 1. National World War II Memorial. Photograph by author.

on the Mall for various aesthetic, environmental, and political reasons (Mills 94–104). Debates raged between the various organizations responsible for choosing and funding the design and groups representing the preservation of the Mall; the latter was especially concerned that the sight line between the Lincoln Memorial and Washington Monument would be interrupted by the new memorial. (This issue was resolved somewhat by putting the plaza, the largest element of the memorial, below ground level.) But at the start of construction not all issues were resolved, and years of heated debate and compromise ultimately were sidestepped when George W. Bush passed Public Law 107–11, "lock[ing] into place the approval for the site and design of the . . . memorial that had already been given to the Commission of Fine Arts and the National Capital Planning Commission" and "declar[ing] that there could be no judicial review of the decisions that had brought the memorial to near completion" (Mills 45). Today, even though the plaza is below grade, the memorial dominates the central Mall area with its fussy and somewhat ostentatious combination of two forty-three foot entrance pavilions; four bronze columns with eagles and victory laurels; fifty six pillars, each seventeen feet tall, representing each state and territory at the time of the war; waterworks in the Rainbow Pool, and on. If the National Vietnam Veterans Memorial gently whispers contemplation, the National World II Memorial, instead, shouts victory and celebration.

If the reactions to the 9/11 attacks suggest how increasingly spontane-ous and instantaneous memorializing has become in the advanced techno-logical age, the World War II Memorial demonstrates the ponderous and divisive nature of contemporary national memorializing. In addition to the public's immediate response to the World Trade Center attacks, ordinary people rushed to memorialize when a bomb killed 168 people at the Alfred P. Murrah federal building in Oklahoma on 19 April 2005: they immediately posted mementoes to the dead on a temporary fence that had been erected to keep sightseers away from the bomb site (Linenthal 2001). Within a week of 31 August 1997—the date Diana, Princess of Wales, died—over one million bouquets of flowers had been left outside her residence at Kensington Palace (Merck 1998). Yet these "vernacular" responses—as John Bodnar calls the social practices of ordinary people—to the media images of the 9/11 attacks, the Oklahoma bombing, and Diana's death contrast with the protracted bureaucracy of national memorializing on the Mall that delays the construc-tion of memorials until, as Bodnar says, "the memory of . . . terrible events [can] no longer be taken for granted" (12).

However it would be too simplistic to suggest that this contrast highlights an opposition between individual memory as instantaneous and institutional memory as belabored; in fact, these two kinds of memorializing are in constant dialogue before, during, and after the construction of any memorial to an officially commemorated event. All forms of public memorializing, according to Bodnar, occur at "the intersection of official and vernacular cultural expressions;" he suggests that while "normally official culture promotes a nationalistic, patriotic culture of the whole that mediates an assortment of vernacular interests, . . . vernacular culture . . . represents an array of specialized interests that are grounded in parts of the whole" (13–14). In the United States, ordinary people participate in all aspects of the planning process of a memorial even if their voices are not always or fully considered. After the memorial is constructed, the future memory of the event is shaped by those who engage with the site. Though the dialogue between official and vernacular cultures is not necessarily equal, the process is generally democratic and symbiotic as the meaning of an event is continually shaped by, and altered to reflect, contemporary attitudes and ideologies.

But how do the memory practices of Vietnam veterans relate to the discussions of 9/11 and World War II memory, to the ideas of national and vernacular commemoration, to the speeding up and slowing down of memory practices? Unlike the immediacy of the event of 9/11 and its remembering, the Vietnam War dragged on for many years. In addition, while returning Vietnam veterans are no doubt comparable to World War II veterans, who "were anxious to get back to 'normal life' as soon as possible" (Mills xxiv), Vietnam veterans who faced many symptoms of post-traumatic stress disorder found great difficulty adjusting to home life. The fact that many civilians did not perceive the Vietnam War as a noble cause or its returning veterans as heroes exacerbated the difficult adjustment process. Compounded with the experience of a protracted war (even if their rotations were limited to twelve or thirteen months) and difficulty readjusting to life on the home front, Vietnam veterans eventually had to come to terms with the fact that they fought in a war that the U.S. ultimately lost. Thus, the specific complexities of their war experiences and the divisiveness of the war demand that veterans must participate in ongoing negotiations of the meaning and significance of the war, reconciling their memories with others' memories and with representations of the war that diverge significantly from their own. Vietnam veterans' contemporary memorializing practices, then, can be positioned at the intersection of the instantaneity of commemoration and the resistance to the "quickening pace of material life and . . . the speed-up of media images and information" (Huyssen 1993: 253), their practices offering insight into the processes of remembering and forgetting, of amnesia and nostalgia, and of the connections between individual, cultural, and institutional memory as well as memory and history. The various intersections of memory are heavily trafficked in the scholarly area of memory studies, but my project is most interested in understanding how and why veterans remember in a milieu where these intersections exist. By suggesting that contemporary memory can be represented by the extremes of 9/11 and WWII memorializing, I wonder what happens—what has happened—to the memories of the Vietnam War and its veterans in this paradigm? But my goal is not to reclaim what has been forgotten from the dusty annals of history, even if some people might think that's where they reside. Rather, by reading Vietnam veterans' memorializing, first, in the context of cultural memory and, secondly, as part of the history of memorializing practices, my purpose is simple: to understand how Vietnam veterans' memory practices are reflective of cultural practices, social trends, and political ideologies of the time in which the practices occur, and to understand how individual veterans—alone or in groups—negotiate these systems in order to remember the war.

MEMORY

Whether commemoration occurs immediately or belatedly, there is little doubt that contemporary society is obsessed with remembering. The processes of remembering, agree contemporary memory scholars in a variety of fields, are never static: they suggest that memory is active and is situated in the present (Bal viii); is continually shaped and reshaped; and is an act of imagination (Bolles), a creative and constructive process. Through various practices of memory, the past is brought into and continually reimagined in the present. Rather than retain memories like "judgment-free snapshots of our past experiences," psychologist Daniel Schacter suggests we hold onto the "meanings, sense, and emotions these experiences provide us" (5). Alan Parkin even suggests, after nineteenth-century psychologist William James, that all conscious experience requires memory.

With 38% of Vietnam veterans experiencing post-traumatic stress disorder (Heberle 11; Shay 168), the experience of trauma is central to the memory formations of veterans, but its oversimplification as a concept has been rightly critiqued. Andreas Huyssen, for example, correctly troubles the suggestion he finds occurring in memory discourse that trauma is at the hidden core of all memory (2003: 8); however, perhaps one central element that can be identified in the object of his critique is an articulation of the relationship between trauma and memory that is not clearly defined or specifically applied. As psychologists have determined, trauma is an overwhelming or extraordinary experience that produces such responses as denial, repression, repetition, or dissociation; these responses can happen over the course of many years. In his first work on trauma, Freud believed that a traumatic event, which was unacceptable to a person's consciousness, would be repressed only to surface again in the form of compulsive or repetitive behaviors (*Studies in Hysteria*; Berger 570). Although in *Beyond the Pleasure Principle* Freud later reconceived this theory and determined that neurotic behaviors were the result of repressed drives and desires rather than traumatic experience (see also Berger 570), practicing psychologists still look to the traumatic event as the cause of an array of interconnected symptoms including, as Judith Herman and Herbert Hendin and Ann Pollinger Hass among others explain, terror, hyperarousal, intrusion, constriction, disconnection, vulnerability, resilience and, in the particular case of post-traumatic stress disorder, nightmares, insomnia, flashbacks, and reactions to loud noise. Literary theorist Cathy Caruth complicates the notion of trauma's cause, suggesting that trauma is locatable not in an event but "in the way that its very unassimilated nature—the way it was precisely *not known* in the first instance—returns to haunt the survivor later on" (4). The trauma cannot therefore be traced back to a particular happening; it cannot be remembered because the trauma, as Caruth describes it, is that part of a psychologically disruptive or altering experience that cannot be comprehended.

Thus, rather than being at the core of all memory, perhaps trauma, whether buried in the unconscious or breaking into consciousness in disruptive and nonlinear ways, cannot really be described as memory at all. This understanding of trauma is not new: again, in *Beyond the Pleasure Principle*, Freud argues that trauma is a repetition of repressed material not its remembering (18–19). In *Acts of Memory*, Mieke Bal describes traumatic reenactment (which takes the form of drama rather than narrative) as "tragically solitary" and suggests that traumatic "(non)memory has no social component" and is "not addressed to anybody" (x). Because trauma must be communicated and integrated, the traumatized individual needs a second person; this interlocutor, according to Bal, "confirms a notion of memory that is not confined to the individual psyche, but is constituted in the culture in which the traumatized subject lives."[3] In Bal's terms, because trauma is private and memory is culturally produced, the expression "traumatic memory" is an oxymoron (viii).

Bal's suggestion that the survivor must communicate her trauma to another person is important, yet such a clear delineation between trauma and memory is not always possible. Trauma and memory are not the same certainly but nor are they opposites; indeed, it may be more useful to understand how they are in fact mutually affective. An individual might experience one or more traumas throughout her life and each trauma will be shaped by memories or experiences that existed or occurred before or after the trauma itself. Or a survivor might suppress a trauma only to have it surface through association with an unrelated memory initially formed around the same time as the traumatic experience. Thus, difficult memories may include traces of trauma just as traumatic elisions will disrupt memories. A more productive reading of the relationship between trauma and memory, then, does not see trauma as the core of all memory, trauma and memory in opposition, or trauma as memory's failure but appreciates how their relationship, like the relationship between vernacular and official memory, is symbiotic.

As a response to the perceived limitations of psychoanalytic interpretations of individual memory, the concept of cultural memory emerged in the scholarly field of memory studies. More precisely, the somewhat simplified reading of Freud's idea from *The Interpretation of Dreams* of the mind as a storehouse for memories was rejected in favor, as Marita Sturken points out, of Maurice Halbwachs' arguments that individual memory is "fragmented and incomplete" (4) and that all memory is socially and culturally produced. But beyond this basic presumption, memory scholars grapple with the specific meanings of "collective" or "cultural memory." Barbie Zelizer's definition of collective memory highlights its negotiated aspects and implies that socially constructed memories are formed through debate and consensus (1995: 214). Because direct interaction is not necessary for the formation of shared memory, other scholars use the term "cultural memory" instead. In speaking of memory's habitual and narrative aspects, Bal uses the term "cultural memory" to emphasize its performativity, the "acts of memory [that] are performed by individuals in a cultural framework that encourages these acts" (xiii). James Young prefers "collected memory," "the many discrete memories that are gathered into common memorial spaces and assigned common meaning," because "a society's memory cannot exist outside of those people who do the remembering" (1993: xi). And Karen Till uses the term social memory to describe the "ongoing process whereby groups map understandings of themselves onto and through a place and time" (2005: 13) and to emphasize the political implications of memory practices. With specific reference to the Vietnam War and the AIDS Quilt, Sturken defines cultural memory as "memory that is shared outside of the avenues of formal historical discourse" (3) and produced through what she calls technologies of memory such as objects, images, and representations. Sturken builds on Michel Foucault's important notion of subjugated knowledges, knowledges that "have been disqualified as inadequate to their task or insufficiently elaborated" (Foucault 1980: 82), but she stresses, in contrast to Foucault's emphasis on what Sturken describes as the "political force" of memory, that cultural memory is not "politically prescribed" and is "not automatically the scene of cultural resistance" (Sturken 6–7). While not always political, she argues, cultural memory is always "entangled" with history, so much so that "it may be futile to maintain a distinction between them" (5). Sturken wishes to emphasize the "entangled" relationship between history and memory in contrast to Nora's suggestion that history and memory are in opposition, to question Nora's argument that "History is perpetually suspicious of memory, and its true mission is to suppress and destroy it" (9).

As a result of the influence of ideas about cultural memory on memory studies, individual memory is often contextualized in a social or cultural framework. For example, Bal suggests that cultural memory has "displaced and subsumed the discourses of individual (psychological) memory and of social memory [because] . . . memory can be understood as a cultural phenomenon as well as an individual or social one" (vii). Like Bal, Sturken suggests that "personal memories can sometimes be subsumed into history," but she also emphasizes, importantly, that "personal memory, cultural memory, and history do not exist within neatly defined boundaries" (5). Yet, Nora acknowledges that the "transformation of memory implies a decisive shift from the historical to the psychological [and] from the social to the individual" (15), and Ulric Neisser "sees the intensification of personal memory as a result of the intersection of personal experience with significant events in collective history" (G. White 294–295; Neisser and Hyman 2000). I would suggest, therefore, that the contextualization of individual memory in a cultural context may not always account for the increasing individualization of memory in contemporary practices such as memoirs, scrap booking, souvenir collecting, weblogs, etc.

Even as cultural memory scholarship responds to the perception that focusing on the individual does not fully account for the various social factors shaping memory, concepts that have emerged from the study of individual memory, particularly those related to the study of trauma, often are used to explain social and national events. For example, James Berger demonstrates how literary and cultural scholars have turned to concepts of trauma as tools to analyze historical catastrophe:

> The idea of catastrophe as trauma provides a method of interpretation, for it posits that the effects of an event may be dispersed and manifested in many forms not obviously associated with the event. Moreover, this dispersal occurs across time, so that an event experienced as shattering may actually produce its full impact only years later. . . . In

> its emphasis on the retrospective reconstruction of the traumatic event (for the event cannot be comprehended when it occurs), a traumatic analysis is both constructivist and empirical. It pays the closest attention to the representational means through which an event is remembered and yet it retains the importance of the event itself, the thing that did happen. (572)

Dispersal happens when traumatic effects occur that seem unrelated to the traumatic event; when an event is experienced as shattering and its impact not felt until many year later, the trauma clearly has been repressed. Thus, in Berger's reading, both the traumatic event and its effects occur temporally and spatially, across time (between the event and its comprehension, if it is ever comprehended) and within and through various spatial forms (forms not always associated with the event itself). In addition, by arguing that traumatic analysis can be constructivist and empirical, Berger suggests that as observers of catastrophe we develop concepts of trauma not just from *a priori* knowledge but also from our own experience and observation. His suggestion that a traumatic event cannot be comprehended when it occurs draws attention to the period of latency between an event and its coming to consciousness (which Caruth discusses), but more importantly it illuminates the intersections of immediate and belabored response to catastrophe. When individuals rush to memorialize an event, they do so without complete cognizance of the event's meaning or consequences; by the time a catastrophe is memorialized officially, through the construction of a memorial or a monument for example, groups and institutions profess a certain level of comprehension of the effects of the event on the national psyche and the importance of it to history.

As I use the term, "cultural memory" reemphasizes the role of individual memorializing practices in the shaping of cultural memory. My use builds on the political aspect of Till's social memory and Foucault's subjugated knowledges as well as Sturken's entangled memories. Underground or forgotten voices can reinforce dominant discourses as well as challenge them even though they may not always enact cultural resistance. Because these are individual voices constructed in politicized space, cultural memory, as I see it, is necessarily political even if it is not oppositional, and it is shaped by the on-going dialogue among individuals, culture, and history. By troubling the dichotomy between individual and cultural memory and illustrating a symbiotic relationship between memory, trauma, and history, my goal is not to revert to a simplistic understanding of the individual and his or her memory practices. Rather, I wish to build on this symbiosis in order to understand

how it shapes and is shaped by individual memory. In this process, I complicate the idea that individual memory is only personal; I also recognize that
defining individual memory as cultural memory's "Other" ignores the lived
practices of contemporary memorializing, which are increasingly individualized. Ultimately, I would suggest it is because of the fragmented nature of
individual memory that individual memorializing practices and their structures—as affected by the experience of trauma; the various social, cultural,
and historical forces; and the physiological decline of memory—should be
considered some of the most significant elements of the practices and structures of cultural memory writ large.

My definition of cultural memory, like that of many other scholars,
also emphasizes the importance of forgetting to the process of memory.
Memory and forgetting are "co-constitutive processes," suggests Sturken, and
forgetting is part of a narrative process (8). Referencing Freud, she continues: forgetting "is an *active* process of repression," one designed to "protect
the subject from anxiety, fear, jealousy, and other difficult emotions" (8). In
the context of psychoanalytic support, Adam Philips suggests that "[p]eople
come for . . . treatment because they are remembering in a way that does
not free them to forget" (qtd. in Kermode 91). When trauma survivors seek
the help of psychoanalysis, then, the goal is to attempt a "cure by inducing
the kind of remembering that makes forgetting possible" (Kermode 91).

Vietnam veterans remember the war in a cultural milieu in which
information about the war is available, in representational form or in online
archives for instance, while many specific details have been forgotten, erased,
or revised in representations as well as in individual and institutional memories of the war. Veterans struggle to remember in an environment that vac-
illates between forgetting and remembering, one that blurs the boundaries
between their own memories and the various representations and narratives
of the war. This struggle has psychological as well as social and historical
implications: as Judith Herman suggests, individual veterans need to forget,
while both individually and collectively they feel the pressure to remember (1). Individually, they may be overwhelmed with traumatic effects that
make them involuntarily recall and repress the memory of painful events.
As a community, veterans are concerned that their experiences will be forgotten by themselves, their fellow veterans, and postwar generations. This
concern is not, as it is with Holocaust "post-memories," to use Marianne
Hirsch's term, that the next generation may not remember correctly or
fully, but rather that there will be no post-memory at all, no passing on of
remembered narratives that are "distinguished from memory by generation
distance and from history by deep personal connection," as Hirsch defines

her term (8). Vietnam veterans' memories are what Andreas Huyssen calls twilight memories: "generational memories on the wane due to the passing of time and the continuing speed of technological modernization, and memories that reflect the twilight status of memory itself . . . that moment of the day that foreshadows the night of forgetting, but that seems to slow time itself" (1995: 3).

When veterans' traumas or individual memories are communicated—culturally produced and enacted—they contribute to the history of the war, broadening history to include the subjective, lived experiences of individuals in addition to the traditionally detached and objective writings of historians. But the relationship between the two, between memory and history, is "entangled," as Sturken suggests. For example, veterans' individual and cultural memory practices might be influenced by pervasive histories of the war and the era, and historians' attempts at objectivity might be affected by their own memories and by dominant cultural memories. Historians also may strive for a coherence in their writing that may be lacking in actual events: in "The Narrative of the Form," Hayden White suggests that the "value attached to narrativity in the representation of real events arises out of a desire to have real events display the coherence, integrity, fullness, and closure of an image of life that is and can only be imaginary" (24). Because of their suspicions about any historiography that strives for completeness or coherence and a desire to have their own experiences be recognized, veterans in their various memory practices may reject official forms of history and produce another type that is at once more specific and experiential yet at the same time more partial and incomplete than its traditional form. Veterans' memoirs, for example, strive for coherence but also represent the incoherent aspects of the war, offering a way to understand how history can be based on subjective memory and individual experience. While positioning experience as evidence problematically serves, Joan Scott argues, to accept rather than understand how experience is privileged, for many veterans personal experience becomes the unquestionable perceived truth, the evidence that is used to justify the validity of their subjective memory-narratives about the war. It is difficult for someone who did not serve in Vietnam to question a veteran's claim to authenticity, his or her declaration "I know because I was there," but as observers of the war's memory practices, we must try and understand how knowledge shaped through experience, pervasive discourses, and the active processes of memory gets to count as the truth of the war.

The completion of the National World War II Memorial and its placement at the center of the Mall, equidistant between the Lincoln Memorial and Washington Monument, declares this war as the definitive turning point in our nation's recent history; now the Vietnam War, along with the Korean War, is relegated to a sidebar in history. And Mills supports this arrangement: "In the Mall's visual continuum it is World War II that is now officially linked to the Revolutionary War and Civil War, and by extension it is the classicism of the National World War II Memorial's design, not the stark modernism of Maya Ying Lin's Vietnam Veterans Memorial, that is put forward as the architectural language most suited to expressing the values that lie at the root of American life" (218). So, while some perceive World War II as the defining war of the twentieth century, others suggest that the World Trade Center attacks ushered in a new era of memory and memorializing in the twenty-first, even as the extent to which the events and responses to 9/11 reveal new or altered memory practices still needs to be completely evaluated.[4] In this milieu, the importance of the Vietnam War to American cultural memory practices is waning somewhat. But, because of this, Vietnam veterans' memory becomes even more important to study: if veterans' practices originated through a desire to counteract the national forgetting of the war, what happens to that memory now that World War II has become the defining conflict of the era and 9/11 has become America's most recent national trauma? If, as many scholars argue, the emergence of the Wall marked a fundamental change in American memorializing practices, what role does that memorial now have in contemporary conversations about remembering?

The scholarship on memory shows us that memory is not static, that it is constantly being reimagined and renegotiated in the present; even if the Vietnam War's significance is fading, even if veterans' psychological faculties are waning, they continue to remember—privately and publicly. Because of this, the content, structure, and practices of memory—and this is not limited to Vietnam veterans' memory, of course—continually alter as social attitudes and political ideologies, as well as the individual's capacity to effectively recall, change. Perhaps what's most important about these features of memory is that we are able to observe them. We can do so because the individual, to greater or lesser extents, has control over how he or she memorializes, because he or she performs these practices in public or records them in other forms (in photographs, journals, memoirs, weblogs, etc.) Despite the increasing occurrence of these practices partly as a result of advances in technology that enable easier access to the past, this democratization of memory has been developing for the past 250 years. Surveying the history of western memorializing with an emphasis on commemorating war, I discuss in the next section how a series of factors—ranging from eighteenth-century revolutions and changes in the methods of recording history to, more recently, the development of the concept of a global society as well as various techno-logical advances—has altered all individual and cultural practices, including those that enable public and private remembering.

MEMORIALIZING

The ways individuals and communities perceive their connections to the past and generate memories and traditions in the present have changed over time and within and through spaces. In the introduction to *Commemorations*, a collection of essays on the intersections of memory and identity, John Gillis identifies three overlapping temporal phases in the history of commemora-tion as it relates to national identity: "the pre-national (before the late eigh-teenth century), the national (from the American and French revolutions to the 1960s), and the present, post-national phase" (5). The pre-national phrase corresponds generally to the period Nora describes as *les milieux de mémoire*, environments of lived, "true" memory, unmediated and spontaneous, when, as Gillis describes, "ordinary people did not feel compelled to invest in archives, monuments, and other permanent sites of memory" (6). At this time, individ-uals experienced living memory without a specific sense of national identity or separation from the past and, Gillis continues, were "content to live in a present that contained both the past and the present" and "did not feel com-pelled to invest . . . in permanent sites of memory" (6).

These conditions began to change after the political and economic revolutions in the late eighteenth century when the middle and working classes started to demand commemoration as part of a general movement to narrow the gap between the popular and the elite (Gillis 7). At the start of this national phase of commemoration, revolutionaries in both America and Europe created a "cult of new beginnings" that generated a "whole new set of memory practices and sites" (Gillis 8; Ozouf 1988); these, in turn, fostered a sense of national identity and unity (8). The cult both necessi-tated the mythologizing of the past and the creation of national commemo-rations—most notably Fourteenth of July, Bastille Day, in France and Fourth of July, Independence Day, in the United States—to construct a perception of "themselves as standing at the starting point of a new era" (8).

In the United States, the diversification and democratization of com-memorative practices continued into the nineteenth century. As John Bod-nar discusses, by the 1820s and 1830s economic growth and the rise of the Democratic Party increased tensions among classes, ethnicities, and regions (26). These developments led to a greater diversity of public commemora-tion practices (26). A joint "decline in the singleminded focus on patriotism and national unity that had reached a peak in 1825" (21) and an increase in "more commemorative attention [being] given to local, state, and regional pasts" resulted in people pursuing their own interests and activities during time that was designated for commemoration (26). So, for example, by the 1830s and 1840s more people were using the Fourth of July holiday as an opportunity to pursue leisure activities rather than patriotic commemoration, with "tavern frolics" and "disorderly, political picnics" in danger of overshadowing the "serious orations about moral and civic values" that also took place (26–27).

Despite the increased involvement of ordinary people in commemorations at various sites of memory, nineteenth-century memorializing was "largely for, but not of, the people," as only kings, leaders, and generals were memorialized and the ordinary participants in wars or revolutions were not (Gillis 9). By the beginning of the twentieth century, however, the "cult of the dead had become democratized," with officers and ordinary foot soldiers being buried side by side (11). As both George Mosse and Thomas Laqueur discuss, when the British Red Cross and shortly thereafter the Graves Registration Commission took control over identifying and burying the British war dead and later commemorating World War I, the names of the soldiers were now recorded and for the first time their graves were marked (Mosse 7, 81; Laqueur 150–167). At the same time in Germany, the Officers in Charge of Graves (*Gräberoffiziere*) were looking after individual graves (Mosse 81). Previously, war monuments, obelisks without reference to individuals, were chosen to memorialize the dead, but now the names of the dead were inscribed on war memorials built in small towns across the United States and Europe (Mosse 99).

Nora offers an expansive explanation for the changes in memory practices in this national phase of commemoration, between *les milieux de mémoire* and *les lieux de mémoire*. In the new phase, *lieux de mémoire*—deliberate sites of memory—the past is organized by historians and others into modern memory sites that "rel[y] entirely on the materiality of the trace, the immediacy of the recording, the visibility of the image" (13). Nora identifies the intersection of the development of a historiographical consciousness in France and "the end of a tradition of memory" as what led to the creation of the new environment (11). More specifically, Nora points to France's defeat in 1870 in the Franco-Prussian War and to the introduction of scientific methodology in the scholarship of history as well as, more broadly, to a movement toward democratization and mass culture as explanations for the shift to *lieux de mémoire*. Sites of memory emerged because remembering can no longer be taken for granted and people must "create archives, maintain anniversaries, organize celebrations, pronounce eulogies, and notarize bills because such activities no longer occur naturally" (12). The sites can be material (such as an archive), functional (such as a testament or reunion), or symbolic (such as a commemoration) although, of course, these features often interrelate. And they can be situated in physical locations, they can be portable, and they can be abstract. Even though Nora's description of *lieux de mémoire* was written through a cloud of nostalgia for the "true" unmediated memory of the earlier *milieux de mémoire* and the concept pertains more appropriately to the French context, it has become an incredibly useful way to understand the democratization, individualization, and materialization of contemporary memorializing practices in the United States.

During this national phase, new memories required collective amnesia, in Benedict Anderson's terms, willful forgetting of the past that Sturken defines as "highly organized and strategic" (7). As explanation for deliberate forgetting, Gillis suggests that economic and political changes "created such a sense of distance between now and then that people found it impossible to remember what life had been like only a few decades earlier" (7). Gillis highlights forgetting as a feature of post-World War II memorializing, pointing specifically to a rejection of the cult of the dead in Germany and Japan, reflected in a refusal to build memorials and a desire to forget the recent past. Yet, I would add, even the war's victorious countries desired to selectively forget elements of the war—the living memorials movement in the United States, for example, symbolized how most Americans, as Andrew Shanken suggests, "experienced a compelling drive to move on and to forget" (130). The movement, which emerged after World War I but came to fruition after World War II, promoted civic building projects such as community centers, parks, and hospitals, rather than traditional war monuments. Spearheaded by *American City* magazine and architects such as Philip Johnson, the movement emphasized, among other things, that traditional war monuments were "the 'white elephants' of an unusable past" (Shanken 130); more positively, they also stressed finding a place at home for returning veterans (Gillis 13).

Even though challenges existed to traditional commemoration prior to the Vietnam War as the living memorial movement indicates, Gillis and Huyssen suggest that cultural memory and public commemoration altered as the Vietnam War was ending. Gillis proposes that western society entered the post-national era of commemoration. In several of his works, Huyssen is concerned with noting changes in cultural practice since the 1970s that may help explain changes in memory and memorializing. In the post-national phase of commemoration, according to these scholars, memory has become yet more democratic but simultaneously more burdensome. While everyone who wishes to participate in memory practices can do so, and the forms of memory practices are increasingly heterogeneous, individuals also feel a greater pressure to "record, preserve, and collect" (Nora 14). In addition, memory practices are simultaneously more global and more local, as distinctions between different times and places collapse and we are "more likely to do our 'memory work' at times and places of our own choosing" (Gillis 14).

For these and other scholars, the National Vietnam Veterans Memorial is exemplary of the changes in memory practices occurring in the post-national phase, its construction described as the most significant turning point in American memorializing of the twentieth century. In the early 1980s, shortly after the Wall was dedicated, writers extolled the Wall's significance or debated its controversial design (see Hess, Griswold, and Wagner-Pacifici and Schwartz). By the early 1990s, scholarship focused on the objects being left at the Wall (Palmer, Hass). At this time, commentators were positioning the Wall in the context of American cultural memory or identifying the Wall as one of the key sites for the reimagining of nation identity. To give some examples: Gillis juxtaposes the Tomb of the Unknown Soldier in Arlington National Cemetery with the "anarchy of memory" at the Wall to mark the onset of the post-national phase. George Mosse ends *Fallen Soldiers* by suggesting the Wall's emergence is the sign that the "myth of the war experience" is dead: while belief in camaraderie and even the ideal of manliness has some continued resonance in the era of post-national memory, the "cult of the war dead"—the idea that dying was actually "sacrifice and resurrection"—and the "cult of the nation" do not (Mosse 73, 224). Mosse points to the popularity of the Wall over Frederick Hart's "Three Servicemen" sculpture as an illustration of people's preference for a new way of commemorating the dead, as well as the loss of the old myth's power (224–225). In a similar move, Bodnar opens *Remaking America* with a prologue on the Vietnam Memorial to highlight how, as he says, "the shaping of a past worthy of public commemoration in the present is contested and involves a struggle for supremacy between advocates of various political ideas and sentiments" (13). Also, Sturken argues that in the context of the "rescripting" of the history of the war, "the Vietnam Veterans Memorial has become a central icon in the process of healing, of confronting difficult past experiences," and "it has played a significant role in the rehistoricization of the Vietnam War" (45).

But if the Wall's emergence marks a change in commemoration, the Wall's perceived message—its refusal to make any political commentary and its fostering of a diverse range of memory practices—has not been replicated in war memorials emerging in its wake. Even if many memorials built subsequently reference the Wall's aesthetic, particularly its simplicity and use of names, they rarely challenge the notion of war as noble cause as the Wall's does with its listing of names and its below grade position. The *National Review* argued this aesthetic "makes the [deaths] individual [ones], not deaths in a cause [and] . . . symbolizes the 'unmentionability' of the war" (Sturken 52; see Chapter Three for further discussion of Wall replicas).[5] In fact, it may be the case that rather than marking a watershed moment in the history of memorializing, the Wall was simply an anomaly in that history. Nevertheless, as the Wall's planning and construction occurred concurrently with the start of the post-national era of commemoration, so it has become exemplary of the memory practices of the era although not, I would suggest, the cause of them.

Regardless of the extent to which the Wall has influenced contemporary features of memory, memory scholars have suggested a range of social and cultural traits that effectively describe the contemporary, post-national era of memorializing. Danger in oversimplifying lies in any attempt to define an era by identifying its characteristics, of course; thus, while I draw on these descriptions to contextualize Vietnam veterans' memory practices, I am cognizant of, and I attempt to point out, their limitations. In *Twilight Memories*, Andreas Huyssen examines the materiality of memory in contemporary culture, noting how he was "struck by the surprising popularity of the museum and the resurgence of the monument and the memorial as major modes of aesthetic, historical, and spatial expression" (1995: 3). In "Monument and Memory in a Postmodern Age," he wonders if the tension he identifies in memory practices between historical amnesia and the public's "veritable obsession with the past" can be described as postmodern.[6] The "ever quickening pace of material life" and the "speed-up of images and information" alters people's sense of historical continuity; the result is that instead of having a sense of before and after, there is a "simultaneity of all times and spaces readily accessible in the present" (1993: 253). Huyssen suggests that because ordinary people have access to information about the past and the present at all times and in all places, an "allatonceness" as Marshall McLuhan puts it in relation to the onset of mass media, they lose their perception of history (Huyssen 1993: 253; McLuhan et al 1967). In comparison, Gillis points to other features of the postmodern era—global markets working around the clock and the speed of communications—to locate our "shrink[ing] . . . sense of distance" between past and present (14). And James Young speculates about the effects of aspects of contemporary society on memory practices in terms of the increased interest in memory itself: "In this age of mass memory production and consumption . . . there seems to be an inverse proportion between the memorialization of the past and its contemplation and study" (1993: 5). These perspectives suggest that the accessibility of information from all times and spaces creates historical amnesia (i.e., because we are presented with so much information, we become numbed to it) and fosters a fascination with the past (as embodied in a range of places and practices such as heritage tourism, museums, retro fashions, antiquing, and memoir writing), although the perspectives do not account for those unable to access technology or for those who choose to or otherwise resist it. Tim Edensor, for example, defines as hyperbolic the insistence "that the social world is inevitably speeding up," a claim he suggests "neglects slower processes [and] divergent rhythms" (125; Highmore 2002: 175).

If the availability of information creates historical amnesia, Huyssen argues society's current obsession with the past implies a rejection of technology. Ultimately, Huyssen contrasts the nostalgic material world with the technological virtual one and argues that renewed interest in museums and historical items are attractive to "a public dissatisfied with simulation and channel-flicking," and that the museum is the "key paradigm in contemporary postmodern culture" (1993: 253, 255). With reference to the way "mass media, even television, have created an unquenchable desire for experiences and events, for authenticity and identity which, however, television is unable to satisfy" (1995: 32), Huyssen suggests the museum can meet this desire because artifacts "carry a register of reality"—the promise of an authentic experience. Huyssen's argument implies that people seek authenticity in the material that they cannot find in the virtual, and they seek it in the past because they cannot find in the present. But I would suggest that individuals increasingly seek authenticity and identity as much in virtual interactions as they do in material objects. Writing even as recently as 1995, Huyssen could not have predicted the extent to which individuals are able to conduct almost every aspect of their lives online, from work, to leisure, to personal relationships. While some lament the loss of tactile sensation or personal connection in the virtualization of everyday life, others can have perceived authentic experiences, aided by technology, that they would not be able to achieve in the material world. For example, museums increasingly enhance their visitors' experiences with technology, providing ever more realistic yet virtual reenactments of ancient times or distant lands that visitors would never, or most likely never, be able to access in their own lives.

Increasing virtualization of ordinary life notwithstanding, contemporary society's obsession with the materiality of memory may bespeak a rejection of modernism's aestheticism and obsession with temporality. As early as 1939, Clement Greenberg noted how the "new urban masses" were turning toward quotidian and mass-produced items as a "rear-guard" reaction against the avant-garde's pure aestheticism (11). Kitsch, which used "for raw material the debased and academicized simulacra of genuine culture" (12), resulted from the pressure of the masses "on society to provide them with a kind of culture fit for their own consumption" (12). At one level, I would question the relevance of an artifact's kitschiness to those who leave items at the Wall, at which objects are left there not because of their aesthetic appeal or the uses for which they were made but because of the meanings the objects have taken on within specific familial, cultural, or social contexts (see Chapter Four for a further discussion of the acquired meaning of objects). However parallels between the rise of kitsch and the obsession with the material items of memory imply how both products and memories are, like marketable goods, available for purchase and consumption.

The commodification of memory, which Gillis and Young imply, is apparent in the proliferation of books, films, museums, and memorials related to contemporary national and international traumatic events such as the Holocaust; in the sale of memorial souvenirs such as pieces of rubble from the Berlin Wall or ground zero at the World Trade Center; and in the burgeoning memoir and scrap-booking industries. The memorializing of the Vietnam War is no exception: commodification occurs not only in the production and distributions of filmic and literary representations of the war but also in particular practices that are this book's focus, such as the sale of Prisoner of War/ Missing in Action bracelets, the business practices of wall replicas, and the tourist industry for veterans to Vietnam. While the exchange of goods for cash in the market place suggests a communal activity, purchasable aids to memory—for instance, souvenirs from every imaginable location and event or subscriptions to ancestry or memorial websites—are usually sold to facilitate memory practices that are likely to be enacted by individuals at home and/ or in private.

Thus, within the context of the increasing globalization, materialization (and virtualization), and commodification of memory, memory has become increasingly individualized. Since the 1970s, Gillis suggests that a "radical critique of older institutional memory" has circulated, with one result being that collective forms of memory have declined, and an increasing burden is placed on the individual to remember (15–16). Today, the onus is on individuals to remember in increasingly archival and site specific ways. Gillis suggests most people have trouble remembering without referencing material items, such as "mementoes, images, and physical sites" (17). Through these artifacts, individuals have access to their own familial and cultural pasts in ways that have never been possible before. This accessibility makes aspects of the past immediate while, at the same time, makes connection to the past seem even more difficult. Now, everyone is compelled to record his or her experiences into memoirs, to become his or her own historian, and archival obsession and genealogical research mark the contemporary age (13–15; see also Derrida 1995). Thus, while the increasing availability of collected or purchased artifacts makes memory practices easier, their availability produces a concomitant burden to effectively manage memory.

A picture emerges here of the contemporary era as both obsessed with and disconnected from the past, as saturated with information yet unaware of how to sift through it all. If *milieux de mémoire* no longer exist as Nora argues, then *lieux de mémoire* occur in what I call, building on this terminology, *milieu du temps passé*, an environment in which the past is always available and present. If they used the term, Huyssen, Gillis, and Nora would argue *milieu du temps passé* is symptomatic of the technological age, which for those who have access makes representations of the past and information from around the world readily available at all times and places. In this milieu, Huyssen would argue that citizens feel nostalgic for perceived simpler times, but they also experience the speeding up and overlapping of remembering and forgetting. If, historically, memorializing occurs when an event is in danger of being forgotten, the most salient feature of contemporary memory in the *milieu du temps passé* is how immediacy and contemplation intersect, how remembering and forgetting can happen instantaneously, yet at the same time the process of deciding how to memorialize national events can span many years.

Today, in the contemporary era of memorializing, while the "nation is no longer the site or frame of reference for most people" (Gillis 17), patriotism continues to shape how ordinary people remember. In *Carried to the Wall*, Kristin Ann Hass argues against Gillis and suggests that the Wall "is a reminder of the potency of the nation in the imagination of grievers at the Wall" (102). I would suggest, however, that the Wall invites rather more individualized interaction, and that patriotism, as Wilbur Zelinsky defines it, can be limited to the "personally perceived action-space an individual encounters in his or her everyday life" (4). This patriotism is informed by public and official discourses but fostered in homes and communities across the country. Post-9/11, public commemorations often are marked by a fervent, sometimes even aggressive, patriotism. After the World Trade Center attacks, rhetoric of unquestioning patriotism swept the nation, commencing with the "sea of American flags, . . . the memorial displays around the world" (Dudziak 2) and resulting in the Patriot Act. Today, the ongoing remembering of the Vietnam War by its veterans occurs in this milieu. In

The Culture of Defeat, Wolfgang Schivelbusch wonders if the attacks "uncovered the suppressed remains of Vietnam" and if the post-9/11 fervor is "really a response to an earlier and unresolved defeat" (294). While it may be difficult to directly link the loss of the Vietnam War to the current wave of patriotism, certainly the current zeal offers an opportunity to reimagine the Vietnam War through a patriotic lens that downplays oppositional perspectives in order to present the war as a noble cause worthy of unquestioning patriotic commemoration.

With social changes that have increased access to information, particularly through technology and globalization, contemporary memory is defined, by Huyssen, Gillis, and Nora among others, as a paradox between historical amnesia and obsession with the past; as archival, deliberate, and site specific; and as simultaneously global and local. Above all, contemporary memory is increasingly materialized, commodified, and individualized. In the rest of this book, I examine these complex features of contemporary memory using case studies of its most visible and significant sites: the memoir, the memorial, the museum, and tourism. I start with the memoir because, as I argue in the next chapter, it is the key paradigm of postmodern memory, the most significant literary mode of the post-Vietnam generation. The contemporary burgeoning of self-reflective personal narratives in which, as Nora puts it, everyone becomes a historian, has its roots, I argue, in the recognition in 1980 of post-traumatic stress disorder that directly and indirectly spawned a generation of individuals searching for and writing about their own personal traumas. Vietnam veterans' memoirs are at the forefront of this trend, but they also resist its most clichéd aspects.

In the *milieu du temps passé*, where the instantaneity of remembering 9/11 coexists with the 50-years-in-the-making World War II Memorial, is focusing on Vietnam War memory irrelevant? Vietnam War memorializing so often exemplified in the National Vietnam Veterans Memorial did not singularly transform contemporary memorializing, nor does the Vietnam War have the cultural and political resonance it did during the war and for several years after it. But how it continues to be memorialized by veterans and loved ones throughout the United States and Vietnam reveals the future of American memorializing as it is practiced in the present—memorializing that has become increasingly "entangled" not only with history but also with commodification, individualism, and patriotism.

Chapter Two
Trauma, Metaphors, and the Body

> Our legs and our arms are full of torpid memories.
>
> —Marcel Proust

On 22 April 1971, Vietnam Veterans Against the War executive committee member and national coordinator John Kerry spoke to the Senate Foreign Relations Committee using testimony from the VVAW's Winter Soldier
Investigation.[1] At the Winter Soldier proceedings two months earlier, recently
returned soldiers publicly gave evidence about the atrocities they had committed or seen committed by the U.S. military in Vietnam. In his speech,
Kerry drew on the bodily experiences of soldiers to counteract what the antiwar organization felt was the administration's refusal to acknowledge the soldiers' sacrifices in Vietnam. In a frequently cited passage from the speech,
Kerry proclaims: "In their blindness and fear [the administration has] tried
to deny that we are veterans or that we served in Nam. We do not need their
testimony. Our own scars and stumps of limbs are witness enough for others
and for ourselves" (Bibby 146; Thorne and Butler 24). Kerry's speech pits the
administration against veterans in physical terms. The administration cannot
"see" veterans' "scars" and "stumps," but ultimately this "blindness" doesn't
matter because veterans' testimonies, until this point marginalized, exist in
spite of attempts to deny them. In Kerry's terms, the veterans' wounded bodies attest to war experiences and speak out against the war.

In this chapter, I explore the ways veterans' personal narratives reveal
how the body remembers and conveys war experience. Working with five
Vietnam veterans' memoirs that both chart and mirror changing national
perceptions on the war, I examine veteran memoirists who write bodies
into their texts using metaphors of the physical to testify to traumatic war
experience or to protest the war. Ron Kovic's *Born on the Fourth of July*
(1976) and Michael Herr's *Dispatches* (1977), both canonical works in the

Vietnam War literature genre, foreground the authors' wounded bodies (real or imagined) as testimony to their authentic war experience. In John Balaban's *Remembering Heaven's Face* (1991) and Tim O'Brien's "How to Tell a True War Story" (1990), the focus shifts to the wounded bodies of others, to which Balaban and O'Brien bear witness; and in *The Circle of Hanh* (2000), Bruce Weigl reconciles with his body and his war experience, embracing an alternative concept of healing and recovery shaped by non-western spirituality.

Hundreds of veterans' memoirs have been published, many within ten years of the war's end, during a period when Vietnam-themed works were earning literary awards and outstanding reviews and the public was still interested in finding out "the truth about America's role in Vietnam" (O'Nan 116). Many early memoirs like Philip Caputo's *A Rumor of War* (1977) or Ronald Glasser's *365 Days* (1986) used novelistic techniques such as writing in the third person, whereas Kovic's memoir challenges this third person voice by switching back and forth from first to third. More recently, the most prominent memoirs have been those written by politicians drawing on their experience in Vietnam to explain their suitability for office; for example, John McCain's *Faith of My Fathers* (2000) and *Worth the Fighting For* (2002) or John Kerry's *A Call to Service* (2003), the latter of which charts the author's rise from VVAW activist to Democratic Senator for Massachusetts. But because they are written to further the authors' political careers, these works often gloss over the most difficult aspects of their war experiences.

So, while hundred of memoirs exist, I have chosen to focus on five particular works for several reasons. Perhaps most importantly, all the writers reject straightforward fiction techniques in favor of a combination of experimental narrative forms and conventions from the nonfiction genre to portray what they believe is the truth of Vietnam. (The truth they suggest is not found in the facts of the war but in its visceral reality, as they experienced it. But, as O'Brien puts it, even in experience "truths are contradictory" [*The Things They Carried* 80.]) In addition, these memoirs reflect upon the difficulties of constructing creative nonfiction: the tensions among fictionalizing one's experiences for readers' interest, telling it "like it was," representing the war's messy and incoherent aspects, and presenting facts as they happened. I focus on five prominent memoirs in order to examine how their war narratives align with dominant public discourses of the war. While I could have discussed other important memoirists—W.D. Ehrhart and Tobias Wolff are certainly omissions here, though I do discuss the first writer in Chapter Five—I chose these particular memoirs because of how they use content and form to present lived experience, challenge dominant myths about the war, manifest the practices of memory in their works, and use metaphor to present their traumatic experiences.

While exceptions exist, the memoir generally offers a sustained examination of the writer's involvement in war, usually resulting in a more nuanced and sophisticated narrative than is produced through the other kinds of memorializing practices examined throughout this work. Sometimes this self-examination leads to the writer "animating his guilt," to use a term proposed by war-era psychologist Robert Jay Lifton, or more generally to a questioning of or opposition to the United States' involvement in Vietnam. While the war experience might be romanticized in some cases, in the most developed veterans' memoirs, the critique of war is sustained. Like online postings on memorial websites or veterans' art, memoirs put on display personal thoughts and difficult experiences for all to see. Always, they involve a great deal of soul searching. While they generally produce more sophisticated, or at least more elaborate, narratives of the war as well as illustrate the general trend toward the individualization of memorializing, memoirs written by the most prominent veteran writers are burdened with the expectation that they should speak on behalf of, and represent, all veterans.

There exists no clearer physical manifestation of memory than the body, which, along with the memoir, inhabits the intersecting domains of public and personal memorializing. As custodians of the most intensely private memories and difficult traumas, bodies and memoirs are material and, therefore, public expressions of personal memory. When a soldier or civilian is wounded in combat, the war's violence is inscribed on the body, often in highly visible ways (for example, a wheelchair using amputee of a certain age would more likely be assumed to be a Vietnam War veteran than, say, a victim of a car accident). In veterans' memoirs, wounding is inscribed on the page in at least two ways—in the retelling of traumatic incidents and in the structure of the work itself, as disruptions in the text.

In later chapters, I examine how individual veterans and institutions interact to produce new meanings and memories of the war. These new versions bespeak veterans' authentic memories, but they can also distort the realities or the facts of the war, such as when politically conservative veterans' groups use war memorializing to celebrate patriotism while ignoring the war's historical contentiousness, or when institutions erase or rewrite important aspects of the war, "depoliticizing the past in order to achieve at least the illusion of consensus" as Michael Kammen suggests (662). In public discourses, elements of the war are erased for political purposes—to rewrite the war as a noble cause or to reconstruct the veteran as a victim. While memoirs also erase details of the war, the reason for doing so, at least among the memoirs examined here, highlights a key difference between memoirs and other forms of memorializing: in memoirs, the erasure of specific details of the war may be explained by the experience of trauma, which disturbs the survivor's ability to recall completely or coherently. Memoirs tread a fine line, however, between being the product of the writer's traumatic experience and his simulation of it for readers' interest, between "self-revelation" and "deliberately contrived trauma writing," a comparison Mark Heberle draws in his work on Tim O'Brien, *A Trauma Artist*.[2] In its contrivance, a memoir may deliberately leave out or alter elements of a story in order to mimic the effects of trauma. Because the reader cannot always determine the difference between effect and performance, I discuss trauma only in terms of its production, which may be deliberate or unconscious depending on the actual experience of the writer. In other words, I do not examine residues of trauma to argue that veterans are still affected by the war—that much is obvious. Rather, I am interested in how veteran writers perform trauma in their works, in how the writers present themselves as survivors of trauma whether or not that traumatic experience is fact or fiction. Memoirs are thus what Pierre Nora calls *lieux de mémoire*, constructed sites of memory and, I would add, of trauma.

But the memoir also is the key paradigm of postmodern memory because it presents the tensions between historical amnesia and obsession with the past, between the individual's burden to remember and the therapeutic need to forget, and between the individual's need to identify as a veteran and society's need to ignore veterans as reminders of a lost war. Memoirs give us insight not just into the lives, psychology, and memorializing practices of the memoirists but also the lives, psychology, and memorializing practices of society. I'm not arguing here that memoirs are microcosms of society, although they can be; rather, I'm suggesting that the structure of memoirs helps us understand how memory functions writ large.

In the chronological progression of the memoirs examined here, bodies of soldiers or civilians become increasingly absent as do specific details of the war itself. As the physical manifestations of war—particularly those experienced in the body—fade, as temporal distance increases between the veteran's time in-country and the writing of the memoir, the writer becomes increasingly preoccupied with conveying the long-term psychological, emotional, and intellectual effects of the war. But the gradual shift in focus from the physical to philosophical, even spiritual, is complicated in all the memoirs I examine by the representation of trauma, which appears most often through the use of metaphor and experimental, fragmented, or interrupted textual structure. The interplay of the body and trauma in these works poses difficult questions: if trauma is known and experienced in the body, does it become disembodied when put into words? Or do representations of the body "speak" trauma, as John Kerry's speech implies? What follows is an attempt to get at the complex relationship between trauma and the body and specifically at how these memoirs use metaphors to communicate the experience of trauma as it is felt in the body.

In *Beyond the Pleasure Principle*, Freud argues that traumatic neurosis has two main characteristics: it is primarily caused by an act of fright or surprise, and it is forestalled by physical wounding. Roberta Culbertson, complicating Freud's dichotomy between neurosis and injury, marks wounding not as the prevention of trauma but as the start of it. In "Embodied Memory," she points out how physiological responses to wounding, such as increased blood pressure and heart rate caused by fright-induced surges of adrenalin, are retained in the body as memory of the event (174). Drawing on the vocabulary of Holocaust survivor Charlotte Delbo, Culbertson differentiates between "external memory" and "deep memory." External memories are recollections of what the survivor thought or witnessed at the time of the traumatic event, or they are the pieced-together remembrances of the traumatic event that can be readily communicated to others. But Culbertson argues that the "truth" of the trauma is not found in external memory but only in the memory of the body's own response to threat and pain. Culbertson points out, however, that by necessity these deep body memories must be rendered "tellable;" they must be "order[ed] and arrang[ed] in the form of a story, linking emotion with event, event with event, and so on" (179). Through this process the survivor can reestablish his or her connection to the world and can become, again, "socially defined" (179). In effect, as Culbertson puts it, this process of telling "disembodies" and "demystifies" memory; however, because body memories exist and are only known in the body, they can never be accurately rendered without losing something of their full and original meaning.

Addressing the translation of trauma into language, Kalí Tal acknowledges that textual representations, mediated through language, lack the impact of the traumatic experience itself, but she moves toward resolving this mediation problem by explaining how the traumatic experience is inscribed through metaphor (15). Tal argues that both trauma survivors and those without experience of trauma are equipped with the same set of signs, but the traumatic experience "catalyzes a transformation of meaning in the sign's individual use to represent [the survivors'] experiences" (16). "Words gain new meanings within the context of trauma," and survivors develop "the metaphoric tools to interpret representations of traumas similar to their own" (16). Metaphors are analogies that allow us to view one concept through the lens of another unrelated one, thereby understanding the first concept in a different way (see Veale, Abrams). They aid the comprehension of language and the representation of meaning. As I understand Tal, then, one survivor will understand the metaphoric meaning of another survivor's description of trauma; in effect, metaphors are like codes that give survivors special access to each other's traumas. Take for example a particular metaphor used by John Balaban, which I discuss in greater detail later in the chapter. On hearing the news of the destruction of a village he knew in Vietnam, he comments: "I felt like I would explode with grief." The subject or tenor, Balaban's feeling of grief, is described using the metaphoric vehicle "explode." Metaphors and memories both work through a process of association; metaphors help survivors communicate an experience (in Balaban's case, ever intensifying grief) by associating it with a vivid image (explode), and, through metaphors, memories become active through the association of experiences and images (in Balaban's case, reading a newspaper article reactivated his grief memory). Tal suggests that survivors will understand the tenor (trauma) no matter what the vehicle (figurative words used to describe the trauma). Because trauma survivors may find it impossible to describe their traumas, metaphors are one way to bring them into language; although metaphors do not describe trauma itself, they enable it to be communicated by comparing it to something else. (Elaine Scarry's suggestion, in *The Body in Pain* [1985], that pain lacks "referential content" is an instructive model for understanding the difficulty of putting traumatic memory into language.) Tal's suggestion, however, excludes those without experience of trauma, but metaphors surely enable those people to understand trauma too; although, because they have not experienced trauma physiologically, their understanding of it may be more intellectual than visceral.

While metaphors can increase comprehension of traumatic experience, they can also obscure meaning. Norman Podhoretz argues that the metonymic term "Vietnam" as shorthand for the war and the era has become perhaps the most negatively charged political symbol in U.S. history, with the word registering "a complex of meanings, devoid for the most part of any cultural or social referents to a particular country or nation" (Balogh 36; Sullivan 176). In unofficial military parlance, vague metaphors are used to describe death: soldiers do not die, they "fall;" they are not killed, they are "greased." The "inevitable and total reduction of the war to metaphor" is a trap literary theorists often fall into, argues Tal (223). But survivors avoid this pitfall by using metaphors to illuminate, rather than defer or obscure, their knowledge and experience of the war. Metaphors, then, become important tools for individual recovery and for the communication of memory and experience in ways that potentially build truthful cultural memory of the war; the veterans' memoirs I examine here use specific metaphors to counteract ahistorical or obscure ones used uncritically in popular and military discourses.

In sum, the need to render body memories tellable emphasizes the concomitant urgency and difficulty of translating body memory into language. For Culbertson, telling is necessary for the survivor to rejoin society; for Tal, writing trauma makes it "real both to the victim and to the community" and "serves both as validation and cathartic vehicle for the traumatized author" (21). Focusing on the physical mutilation of the body more so than the body's experience of trauma, Michael Bibby also highlights the importance of telling for veterans themselves. In *Hearts and Minds*, Bibby examines poetry from the GI antiwar movement to illustrate how "representations of mutilation . . . bear witness to the atrocities of war" (136). Like the John Kerry quote that opened this chapter, Bibby argues veterans' writings make the mutilated body a vivid and potent antiwar symbol. If the military through its basic training constructs the ideal of the male soldier as an "impenetrable body" (Bibby 126), antiwar veterans expose this as a lie by foregrounding their wounded bodies. Robert Jay Lifton argues their willingness to expose their war wounds turned antiwar veterans into heroes during the war years: American society was "haunted by the specter of a new kind of hero-prophet who turns his fleshly knowledge of violence into a rejection of that violence. . . . His 'hero-deed' is not what he did in the war but his rejection of that war" (325–326).

Bibby focuses on how the GI antiwar movement used poetry to protest the war by publishing it in the antiwar underground press, distributing it among veterans, and reading it at antiwar gatherings. Similarities exist in the content of GI antiwar activists' poetry and veterans' memoirs published shortly after the war ended. In particular, both genres either foreground wounded bodies or metaphors of them in order to convey the urgency of remembering and testifying. While both poetry and memoirs were written both during and after the war, because of its immediacy in terms of production and delivery, poetry has become the exemplary genre of the war era. Soldier-poets, student activists, and other writers and performers used poetry as a quick and efficient way to convey antiwar messages that, through rhyme and repetition, became persuasive and memorable. If poetry reflects the immediate response to the war as events were happening, memoir expresses a more contemplative one. In this way, the memoir has become the exemplary genre of the postwar era, a period of great soul searching when the public questioned the motivations of leaders, and veterans sought to examine exactly what happened to them in Vietnam.

Although, of course, it pre-dates the Vietnam War era (some argue going back as far as Augustine's *Confessions* of 398 AD), the memoir burgeoned during and after it. In "Modern American Autobiography," Albert E. Stone proposes that "the past half-century has seen a remarkable efflorescence of personal histories by a wide spectrum of amateur and professional writers" (97). Stone describes how the autobiographical genre has shifted and expanded:

> From bibliographies and other channels (ranging from *Publisher's Weekly* and Sunday book reviews to women's reading clubs and word-of-mouth advice from college-age children fresh from courses on American autobiography), present-day readers have in large numbers been attracted to autobiographies. Increased self- and group-consciousness among women and blacks, the paperback revolution since World War II, book clubs, and other new sales outlets have encouraged the spread of this consumer group, whose common denominator is an interest in others' lives and storytelling styles. These accounts appear now in a variety of conventional forms and new narrative modes: memoirs and confessions, testaments and apologies, diaries and journals, collaborations and collections of letters. (97–8)

The ordinary person's memoir, in fact, is a peculiarly late twentieth-century phenomenon that, I would argue, is the most significant literary mode of the post-Vietnam generation, reflecting the democratizing of the genre in an era when official representations of war, often distorting the facts of it, became the focus of ever increasing skepticism. In particular, the scope and form of the genre enables veteran writers to examine at length their own complicity in atrocities committed during the war, to bear witness to atrocities committed to and by others, and to examine how memories of complicity and witnessing change over time. The memoir, then, is both confession and testimony.

In light of the well-documented feelings of guilt that accompanied Vietnam veterans' return to the U.S. and the psychological support that encouraged them to come to terms with their guilt, an interesting correlation exists between the rise in popularity of confessional apology as a mode of autobiography or memoir and the increasing number of veterans producing personal narratives. These increases can be explained, at least in part, by the acceptance of post-traumatic stress disorder (PTSD) as a legitimate illness. PTSD was diagnosed for various combinations of traumatic symptoms but was officially recognized by the American Psychological Association as an illness in 1980, five years after the war ended; subsequently, almost 38% of veterans have met all the criteria for PTSD, and more than 70% have suffered at least one of the most common symptoms (Heberle 11; Shay 168). Its acceptance as a psychological illness and the avowed effectiveness of "talking cures" as treatment for PTSD has undoubtedly led a large number of veterans to write their experiences of the war into personal narratives and memoirs.

Lifton was the first psychologist to link veterans' recovery with the need to acknowledge feelings of guilt. He analyzes their postwar recovery from a psychohistorical approach, which he defines as an application of psychological principles to historical events (15). Summarizing his analysis of veterans' recovery process, Lifton states that "Vietnam's atrocity-producing situation and counterfeit universe created an extraordinary constellation of mutually reinforcing guilt and numbing; which in turn blocked and undermined the kind of meaningful survivor formulation and mission that could animate the guilt and initiate a reordering process" (396). Lifton gives an example of how this counterfeit universe was constructed: when soldiers experienced moral and spiritual uncertainty about what was going on in Vietnam, they would often seek the counsel of Army chaplains or psychiatrists. But more often than not, these counselors excused atrocities the soldiers hoped they would condemn (166–167). Because "spiritual-psychological authority was employed to seal off any . . . alternatives," the soldiers were forced to exist in a "counterfeit universe" in which "all pervasive, spiritually reinforced inner corruption bec[ame] the price of survival" (167). As the soldiers learned to numb themselves to atrocities, they also suppressed their feelings of guilt, and Lifton's work with veterans helped them to articulate the difference between "static guilt," which prevents recovery, and "animating guilt," which aids it. Animating guilt, according to Lifton, "is characterized by bringing oneself to life around one's guilt;" it "propels one toward connection, integrity, and movement" (127–8).

One of the simplest ways veterans moved toward animating guilt was by connecting with other veterans, a gesture Lifton facilitated in his "rap groups" during the early 1970s, which used the consciousness-raising model developed in students' and women's groups in the 1960s. In these sessions at antiwar meeting places, veterans could tell their stories and feel connected to others who had experienced similar traumas in Vietnam. For many veterans, these talking cures became writing cures; one of the most prominent examples of this transition in practice is *Winning Hearts and Minds: War Poems by Vietnam Veterans*. The editors—Larry Rottman, Jan Barry, and Basil Paquet—were active in antiwar groups and initially conceived this volume of poetry as a VVAW project. According to Michael Bibby, the volume appeared in 1972 "as a culmination of the antiwar activism centered around the Winter Soldier Investigation" (215). This volume and others like it illustrate how veteran poets worked through many of the same issues as veteran memoirists. While poetry also addresses guilt or trauma, as I have been suggesting, the practice of writing and reading memoirs enables the kind of sustained examination of complicity in war that animates personal or facilitates collective guilt about American involvement in Vietnam. Nevertheless, poetry functions as an important stage in that process; as the editors of *Winning Hearts and Minds* suggest, "What distinguishes the voices in this volume is their progression toward an active identification of themselves as agents of pain and war—as 'agent-victims' of their own atrocities" (v).

In this self-identification as agent-victims, veterans are remarkably well placed not just to confess to their own participation in atrocities but also to record the participation of others, to create texts that function as both confessionals and testimonials. Psychologist Dori Laub, a medical doctor and co-editor with Shoshana Felman of *Testimony: Crises in Witnessing in Literature, Psychoanalysis, and History*, describes the relationship between the listener, which Laub calls the hearer, and the survivor: the hearer is "the blank screen on which the event comes to be inscribed for the first time" (Felman and Laub 57–74). But the hearer also has agency and works hard to maintain his perspective while, at the same time, shares in the survivor's struggles to preserve and maintain his own traumatic memories (58). The hearer must participate in validating the reality of the traumatic experience in order to help "reexternaliz[e] the evil that affected and contaminated the trauma victim" (69). To reexternalize means, as Culbertson and Tal reminds us, to render body memories tellable—to bring them out of the body and into the world. In the interaction between the survivor and the hearer, testimony is produced (Felman and Laub 1–56).

In Felman's description of it, testimony retells the experience of an event but in a way that admits—either consciously or unconsciously—to its own lack of full understanding of the event about which it speaks. It presents acts not fully assimilated by the survivor, translating trauma into language without full cognizance of what the trauma means. Testimony parallels metaphor to the extent that both communicate trauma without trying to fully understand it. However, while often the goal of testimony is to externalize and articulate trauma's incommensurability, metaphor strives to make trauma more comprehensible. Testimony is not offered by the survivor or hearer as definitive or complete, and yet it is offered for several possible reasons—to validate or authenticate the experience of the speaker, to help the speaker work through traumatic experiences, and to ensure that the memory of something will not be completely lost.

Through the process of confessing and bearing witness, veterans animate their guilt. Like Holocaust survivors, who have written or been the subject of much of the scholarship on testimony and witnessing, Vietnam veterans are survivors and victims; unlike Holocaust survivors, they are also killers and persecutors. With this dual burden, they must admit their guilt before being able to testify about their own experiences and bear witness to the experiences of others. In these memoirs, I suggest, veterans use the body or metaphors of it to negotiate the terrain of confessing and bearing witness, but how they do so has changed over time. In the years immediately following the war, when *Born on the Fourth of July* and *Dispatches* were produced, veterans believed their own "scars and stumps of limbs [were] witness enough for others and ourselves," as Kerry's powerful words suggest. But as time passed after the war ended, works like *Remembering Heaven's Face* and "How to Tell a True War Story" let others' bodies testify. In Weigl's reconfiguration of memory in *The Circle of Hanh*, his spirituality takes him beyond—it transcends—his physical bodily experiences of the war.

I have divided my analysis of these memoirs into three groupings with the headings "Wounding," "Witnessing," and "Recovery" to illustrate the progression in the memoirs from the immediacy of the war, toward a reconciliation with its memories, and into a semblance of healing from it. Perhaps the writers move away from the body because as the years pass they become increasingly successful at finding the language to communicate their body memory, or because their hyphenated identities as agent-victims are slowly replaced with new identities as veteran-writers.

WOUNDING

Despite their significant differences, I start by bringing together Ron Kovic and Michael Herr because both works try to capture the war's immediacy, brutality, and excitement by foregrounding their own woundings or imaginings of them. Kovic was a Marine paralyzed on his second tour of duty who later rose through the ranks of Vietnam Veterans Against the War; Michael Herr, a war correspondent, was never physically wounded, but he also came to oppose the war. The writers present the viscerality of war not only to describe their own experiences but also to provoke responses from their readers: Kovic attempts to instruct his readers in the devastating effects of war, while Herr recreates for his readers what he believes is an accurate depiction of Vietnam. Through this comparison, I do not wish to privilege the traumatic experiences of the combat grunt over those of the correspondent. Nevertheless, the implications of the comparison are clear: the staggering critical acclaim of *Dispatches* and popularity of Oliver Stone's film version of *Born on the Fourth of July* (1989) suggest both that fictionalized representations of the war are more palatable to critics than the facts of it, and that, as Tim O'Brien says in another context, story truths may be truer than happening truths (*The Things They Carried* 179).

Ron Kovic's *Born on the Fourth of July* portrays one young man's emotional and psychological struggle to reconcile his behavior in Vietnam with his growing opposition to the war, a course of development that mirrors the evolving disillusionment about the war felt by many veterans and the nation. The memoir, while focused primarily on the war, spans his whole life from childhood to political activism; in this way, the work is a Bildüngsroman, a work of education that charts the development of the self, universal in its message and appeal. As testimony, Kovic's narrative presents a tension between the search for meaning and coherence in his life and the disruption trauma causes to it. As literary text, a site of memory and trauma, the memoir dramatizes traumatic recall in at least three ways: it translates deep memories into metaphoric language, foregrounds the moment of traumatic injury, and performs the interruption of repressed memories through its narrative structure. In effect, while Kovic's life story follows the Bildüngsroman pattern (linear and progressive), its narrative structure is traumatic (disrupted and repetitive).

Published in 1976, *Born on the Fourth of July* tells the story of Ron Kovic from Massapequa, New York, who went to Vietnam in September 1964 with the naïve belief that he was going to fight communism and serve his country honorably. He returned to the U.S. after two tours of duty with his ability to walk, his sexual function, and his belief in the war's purpose permanently destroyed. The memoir's structure is nonchronological but psychologically progressive, opening not when Kovic joins the army or when he first plays with guns as a child but in combat at the exact moment he is paralyzed. This pivotal incident divides Kovic's life into a before and after, and its placement at the book's beginning shapes Kovic's memoir as definitively as it shaped his life. The second chapter continues chronologically from Kovic's wounding and describes his various stages of recovery at under funded and unsanitary Veterans Administration hospitals, where his antiwar beliefs slowly take shape. Only in the third chapter does the memoir refer, for the first time, to his life before Vietnam. Here, Kovic discusses the social climate of the 1950s when boys played with guns, wanted to be like their fathers (who fought in World War II) or like heroes of the era (such as John

Wayne and Audie Murphy), and shared an uncomplicated view of service to one's country. Although Kovic portrays this simpler time with some irony, he wants to emphasize the contrast between his idyllic childhood and credulous teenage values on one hand and the shock of war and the horrific wounding he suffered on the other.

Although the memoir starts with the moment of Kovic's wounding, he does not address the traumatic effect of this injury until later in the text, when he realizes the full impact of his loss of sexual function and its connection to the patriotic ideology that sent men to Vietnam in the first place. To describe this trauma, Kovic must turn to metaphor:

> They have taken it, they have robbed it, my penis will never get hard anymore . . . I never dreamed that this could possibly happen, that this part of me . . . has gone, has suddenly disappeared. Gone. And it is gone for America . . . . I have given my dead swinging dick for democracy. . . . It is gone and numb, lost somewhere out there by the river where the artillery is screaming in. Oh God oh God I want it back! I gave it for the whole country. I gave it for every one of them. Yes, I gave my dead dick for John Wayne and Howdy Doody, for Castiglia [his friend who died in Vietnam] and Sparky the Barber. (85–6)

In this excerpt, two experiences of trauma are described: the actual moment of injury and Kovic's discovery of his loss of sexual function. To articulate both experiences, he dramatizes discovering the loss of sexual function ("my penis will never get hard anymore") by locating his bodily damage in Vietnam ("lost somewhere out there by the river") and bringing the metaphoric loss of his penis in Vietnam together with his present traumatic experiences at home. It is important to recognize that the loss of penis is described metaphorically: rather than refer to the actual injury that caused his impotence (a bullet in his spine), he fictionalizes damage he did not literally sustain (the severing of his penis, flung into the river) in order to dramatize the retelling of both traumatic experiences (the injury and discovering his impotence).

Later in the text when his leg is threatened with amputation, he fights to ensure that the metaphoric fate that befell his penis will not literally befall his leg. Even though (like his penis) his leg is "numb and dead," he wants to retain it because (unlike his penis) it "still means something to me. It is still mine" (100). His leg is important, in part, because he understands the political value of his broken body: "I could see this thing—this body I had trained so hard to be strong and quick, this body I now dragged around with me like an empty corpse—was to mean much more than I had ever realized. . . . Yes, let them get a look at me. Let them be reminded of what they'd done when they'd sent my generation off to war. One look would be enough—worth more than a thousand speeches" (114). Even though he compares it to a corpse, Kovic knows that the political efficacy of his body relies, ironically, on the visibility of his "lost," withered legs on the one hand and the invisibility of his penis—so ceremoniously discarded previously in the text—on the other. Even though his legs do not function, he would be admitting defeat to allow their amputation after working so hard and so long to keep them. As a spokesman for VVAW, Kovic foregrounds his broken body as an authoritative symbol that speaks out against the war in remarkably similar ways to John Kerry's speech to the Senate Foreign Relations Committee that opened this chapter.

In *Born on the Fourth of July*, Kovic's traumatized body becomes a cogent antiwar symbol. Interruptions in the narrative, however, appear to complicate the resolution Kovic reaches with his damaged form. The memoir opens with his wounding and closes with a full confession regarding his accidental shooting of a young corporal from Georgia. Until this confession, Kovic models his process of repression, denial, and numbing by having fragments of memories of the shooting interrupt the text in many places. In statements that often are never elaborated and seem misplaced, the memory of the corporal's death emerges in comments like: "I think the war has made me a little mad—the dead corporal from Georgia . . ." (28); "the dead corporal from Georgia and all the other crazy things" (32); "I am dreaming too often of the dead corporal" (98); "the dead corporal was finally catching up with me" (122). In one of several stream of consciousness passages in the memoir, Kovic progresses quickly through a series of emotional responses to the corporal's shooting that range from justifying his death ("he probably hated niggers" [131]), pleading for him to be alive again, and finally to confession. Kovic's memoir presents how traumatic repetition disrupts narrative but also, as importantly, how admitting to guilt can help him come to terms with the trauma. In the memoir's progression, only after Kovic addresses his wounding in metaphorical terms does he begin to process the guilt he feels about killing the corporal. Bringing his body memories into language—letting the metaphors testify to his experience—appears to animate his guilt.

However, this positive progression, coming to terms with trauma and guilt, is repeatedly counteracted in the text's narrative structure. Unlike the last scene of Oliver Stone's filmic adaptation of the memoir, when loved ones and supporters surround Kovic as he makes his way onto the stage at the 1976 Democratic Convention, a pivotal culmination to his successful career as an antiwar activist, the book ends where it starts: at his moment of wounding. In fact, the book presents two conclusions. The first ends with the moment of wounding, of which Kovic says, "All I could feel was the worthlessness of dying right here in this place at this moment for nothing" (170). After this denouement, which brings Kovic back to the beginning of the memoir, he adds a stream of consciousness epilogue about a 1950s backyard that ends, "It was all sort of easy. It had all come and gone" (172). By returning to this pre-war idyllic scene, Kovic reconstructs a different memory of the past, but coming at the end of a confessional memoir about wounding, killing, and guilt, the reader knows this memory is a fallacy. His nonchalance masks the wounds and traumas that continue to disrupt the memoir and his life narrative.

In *Dispatches*, Michael Herr's control over the text also is in tension with the way traumatic recall disrupts the narrative. Published one year after *Born on the Fourth of July* and two years after the metaphorically named "fall" of Saigon, *Dispatches* is often recognized as one of the most prominent works on the Vietnam War. This accolade emerged partly because, in this work, Herr skillfully blends experimental narrative structure with "grunt" language in order to graphically simulate the chaos and complexity of the war. In one example from the first chapter, "Breathing In," Herr intersperses words from three songs—Johnny Cash's "Ring of Fire," Nitty Gritty Dirt Band's "Up on Wolverton Mountain," and Bobby Bare's "Miller's Cave"—with a stream of consciousness passage on lacking sleep and keeping the company of "strungout rednecks" while he waits for a chopper ride to the next assignment (13). Song lyrics juxtapose with scene description—with reference to the first song, perhaps "Ring of Fire" played on a radio somewhere as Herr tried to sleep, waiting for the chopper; or perhaps the lyrics, the burning ring of fire, describe how he feels, trapped with grunts who are "wound too tight," waiting for combat action and ready to combust at any moment. The environment is like purgatory and the sensation is heightened anticipation; the staccato writing, intertextuality, and colloquial language epitomize *Dispatches*.

As he retells it in *Dispatches*, Herr doubted his own journalistic role in Vietnam, being reminded of this doubt every day when inevitably someone would ask him what he was doing there. At one point, Herr admits he never belonged in the jungle (10), and, in fact, he tells much of his narrative from the perspective of the air as choppers whisk him in and out of hot spots. Despite being disconnected from the "dead ground" of Vietnam (4), where the grunts are, Herr uses experimental techniques to establish his membership with a community of soldiers and to depict his time in Vietnam in dramatic or glamorous ways; in effect, Herr portrays his experiences in Vietnam by metaphorically constructing himself as a soldier.

Herr watched the camaraderie between grunts but as a journalist always felt like an outsider, a feeling of alienation symbolized by the juxtaposition of the foot soldiers in the jungle with Herr always in a helicopter. Yet his desire to feel what the grunts felt underpins the entire work. Sometimes, he suggests his experiences were aligned with those of the grunts: when he talks of "[y]ears of thinking this or that about what happens to you when you pursue a fantasy until it becomes experience, and then afterward you can't handle the experience" (68), he models the clichéd dream of young boys who want to go to war. At other moments he adamantly marks the distance between the soldiers and himself: "I stood as close to them as I could without actually being one of them, and then I stood as far back as I could without leaving the planet" (67). Clearly, Herr is both attracted to and repulsed by the war and the grunts fighting it, but always he wants to understand, to retell, and to feel their experiences.

Also blurring the distinction between his own experience and that of the grunts is Herr's experimental blending of fact and fiction into a new journalism style neologized by Norman Mailer as "faction." Susan Jeffords observes how Herr brings fragmented "dispatches" together into one narrative in a way that "creates the appearance of a whole as if these disparate pieces all fit together as a unit" (25). Implicit in her comment is a criticism that Herr, by gathering fragmented experiences and stories into the unity of *Dispatches*, lords his authority over various perspectives on the war and appears to give the war a level of coherence it did not have. Jeffords is correct to critique any attempts to portray coherence when it was clearly lacking, but because *Dispatches* prides itself and its presentation of Vietnam as incoherent and fragmented, by gathering his daily reports into one unit, I suggest Herr creates not the façade of coherence but a text that foregrounds its technique of combining disjointed narrative fragments of experience and attempts to create understanding and meaning. Indeed, writing in a period when facts of the war were deliberately hidden from the public and from ordinary soldiers, when in-country journalists termed the daily military briefings "The Five O'clock Follies," Herr would claim his experimental faction represents the war more truthfully than writing that claims to be factual.

To connect with the soldier community, Herr retells his war experience using combat metaphors. Reflecting on his time in Vietnam, Herr describes a recurring memory: "[o]ne night, like a piece of shrapnel that takes years to work its way out, I dreamed I saw a field that was crowded with dead" (68–9). Without the simile "like a piece of shrapnel," this sentence could just refer to a dream that happened "one night," an anomalous nightmare without significance. However, the shrapnel image, which indicates the dream takes "years to work its way out," suggests a difficult recurring nightmare. In the contrast between "one night" and "like a piece of shrapnel that takes years to work its way out," hints of traumatic experience emerge. The shrapnel conveys unresolved traumatic recall that will create fresh tears and wounds each time it occurs. As a simile that helps us understand Herr's experience, shrapnel conveys both repressed memory and its possible assimilation: the meaning of Herr's dream—like shrapnel—comes slowly to consciousness (psychologically) or to the surface (physically), suggesting it might take years to comprehend. And yet, pieces of shrapnel often do work their way to the surface of the skin, sometimes over a period of many years; thus the image may imply that Herr eventually does at least accept, if not fully understand, the dream's meaning.

Later in the book, Herr reflects on the lives of fellow correspondents after Vietnam: "some fell into bureaus in Chicago or Hong Kong or Bangkok, coming to miss the life [in Vietnam] so acutely (some of us) that we understood what amputees went through when they sensed movement in the fingers or toes of limbs lost months before" (244). On first reading, Herr seems to be mourning the loss of his lifestyle in Vietnam, but this impression is quickly complicated by the comment that only "some of us" felt this loss. The parenthetical aside simultaneously suggests and denies his own feelings, making it unclear if he is including himself in the designation "some." Yet at the heart of his ambiguous expression of loss lies a simile connecting it with the physiological sensations that follow amputation. This parallel between experiential and bodily loss makes Herr's memory of Vietnam visceral and calls attention to the process of memory itself: the meshing of the amputated limb and terminated tour of Vietnam highlights two kinds of memory—one habitual, the other psychological. Amputees experience the phantom limb sensation because their brains are "hard wired" into sensing that the limb is there, but this physical explanation alone does not explain the additional psychological loss of Vietnam that Herr describes.[3] Physically, Herr describes an experience of war that is gone forever; the memory, part habitual part traumatic, continues to trick the body into thinking that it is still in Vietnam and still at war. Psychologically and emotionally, Herr and his colleagues clearly sense the loss of a conflicted lifestyle to which they had become accustomed in Vietnam.

By using "dreams like shrapnel" and "lost experience like lost limbs," Herr connects his own memories with the physical experience of the war wounded. Describing an incident when he believed he had been injured, Herr quickly compares it to combat injury: "some hot stinking metal had been put into my mouth, I thought I tasted brains there sizzling on the end of my tongue, and the kid was fumbling for his canteen and looking really scared, pale, near tears, his voice shaking" (31). But, as the narrative eventually reveals, the grunt's scared appearance is not because Herr sustained a combat injury (in fact, he fell and the soldier accidentally kicked him in the face) but because he's embarrassed that he kicked a journalist. In this instance, Herr converts an incident that illustrates the distance between him and the grunts into one that aligns him with them. By using metaphors of wounding to retell his traumatic nightmares and imagining stories of physical wounding, Herr creates privileged access to the grunt community in the text in a way that has been denied him in the jungles of Vietnam or in the air above them.

One consequence of performing traumatic experience is that Herr, by asserting his membership in the grunt community, constructs a masculinized soldier identity in the text, an identity often shaped, as David Morgan suggests in "Theater of War," by the relationship between hegemonic masculinity, men's trained bodies, legitimated violence, and individual heroism. But the extent to which this construct challenges or undermines this identity is complicated by Herr's rhetorical choices. On one hand, describing his trauma through association with the war wounded reaffirms a hegemonic notion of heroicized masculine identity. But on the other hand, one of the injuries he imagines—amputation—demands an alternative conception of heroism. As Michael Bibby and John Kerry suggest, the mutilated body was a counter image to the military's impenetrable body of the male soldier; in addition, those who foregrounded their wounded bodies were, in effect, signaling their disgust at being involved in a war they felt was an abomination. Thus, Herr's imaginary wounds express a paradox: by wounding himself, he chooses to become a metaphoric soldier, creating *a priori* an identity that unquestioningly supports service to his country; however, by foregrounding the wounding, his (metaphorically) mutilated soldier body has the potential to symbolize opposition to the war.

Herr appropriates physical injury that he did not sustain to assert his affiliation with a community of physically and/ or psychically traumatized veterans. The slippage between these two ways of identifying—as with all other blurring of binaries in *Dispatches* (fact/ fiction, journalist/ grunt, physical/ psychic trauma, Vietnam/ America)—illustrates how Herr uses narrative techniques less to represent the war than to reconstruct it. And in order to simulate the experience of war, he needs to do more than tell the grunts' stories—he needs to be one of them. Herr reconstructs the war for at least two reasons: to share with his readers the traumatic experiences of soldiers and to align the journalistic experience of war with that of the grunts' war experiences. By using metaphors to align experiences, Herr presents himself as a metaphoric soldier, but the scheme also allows his readers to understand the cognitive, visceral, and emotional experience of war.

Herr's and Kovic's memoirs epitomize the first stage of Vietnam veterans' memoirs—those written during or immediately after the war that struggled to represent as yet unassimilated memories of their experience. The texts are unresolved, immediate, and visceral and represent the character fully immersed in the war. Julia Kristeva reminds us that wounding is a "violation of the seal of the surface of the body that, through trauma, destabilizes the subject" (*The Powers of Horror* 53). Metaphors of wounding in these memoirs depict the physically violated, psychologically destabilized subject, in short, traumatized because of the war. Writing trauma through memoir shows the writer's attempts to reconstruct his subjectivity, not to become "impenetrable" but to begin healing.

In Herr's and Kovic's works, a sense of urgency exists: their stories must be told and their bodies must speak for them. John Balaban's and Tim O'Brien's memoirs focus more on contemplating and complicating what it means to remember the war through writing, and they are more self-conscious in discussing the relationship between remembering and retelling. All four memoirists have as one of their ultimate goals the desire to retell their experiences viscerally for the benefit of the readers in order to, as O'Brien says, make them "feel what I felt" (*The Things They Carried* 178), and all four writers use metaphors to bring bodily trauma into language. But in Balaban's and O'Brien's works the body is written into the memoirs for somewhat different purposes, not just to promote self-healing but also to bear witness to the suffering of others.

WITNESSING

It could be suggested that Balaban and O'Brien experienced two different wars. Balaban spent two years in Vietnam as a conscientious objector during which time he worked for an organization that sought overseas medical aid for war-injured children. O'Brien, in contrast, served as a foot soldier in Quang Ngai province, close to Danang. In the sections examined here, Balaban bears witness to the bodies of Vietnamese whereas O'Brien witnesses the death of a fellow soldier. Their works are as much about describing the physical wounding of others as they are about finding the language to effectively bear witness; to that end, the importance of the authors' own physical experiences, the importance of their bodies, is lessened. Nevertheless, writing of and through the bodies of others, both writers also necessarily explore their own traumas, address their own guilt about participating in war, and confront anxieties about getting the story right.

In *Remembering Heaven's Face: A Story of Rescue in Wartime Vietnam*, John Balaban is the cautious hero of his own memoir, a conscientious objector who chose to spend his two years of alternative service in Vietnam. Reflecting on this choice in the first section of the memoir, Balaban recalls his naïve desire "not to bear arms but to bear witness" (17). In the memoir as a whole, Balaban seems to ignore his own woundings—his psychological and physical discomfort—in order to bear witness to the wounded bodies of Vietnamese children. As a fluent speaker of Vietnamese, a noncombatant in Vietnam, and a student of Vietnamese history and culture, Balaban gives his readers more access to the experiences of ordinary Vietnamese than we get in most writings of American combat veterans. But throughout his time in Vietnam, as it unfolds in the memoir, Balaban realizes all of his experiences are useless if he cannot find the language to truthfully and effectively bear witness to what he sees there. Only by struggling to tell the stories of injured Vietnamese children does Balaban become aware of the limitations of bearing witness, of his own difficulties dealing with the incomprehensible nature of what he witnesses, and of the failure of language to express the incomprehensible.

In one section of *Remembering Heaven's Face,* at a point when Balaban starts to realize these limitations, two testimonies coexist: the story of Balaban's experiences while working for The Committee of Responsibility to Save War-Burned and War-Injured Children (COR), a U.S.-based organization responsible for identifying at risk war-wounded Vietnamese children who required medical treatment not available in Vietnam, and the medical testimonies of these injured children as recorded by COR. Initially, Balaban simply reproduces the medical testimonies in their original form, as clinical case biographies written by a COR doctor. In the case biography of Huynh Van Tien, for example, an alleged child member of the Viet Minh who was wounded by an M-16 rifle during the Tet Offensive, Dr. Richard Bowers strives for objectivity: "On the 4th of February his abdomen was explored and he was found to have a large retroperitoneal hematoma" (148). Because the American authorities refused to evacuate Huynh due to his Viet Cong connection, reprinting the objective biography serves a political purpose for Balaban: he presents the refusal as an illustration of the authorities' double standard—agreeing to help the wounded but not if they are perceived to be the enemy. The medical testimony's objective style also confirms for Balaban the necessary emotional distance for his work, and the content conveys the urgent need for treatment. The author notes that he was so concerned with the immediacy of the crises in Vietnam he had to set aside his own personal feelings: "[w]hen I could prepare myself, I could look at anything. And when I considered that my discomforts were a necessary part of the rescue, they seemed small and bearable" (189). Yet Balaban comes to realize that because these testimonies omit both the children's and the COR workers' responses to the injuries, they fail to evoke a visceral response from his own readers— necessary, he feels, to provoke action.

So when the author has to write case biographies himself, the narratives become more subjective. When Edward Kennedy's Senate Subcommittee on Refugees, Escapees, and Civilian Casualties invites him to prepare testimony on civilian casualties because, as he describes it, he is "an expert in Vietnamese misery" (203), Balaban describes six cases in more detail. Here is an excerpt from one of them:

> Case 75: A 12-year old boy found by the roadside near Saigon with his hands destroyed and both eyes and ears perforated by grenade fragments from a blast of unknown origin. He cannot speak, see, or hear. No one knows where his family is. Until our discovery of and interest in this boy, he had been chained to a bed in a large orphanage near Saigon. Although there are two Vietnamese ophthalmologists in Saigon, the child had never been referred to them. (205)

In comparison with the biographies produced by the doctor, Balaban's version is much less clinical, although, of course, Balaban writes this testimony for a different purpose than Bowers writes Tien's, as he wishes to provoke Ted Kennedy's Senate Subcommittee to action, to save the lives of war-injured Vietnamese children. Both testimonies express uncertainty about how wounds were inflicted, but Balaban conveys additional doubt regarding the whereabouts of the boy's family. Even here, Balaban realizes his subjectivity does not go far enough, and the comments he adds when writing the memoir illustrate the limitations both of the prepared testimony for Kennedy's committee and of bearing witness more generally:

> Even as I typed these awful bios on our office's ancient Royal, I knew I wasn't saying enough. I wanted to say what it *felt* like to encounter the first boy, who was dying of malnutrition because he couldn't get enough food through the small, hard, jawless hole that was now his mouth as he lay on a floor in the orphanage spooning in gruel, holding a hand mirror to see where it was going, because he didn't have any feeling there anymore. What it *felt* like to unlock the second boy from his bedstead

under the hateful glare of an evil and stupid Vietnamese Catholic nun
who had chained him there because she had thought him crazy. . . . I
wanted my words, like the infections raging in that boy's ears, to inflict
pain on any American who heard them. (205–6)

The first testimony, written for Kennedy's committee, records that one boy
had been "chained to a bed in a large orphanage near Saigon" while these
additional comments, which create a new testimony, reveal how the author
had to "unlock the boy;" Balaban's role clearly shifts from observer to partici-
pant. Describing the nun as "evil" and "stupid" with a "hateful glare," Balaban can no longer remain detached from or unemotional about what he is
witnessing. By placing these two testimonies together, Balaban foregrounds
the failure of the medical biography as testimony as well as the limitations of
his own testimony to the subcommittee.

His comments—"I wanted to say what it felt like" to "encounter
the first boy;" "what it felt like to unlock the second boy;" and "I wanted
my words, like the infections raging in that boy's ears, to inflict pain on
any American who heard them"—express his desire to have the readers of
the testimony experience the equivalent of both the injured boy's physical
pain and the author's outrage. Balaban wants his testimony to speak of the
body of the Vietnamese boy, to sear the minds of his readers and be felt in
their own bodies. Just as Balaban realized that the medical testimony failed
because it did not affect a visceral response in the reader, here he realizes his
testimony to the committee failed because it did not go far enough in presenting his own subjectivity, his own physical and psychological response to
what he witnessed.

As the dramatic present of the memoir shifts from the war period to
Balaban's contemporary life, the author also transitions from foregrounding
the immediacy of witnessing to contemplating the long-term effects of it.
Although this transition underpins the memoir's entire progression, Balaban
only addresses it self-consciously at one point:

Often enough over the years, I have found myself at a window with tears
in my eyes as I suddenly, without expectation, have been greeted by the
naked nine-year-old thrashing on the stainless-steel operating table with
his eardrums blown; often images from my COR days come floating
up on mental backwaters. . . . But somehow, if I believed at all in the
existence of PTS, I thought of it as something that applied to GIs, like
shellshock or battle fatigue. . . . But I hadn't [thought I'd been damaged by Vietnam]. I thought all that flashback stuff was soap opera and

whining. And now, twenty years after these events, I can't imagine how
I could ever have thought I could look on that carnage of children and
not be hurt forever by what I saw. (283)

Here is the first moment in Balaban's memoir when he finally presents the
realization that bearing witness to war-injured children has hurt him. And
only here, finally, does Balaban bear witness to his own physical and emotional experiences in Vietnam, admitting that what he has been experiencing
over the past twenty years could be post-traumatic stress disorder.

However, before this admission, he experiences a moment one morning, before he walks to campus to teach an English class, when his traumatic
memory comes to the fore; not yet fully cognizant of this trauma, he describes
it through metaphor: "One morning . . . I was having breakfast and reading
The New York Times . . . when I read on the fifth or sixth page that the village of Duc Duc had been caught in a crossfire and burned. . . . With my
thoughts sparking like tracers, I finished breakfast, walked up onto campus,
and taught my grammar class. . . . All the while, I thought I would explode
with grief" (218). As a conscientious objector, a man who refused to take
up arms, Balaban's war metaphors—"thoughts sparking like tracers," feeling
like he would "explode with grief"—are extremely powerful. While of course
the metaphors graphically express his immediate response to this news item,
the passage could also be read as testimony to the delayed impact of trauma
after he comes home from the war, his shock at the news of the destruction
of Duc Duc illustrating residues of deep memories—memories that he feels
in his body but has not yet been able to put into language—from his time
in Vietnam. In this way, the news item becomes a "trigger," both literally
and metaphorically, that brings his deep memories to the surface. In addition, the immediacy evoked by the image of "thoughts sparking like tracers"
and "explod[ing] with grief" seems to mimic the way panic is experienced
physiologically (racing thoughts like racing pulse) and how trauma comes to
consciousness (abruptly, in fragments, and without preparation).

Balaban's choice to place this passage before he admits or realizes that
he may have suffered PTSD is particularly significant. The metaphors help
him describe a transitional and cathartic moment when he recognizes the
emotional impact of the war but before he fully understands those emotions
or can completely explicate them in language. Thus, the metaphors work
to render Balaban's body memories tellable. Metaphors work as a conduit
between Balaban's memories of his traumatic experiences and his language,
helping him bring his trauma to consciousness and enabling him, at a later
point in the memoir, to name his experience as PTSD. Like Kovic, whose

metaphors surface before he animates his guilt, Balaban's metaphors emerge before he names and claims his trauma.

The metaphoric images of tracers and explosions also help Balaban establish lines of communication, even camaraderie, with other traumatized veterans. This connection is established through the vehicle and tenor of the metaphor: the specific vehicle, "sparking like tracers," is Balaban's own way of describing his thoughts, but the combat theme of the vehicle, tracers, establishes shared understanding between him and other veterans. While specific details of Balaban's thoughts, the tenor of the metaphor, are unique to him, the metaphoric vehicle establishes a connection between Balaban, a conscientious objector, and any combat veteran whose memories of traumatic experience have later been awakened by a seemingly pedestrian or even unrelated trigger.

In Herr's and Kovic's memoirs, the body's knowledge of war and wounding is central. In *Dispatches*, physical wounding establishes Herr as metaphoric soldier; in *Born on the Fourth of July*, the paralyzed body is a cogent antiwar symbol; and in *Remembering Heaven's Face*, the body's knowledge of war is also central, first in the bodies of Vietnamese children and later in the author's own body. Perhaps because Balaban was a conscientious objector, his "fleshly knowledge" of war, to use Lifton's term, is not as important to him as it is for combat veterans. But Balaban uses the mutilated bodies of Vietnamese children in the same way that GI war resisters used their own bodies—as antiwar symbols that challenge American military leaders' willingness to sacrifice the lives of civilians for increased body counts. Despite foregrounding the experiences of others, Balaban comes to realize, reluctantly and belatedly, that he experienced trauma, which previously he thought could only be experienced by combat soldiers.

One of the key differences between Tim O'Brien's *The Things They Carried* and the memoirs by Herr, Kovic, and Balaban is that while the first three writers use metaphor at certain moments to express specific traumatic experiences, in O'Brien's writing the entire work becomes metaphor. In "How to Tell a True War Story" specifically, songs and sunlight signify and trigger traumatic war memory, war stories are stories about love, and "War Story" itself functions as a metaphor of O'Brien's "ineffaceable trauma" (Heberle 193) at witnessing the death of a fellow soldier. At each level of metaphor, challenges to the meaning of the first element (songs and sunlight, war stories, "War Story") illuminate a new understanding of the second (memory, love, trauma and witnessing).

The Things They Carried is a collection of interconnected stories related to O'Brien's rotation in Vietnam and his attempts to write about it twenty years later. Often, elements introduced in one story later become the focus of another; sometimes passages and ideas in one place are repeated verbatim elsewhere. Like all works examined here, *The Things They Carried* demonstrates the structure of active memory, how memories are continually shaped and reshaped into new ones. *The Things They Carried* uses the techniques of literary nonfiction—self-reflectivity, claiming to present the truth, blurring the distinction between narrator and author, and so on—to construct a fictional story that tells, it grandly claims, the truth of war and of human emotion. Yet O'Brien, even as he clearly uses nonfictional elements, claims in the strongest terms that *The Things They Carried* is fiction. It would be more accurate, therefore, while acknowledging the limitations of labeling, to define the work as metafiction (Calloway 1995), as a work that, by writing about the process of writing, self-consciously critiques the clichéd war story, claiming validity by suggesting that truth can only be found in fiction while protecting itself from complaints of inaccuracy by refusing to acknowledge its nonfictionality.

"How to Tell a True War Story" combines several attempts to tell the story of Curt Lemon's death with the narrator's self-reflective commentary on how "best" to tell a "true war story," ultimately revealing that the whole story is a metaphor that expresses O'Brien's own traumatic recall. In ways similar to *Remembering Heaven's Face*, the narrator tries repeatedly to bear witness to physical injury (in this case, the actual moment of Lemon's death), calling attention to how language inevitably fails to portray the experience of trauma in the body. The first time we come across Lemon in this story he is unnamed and discussed only because his buddy, Rat Kiley, is writing a letter to Lemon's sister explaining her brother's death. A couple of pages later the narrator identifies the subject of the letter: "The dead guy's name was Curt Lemon" (68). This is the first telling of Lemon's death:

> They were just goofing. There was a noise, I suppose, which must've been the detonator, so I glanced behind me and watched Lemon step from the shade into bright sunlight. His face was suddenly brown and shining. A handsome kid, really. Sharp gray eyes, lean and narrow-waisted, and when he died it was almost beautiful, the way the sunlight came around him and lifted him up and sucked him high into a tree full of moss and vines and white blossoms. (70)

In this first telling, the speaker cannot be certain about his other sensory memories, like the noise, and all he can remember and describe are the visual memory of Lemon's movement from shade into sunlight and some specific details about the physical appearance of Lemon and the tree into which his body is blown. With the other sensory elements inaccessible, the traumatic experience of witnessing Lemon's death returns to the speaker as a fragmented visual memory. The sunlight here functions like the flash of a camera might, illuminating a single freeze-frame image of Lemon, capturing and preserving in the speaker's mind a "flashbulb memory," an incomplete memory that "suggest[s] surprise, an indiscriminate illumination, and brevity" (Brown and Kulik 24).

Starting this first telling with "[i]t's hard to tell you what happened next" (70), the speaker is hesitant and cautious yet ultimately convinced this visual memory does not adequately or truthfully tell the story of Lemon's death in a satisfactory way. So he tries again. Determining that a "true war story, if truly told, makes the stomach believe" (78), the speaker then attempts his second telling of Lemon's death: "We crossed the river and marched west into the mountains. On the third day, Curt Lemon stepped on a booby-trapped 105 round. He was playing catch with Rat Kiley, laughing, and then he was dead. The trees were thick; it took nearly an hour to cut an LZ for the dustoff" (78). This same death, differently told, is now much more objective; like Balaban's testimony to the Senate Subcommittee, it is based on the speaker denying his own response to what he witnesses. But the story fails as a true war story because it contradicts the speaker's standards; it does not "make the stomach believe." This second version also fails because it tries to assert definitively that these are the facts, even as the speaker becomes increasingly uncertain about his ability to know the facts. Thus, he decides that "in a true war story nothing is ever absolutely true" and that often "there is not even a point, or else the point doesn't hit you until twenty years later" (82). After asking "Christ, what's the *point?*," the speaker offers up the third telling:

> This one wakes me up.
> In the mountains that day, I watched Lemon turn sideways. He laughed and said something to Rat Kiley. Then he took a peculiar half step, moving from shade into bright sunlight, and the booby-trapped 105 round blew him into a tree. The parts were just hanging there, so Dave Jensen and I were ordered to shinny up and peel him off. I remember the white bone of an arm. I remember pieces of skin and something wet and yellow that must've been the intestines. The gore was horrible, and stays with me. But what wakes me up twenty years later is Dave Jensen singing "Lemon Tree" as we threw down the parts. (82–3)

Here the speaker builds on elements that appear in the first and second tellings. The narrative adds three significant new aspects, however: direct involvement of the speaker with the body (Heberle 194), attention to details of the mutilated body, and a self-conscious comment about how the memory continues to have an impact on the speaker twenty years later. This memory, no longer simply visual or objective, now includes the auditory sense of music and the tactile wetness of Lemon's intestines. Most importantly, the speaker identifies the song, not Lemon's body parts or anything else from the event, as what wakes him up. The song makes the speaker aware of his own trauma—like Herr, he is woken up at night—and this emphasis on a more ephemeral aspect of Lemon's death starts to get at the heart of what is a true story.

The song works similarly to the shrapnel of Herr's story as a vehicle for bringing the speaker's buried memories to consciousness. But the choice of image, song as opposed to shrapnel, has markedly different implications. While the shrapnel image brings us right into combat, the pretty song presents the antithesis of violence and war and associates the war memory with more peaceful times. This association could be a coping mechanism for the speaker as he remembers this moment by deflecting it through the song, but it also calls attention to Jensen's ironic sense of humor, singing "Lemon Tree" as he pulls Lemon from the tree. But while the song helps the speaker explain how Lemon's death continues to impact his memory, it still fails to fully describe the moment of death. So the speaker returns to the image of Lemon's body in sunlight and, with this image at the fore, he tries one last time to retell Lemon's death:

> Twenty years later, I can still see the sunlight on Lemon's face. I can see him turning, looking back at Rat Kiley, then he laughed and took that curious half step from shade into sunlight, his face suddenly brown and shining, and when his foot touched down, in that instant, he must've thought it was the sunlight that was killing him. It was not the sunlight. It was a rigged 105 round. But if I could ever get the story right, how the sun seemed to gather round him and pick him up and lift him high into a tree, if I could somehow re-create the fatal whiteness of that light, the quick glare, the obvious cause and effect, then you would believe the last thing Curt Lemon believed, which for him must've been the final truth. (84)

This image of Lemon in sunlight helps the speaker convey his death most truthfully—not the way his body was blown asunder or his body parts scattered in the tree but, in fact, the last moment of Lemon's life. The change of light captures the "story truth" of Lemon's death. The speaker is not suggesting that the sunlight killed Lemon—he adamantly asserts a rigged 105 round did that—but that Lemon must have surely believed the sunlight was killing him.

This final telling is true, according to the speaker, because a true war story "is never about war. It's about sunlight. . . . It's about love and memory. It's about sorrow" (85). A true war story does not need to capture the visual fragment or recount the obvious facts of war, but it must evoke the visceral experience of it, and it should relate to experiences noncombatants can understand. In "War Story," the recognizable, everyday symbol of sunlight is used as a metaphor to describe the sensory and traumatic experiences of war; the sunlight is a trope for death that makes it simultaneously sorrowful and beautiful. In addition, the entire story, which O'Brien admits is fictional, becomes metaphor for the experience of war and its analogous experiences of love, memory, and sorrow, making the narrative universal in its appeal. In other words, "War Story" is itself a metaphor of how memory works through association and metaphor.

O'Brien is able to represent trauma and its consequences without merely retelling his own personal experiences (Heberle 193). Nevertheless, while the goal of recreating the moment of Lemon's death is to make the reader believe the last thing Curt Lemon believed, the whole story clearly is told through the lens of O'Brien's, or at least the narrators', own traumatic recall. His trauma intrudes in the text in moments of uncertainty and in repetition, in a kind of structural stuttering as the author starts the story over and over again, trying to get it right.[4] Thus, even as O'Brien strives to write himself out of the story of Lemon's death, his trauma is revealed in the narrative structure as well as his admission that twenty years later he still sees the sunlight on Lemon's body and still hears "Lemon Tree." Ultimately, the sunlight and "Lemon Tree" are metaphors that bring O'Brien's traumas into language, but they also are screen memories—memories, in Freud's terms, that simultaneously relate to and displace other more painful memories that have been suppressed ("Screen Memories" 301–322)—that mask the narrator's memories associated with the trauma of Lemon's death.

In Balaban's and O'Brien's memoirs, written approximately fifteen years after the end of the war, representations of their war experiences are complex and reflective. For both authors, temporal distance facilitates self-critical commentary on their ability to get the story right. Both works are less concerned with capturing the immediacy of the war and more invested in representing, finally, how to write their memories truthfully. Both O'Brien and Balaban are concerned with broadening access to the metaphors of war:

O'Brien universalizes the lessons of war to make "true war stories" speak about human conditions—sorrow, love, and memory—to which even those who have never experienced combat can relate. Balaban uses war-themed metaphors to broaden the definition of who can claim to be a veteran and who can suffer from post-traumatic stress. Both authors minimize their own bodily experiences in order to bear witness to the physical injury of others, either Vietnamese children or fellow soldiers. But ultimately, their bodies betray them and refuse to be silent, allowing traumatic recall to surface: Balaban felt like he would "explode with grief," while the song and sunlight bring O'Brien's trauma into the present.

Through the act of writing, memories are continually renewed and combined with new memories of and perspectives on Vietnam, the war and country. In the selections examined from these four memoirs, this renewal happens primarily within the context of the United States. But in the final section of *Remembering Heaven's Face*, Balaban writes about returning to Vietnam. By returning, his conceptions of the country and the war—as shaped by years of remembering, thinking about, and studying it—are altered and renewed. In the third section of this chapter, I examine another return visit to Vietnam—that of Bruce Weigl's, which he discusses in *The Circle of Hanh*. Most veterans realize the psychological and intellectual importance of this return journey and many prominent veteran writers, including all the writers discussed here, have been back. For many veterans, as I discuss more thoroughly in Chapter Five, the return journey offers an opportunity for recovery or closure, a chance to replace difficult or painful memories with ones that are less so. While the journey brings them back to the place where those painful memories were first formed, the temporal distance between first and return visits bespeaks a shift in attitude toward Vietnam, which, as the adage goes, is no longer a war, now a country.

RECOVERY

Nowhere is the process of understanding Vietnam as a country not a war more clearly connected to narrative structure than in *The Circle of Hanh*, the first work of nonfiction prose for Bruce Weigl, a prolific poet and translator of Vietnamese poetry. Published in 2000, the memoir recounts Weigl's journey to Vietnam in 1996 to collect his newly adopted daughter, Hanh. This journey is just one of many for Weigl, who was with the 1st Air Cavalry stationed at An Khe in 1967–68 and then became one of the first American veterans to visit north Vietnam after the war ended, first "as a curious and frightened veteran trying to find the boy I had been during the war" and "then as a writer and translator of Vietnamese poetry" (14). While the work also focuses at length on Weigl's childhood in Lorain, Ohio, an important inclusion that blends the experience of war with other elements of his life, here I look at how Vietnam works as frame and center to the text.

As its title would imply, circularity informs both the content and structure of the memoir. The book starts and ends with Weigl's return trip to Vietnam. Literally and symbolically, the memoir circles back to Vietnam as, both emotionally and spiritually, Weigl returns to the place he calls the "home of my heart." The circular motif is used in at least three ways in this memoir. First, as noted, the memoir circles back at the end of the memoir to Weigl's most recent trip to Vietnam, to his anticipation of the completion of the story's circle—the adoption of Hanh. Second, as he travels back and forth from the U.S. to Vietnam, his circling is both physical and psychological. Finally, calling attention to the writing process, Weigl lets "the story have its way" and allows it to circle "back on itself into the lives of far away people who had never stopped calling to me. It led me back to the circle of Hanh" (7). These circular motifs construct a complex geography of remembering that challenges the linear narrative format as well as perceived notions of veterans' healing process.

Unlike the other writers examined in this chapter, Weigl never directly presents his war experience in Vietnam; rather, he focuses on the "many small befores, and the one irrevocable after" (140) of his life prior and subsequent to this most pivotal event. The work discusses Weigl's tour of duty in anticipatory and retrospective ways, but it deliberately avoids placing Weigl the soldier in the dramatic present of the war. In the progression of the book, one would expect this dramatic present to occur in the chapter that follows immediately after "The Borderline," which deals with the weeks before he leaves for his tour of duty in Vietnam. However, in "Before and After," Weigl rejects this chronology, and the chapter instead jumps back and forth to his life pre- and post-Vietnam. The after is marked, in part, by sleepless nights, fearful parents, and the "need to put my life in jeopardy" by taking drugs and engaging in casual sex (154). Two understated but poignant assertions capture the contrast between his life before and after the war: "In the before we played dead in mock battle. In the after Albright liked to fuck with the dead" (146); "I came back from the after into the before, but it wasn't there anymore" (152). Both comments deny the easy categorization of life before and after, yet they do suggest how, after the war, Weigl and his comrades returned to the U.S. hardened and lost, and they suggest how Weigl's life was temporally and psychologically cleaved in two.

At the symbolic center of the book, "Before and After" denies the dramatic present of Vietnam but offers Weigl's concept of the portal instead.

Weigl suggests this is a concept only Vietnamese and those who experienced the horror of the war can fully understand: "There are portals through which other places may be entered. The Vietnamese know that. The Buddhists in Hue know that. Johnson didn't know it. McNamara, no. Nixon, not a clue. Those who fought and died in the green place knew it; those who'd managed to slip through those doors" (142). In an interview, Weigl talks of having "walked through the portal back to that place,"[5] suggesting that the portal leads to and helps facilitate his acceptance of his difficult experiences in the war. As the memoir progresses, so does the speaker's conception of the portal:

> A long time ago, I walked through one of those portals, one of those doors that have always seemed to lead me to understanding. I have difficulty remembering the order of things since that passage. Time got stupid for me. The borders between the before and the after became blurred or seemed to disappear so that I found myself caught in a swirling immediacy where everything seemed to happen at once. . . . I had done so much traveling in the world of hurt that had been my life that the boundaries we need in order to be human had vanished. I had invented new boundaries. I invented the before and the after. (122)

In this passage, as I read it, Weigl's experiences in Vietnam complicate the idea of a portal as straightforward conduit between before and after. If, prior to the war, the speaker had a simplified conception of the portal as what one passed through from a naïve before to a more enlightened after, the war destroys his belief; it also destroys his sense of time and self that he then has to invent anew. And he does this, in part, by discovering the power of words; more specifically, he constructs a memoir that presents the experience of before and after not as linear but as circular.

In another passage, Weigl further complicates the portal concept:

> I had come to know that it was only the old journeying again that I'd done all my life; that walking in and out of doors, crossing back and forth through portals that hold back the machine of time. When you pass back and forth so easily between worlds, you may see the fresh underbelly of things, and how the righteous and the wretched are one. Sometimes what is revealed fills me with horror and with dread. (155)

The portal's nonlinearity, as it "hold[s] back the machine of time," suggests not that it is passed through at various milestones in life but is, instead, like active memory that he carries with him always. Again, the portal is circular not linear; he does not pass through it from "A" to "B;" rather, he journeys back and forth, continually visiting the past and the future in the present. Passage through the portal both condenses time and space and reveals knowledge that is dreadful even as it is enlightening.

In his memoir, Weigl continually rethinks the meaning of the portal as metaphor to describe the significant experiences in his life, with the war as the absent present at the memoir's center. Like in O'Brien's "How to Tell a True War Story," this rethinking appears as a structural stutter, as Weigl tries and tries again to get the meaning right. If Weigl begins the memoir thinking of the portal as a quick and temporal transition from an unenlightened before to a mature and knowing after, he ends by seeing the portal as, like memory, always existing in the present, a geography of remembering that is physical and psychological, spatial and temporal.

If the war in Vietnam is the portal at the center of the memoir, a swirling hole consisting of memories, the country of Vietnam is the circle that holds the memories in place and gives them meaning and purpose. As metaphors, the portal and the circle appear to present the war and the country in opposition: the portal/ memories of the war are incomprehensible and irresolvable, while the circle/country represents for Weigl coherence, stability, and "home." I would argue, though, that the portal and the circle are not in tension but are, rather, mutually dependent. The hole can only be illuminated by the circle, the circle can only be filled by the hole; in practical terms, Weigl's understanding of Vietnam as a country is shaped by his experience of the war, and his knowledge of the war is informed by Vietnam's history and culture.

Of course, the hole in the middle of the narrative could be read as a traumatic one, specifically performing the period of latency between the occurrence of trauma during the war and its coming to consciousness, as Cathy Caruth would define it. In this traumatic hole, Weigl's memories of the war circulate endlessly, but while they develop they never move toward resolution or complete understanding. Weigl has made his peace with the difficult memories of his experience in Vietnam—they exist in the portal but he does not feel compelled to narrativize them fully. In addition, the omission of details of his war experience does not omit the war altogether, of course, for Weigl's theory of the portal/ circle relationship suggests he has moved toward acceptance of his memories, and that he can clearly separate Vietnam the country from Vietnam the war, even though his idea of one is clearly shaped by his knowledge of the other. Painful memories of the war exist, but for Weigl moving forward with his life means accepting not forgetting them. In this way, Weigl's own experience of trauma holds remembering and forgetting in productive, dialogic tension.

Through the work's narrative structure, its tension between the hole and the circle, Weigl presents two modes of perception that rub against each other at the border where the hole and circle intersect. At this border, two different cultures and belief systems meet. Tracing the circle, Weigl moves toward accepting his difficult memories of Vietnam in spiritual rather than physical ways. Of this acceptance, Weigl, a practicing Buddhist, marks the distinction between the two belief systems to which he has been exposed: "Western science says, 'well, you gotta put that behind you;' whereas Buddhism says, 'it's part of who you are now; make a life from that'" (*Speaking of Faith*). This understanding enables Weigl to integrate his body and mind, to blur the boundaries between his body memories of the war and his lived experience of the country; in doing so, he proposes a nonwestern theory for coming to terms with trauma that accepts rather than resolves, circles rather than progresses, and ultimately integrates the body with words rather than foregrounding or denying the body.

Heberle suggests that "true war stories are not simply about war but are fictions of traumatization that require willing listeners as well as skillful storytellers" (192). All the metaphors created by these writers—lost penis, dreams like shrapnel, lost experience like lost limbs, sparking thoughts like tracers, exploding grief, songs and sunlight, portal and circle—are attempts by them to come to terms with their war experiences and to bring their difficult traumas into language, skillfully confessing and testifying to their listeners, the readers. The memoirs progress from images of the body and combat, to images of the everyday, to images that convey spirituality and acceptance. In this progression, we see how memories of the war are continually renewed and reshaped as veterans move toward some semblance of reconciliation with their traumas. Veterans' memoirs are personal and public sites of memory; they simultaneously perform the experience of traumatic numbing and repetition while they also challenge superficial myths of the war in cultural memory through their sustained examination of guilt and complicity. If memories bring the past into the present, then stories of memories, such as those in memoirs, carry the past and present into the future. As Tim O'Brien tells us: "Stories are for eternity, when memory is erased, when there is nothing to remember except the story" (*The Things They Carried* 38).

In many ways, memoirs complicate the teleology proposed in the progression of chapters in this work: as memorializing moves away from the National Mall, these practices become simultaneously more democratic and routinized even as the meanings the practices produce are increasingly ahistorical and homogeneous. Yet, the memoir form confirms larger trends in contemporary memorializing. Through their sustained examination of personal experience in and responsibility for the war, memoirs vacillate between historical amnesia and obsession with the past; in addition, imbued with trauma, individual, and cultural memories, they illustrate the symbiotic relationships between them. By writing of and through the traumatized body, memoirs confirm the individualization and materiality of memory. And, of course, as cultural products that circulate in the literary marketplace, they are commodities. But even as the memoirs I examine here trouble the rewriting of war narratives for patriotic ends, like the replica walls and museums I examine in the chapters that follow, their goals are always to write the truth of their experience in Vietnam, as they perceive it, and to reproduce the war viscerally.

Chapter Three

Moving Walls

Bobbie Ann Mason's novel *In Country* ends with a journey to Washington, D.C., to visit the National Vietnam Veterans Memorial. Eighteen years old Samantha "Sam" Hughes, her mother, and her uncle Emmett, a Vietnam veteran, drive to the Memorial to find the name of Sam's father Dwayne. When Sam first arrives at the Wall, she notes that "[i]t is massive, a black gash in a hillside, like a vein of coal exposed and then polished with polyurethane" (239). While Sam feels "as though all the names in America have been used to decorate" the Wall (245), she also complains that "the monument and the flag seem like arrogant gestures, like the country giving the finger to the dead boys, flung in this hole in the ground" (240). Mamaw Hughes expresses frustration when she climbs some steps to find her husband's name at the top part of the Wall because all she can see is her own reflection (244).

This passage from *In Country* reveals some of the Wall's elements that most often are discussed by scholars and visitors alike: the diversity of soldiers who went to Vietnam as recorded in the names of the dead; the surprise of being confronted with one's own reflection; and the recognition of an irony—namely, that this uncelebratory memorial is dug into the ground "like a giant grave [with] fifty-eight thousand bodies rotting here behind those names" (239), alongside the Washington Monument, "a big white prick" that symbolizes how the "U.S.A. goes around fucking the world" (238). As discussed in Chapter One, much scholarship has lauded the Wall's innovative design and perceived lack of political commentary, identifying it as the key site for the negotiation of U.S. public memory about the war in Vietnam. Scholars propose that then Yale undergraduate Maya Lin's design marks a watershed in public memorializing in the United States, particularly in the way its reflective black surface and descent into the earth challenge the tradition of white monumental structures that rise into the sky on the National Mall. While in fact nontraditional (or nonstatuary) memorial designs predate Lin's memorial (see Shanken; Griswold 693–696), scholars such as John Gillis suggest all public memorializing since the Vietnam War has been influenced both by the design of the Wall and by the various practices that have evolved around it, that the "Vietnam Memorial, with its wall of names, is generally agreed to represent a turning point in the history of public memory, a decisive departure from the anonymity of the Tomb of the Unknown Soldier and a growing acknowledgment that everyone now deserves equal recognition at all times in wholly accessible places" (13). Even though, as George Mosse and Thomas Laqueur among others discuss, war memorials listing the dead first emerged after World War I and have been popular since, "by aesthetic and social consensus, names are today a kind of reflexive memorial impulse."[1] Without a doubt, the Wall has become the quintessence of the dramatic and overwhelming effect of the names list. In addition, Lin's influence resonates in contemporary memorials that strive to ensure the names of all the dead are listed; as in the case of the planned 9/11 memorial, "Reflecting Absence," her influence results from her direct involvement with the design committee.

Because the Wall has such cultural resonance, many replicas of it exist in the United States, including half-size traveling and online virtual walls. I examine how, as sites of memory, these replicas decontextualize, decentralize, and democratize the memorializing practices that first evolved at the Wall. Generally, in this post-national era of commemoration, as Gillis terms it, memorializing practices are more democratic but also more routinized, learned through observation and often reduced to a routine. Conversely, the meanings generated through those practices have become ever more homogeneous and reactionary, often shaped by a politically conservative ideology; they also have become more privatized and commodified, reflecting the influence of the globalized economic market in all aspects of western society. By detaching memorializing from specific locations, these sites create new narratives of the war that are neither informed by historical fact nor reflective of the actual heterogeneous responses to the war from American citizens during and after the war and at various locations in the United States and beyond. The replicas attempt to reconstruct the experience of the Wall, to bring the encounter between memorial and visitors away from the National Mall and into the metonymic town square and the home via the computer screen. These "moving" walls, then, are portable, sensory, and affective. The replicas reinforce the perception that the Wall is the most significant site for memorializing the war in Vietnam, whether they replicate it, like The Wall That Heals or Vietnam Veterans Memorial Fund's Virtual Wall, or offer an alternative to it, like The Moving Wall or The National Vietnam Veterans Memorial Page. Yet, despite recreating the Wall experience and reinforcing its significance, the replicas, in order to establish their importance separately from the Wall, ultimately engage in various levels of critique and rejection of the national memorial. Because location is crucial to a discussion of these replicas, this chapter charts the physical movement of replicas away from the Mall—from the Last Firebase, the Prisoner of War/ Missing in Action (POW/ MIA) merchandise stands that literally and ideologically confront the Wall; to the small town visited by half-sized replicas of the Wall; to the virtual wall, available everywhere but physically rooted in no one place. The proliferation of replicas indicates, in part, extreme practices of individual memorializing as individual veterans dedicate their lives to bringing replicas to ordinary people across the country, physically or virtually. Ultimately, the replicas reveal a tension between the increasing democratization of memorializing on the one hand and, on the other, the increasing homogeneity of the meaning of the war that circulates at these replicas. The replicas also reveal both the importance of place to memorializing and the perceived dichotomies between the local and the national and the city and the suburb or the rural small town. But the mobility and accessibility of the replicas reveal how these dichotomies are in many ways arbitrary, particularly as the virtual walls blur the distinction between the local and the national by bringing the nationally significant memorial to local communities, crossing or conflating locational boundaries and challenging the idea of place as a fixed and immutable location in space and time.

Locally based memorials and wall replicas emphasize the notion of the Wall's significance as the paradigmatic site and design for memorializing the war. While the realistic statuary monument of the soldier remains very much the norm for war memorializing, many local memorials to the Vietnam War copy the more abstract features of the Wall.[2] By 1989, memorials in fourteen states across the U.S. had incorporated some of the elements first used in the Wall. All these memorials are made of reflective black granite with the names of the local dead etched into the rock and some even have angled or sloping walls that reference the Wall's dramatic shape. For example, the Des Moines, Iowa, memorial is called "A Reflection of Hope" and is made of the same imported granite as the Wall; the Codington County memorial in Watertown, South Dakota, also uses the same granite in a monument comprising three rectangular structures. Another common way these structures reference the Wall is, of course, with a list of names. However, because state memorials are built to commemorate local soldiers who died, they do not replicate exactly the Wall's function or purpose, but they do reference design elements of it. Local memorials remind citizens of the Wall, but they never replace its national significance and stature.

Local memorials exist, in part, because of the importance of physical place in the memorializing process. Group remembrances endure, Maurice Halbwachs argues, "when they have a double focus—a physical object, a material reality such as a statue, a monument, a place in space, and also a symbol, or something of spiritual significance, something shared by the group that adheres to and is superimposed upon this physical reality" (Halbwachs 204; Till 2003: 291). Places of memory, as Karen Till suggests after Doreen Massey, "far from being 'rooted' or stable, . . . are porous networks of social relations that continuously change because of the particular ways they are interconnected to (and in turn shape) other places and peoples" (2003: 297). In Pierre Nora's discussion of the material *lieux de mémoire*— sites of memory that are "concrete" and found in "spaces, gestures, images, and objects"—he differentiates between portable, topographical, and monumental *lieux*. The Tablets of the Law, the Ten Commandments, is an example of a portable *lieu*. Topographical *lieux* "owe everything to the specificity of their location and to being rooted in the ground" whereas monumental sites, in contrast, "owe their meaning to their intrinsic existence; even though their location is far from arbitrary, one could justify relocating them without altering their meaning" (22).

The importance of topographical war sites, such as Lexington Green or Gettysburg, to citizens in the United States is illustrated both by their popularity as tourist destinations and by people's efforts to preserve them, just as the importance of these types of sites to veterans is demonstrated in the large numbers who return, for example, to the World War II memorial sites of Normandy and Ypres. All U.S. locations that are places of memory to foreign wars are arbitrary—chosen through debate, availability of location, or according to tradition. With no topographical *lieux* to the Vietnam War possible in the United States, veterans instead create monumental *lieux*. Traditionally, memorials to foreign wars have been monumental, built at symbolic and sometimes arbitrary locations. (Even the setting of the National Mall on the Potomac is arbitrary—personally chosen by President Washington after fierce debates in Congress failed to reach consensus about where it should be located—though the Mall has become the nation's symbolic place of national memory.[3]) Because the tradition has been to build statuary monuments, rarely are foreign wars memorialized with portable, moveable *lieux*. World War II air shows are one exception: they bring planes used in Europe, and sometimes the aging pilots who flew them, to towns across the country to remind local citizens of their military heritage. Like World War II air shows, traveling and virtual walls are transportable sites of memory, bringing memorializing to local communities across the country.

The locations at which the traveling walls are displayed are directly or indirectly places of memory to the war—they are cemeteries or Veterans of Foreign Wars (VFW) halls, high schools or community centers that sometimes were built as living memorials after World War II. While, using Nora's terms, these locations can be defined as monumental *lieux*, their location less important than their intrinsic being, his theory does not fully account for the relationship between one of these locations and a portable site of memory, such as a traveling wall. When portable sites are temporarily located at monumental sites, their meaning and significance become more layered. For example, if The Moving Wall, a site of memory for the Vietnam War, was located for a week at a VFW hall, a site generally favored by World War II and Korean War veterans rather than veterans of the Vietnam War, The Moving Wall must negotiate the Vietnam War's meaning with veterans of different wars; the negotiation may produce commemorations of war that are more complex (to include the memorializing of wars, such as in Vietnam, that had no perceived noble outcome) but that also are potentially more simplistic (if, for example, all wars are celebrated patriotically without discrimination based on historical difference). At the same time, because portable *lieux* are not permanently located in specific locations, the owners of the replicas are less hindered from reaching consensus about location, design, or symbolic meaning with local citizens, veterans' groups, and state government. Because of this, replica wall owners and visitors may feel freer to map their own narratives about the war onto the site.

With the exception of Vietnam Veterans Memorial Fund's traveling wall, which is a registered nonprofit organization, the material and virtual versions of the Wall are privately owned and operated by veterans. (Vietnam Combat Veterans, which runs The Moving Wall and shares volunteers with the web-based The Virtual Wall, is a registered limited company; others are more informally organized.) Often, the private organizations espouse a conservative ideology, articulating perspectives that are promilitary and patriotic. In some extreme cases, private sites advocate perspectives on the war that are vehemently antigovernment and proreligion, also supporting the idea of government conspiracies against POWs and Vietnam veterans. They also support a revisionary history of the war that does not incorporate the war's divisiveness, the substantial antiwar movement during the war or since, or the heterogeneity of contemporary memory. Instead, informed by a variety of political notions since the early 1980s including President Reagan's declaration that the war was a noble cause (see introduction), President George H.W. Bush's assertion after the end of the Persian-Gulf War that "we've kicked the Vietnam syndrome once and for all," and the rise of the POW/MIA movement—the last of which I examine later—these replicas construct a history of the war uncomplicated by dissent and a contemporary vision of it that is credulously patriotic.

Of course, the intersection of war veterans and patriotism is nothing new or unusual, nor should it be criticized for its own sake. In fact, one might argue, as does Michael Kammen, that the Vietnam War era was somewhat anomalous in terms of the nation's level of patriotism, when "civil rights activism and then opposition to the war in Vietnam caused a dramatic decline in conventional manifestations of patriotism" (645). Between the end of World War I and the early 1960s, ardent patriotism and nationalism were pervasive, at least on the surface, even if apathy was as rampant as enthusiasm for patriotism, and elitism and snobbery sometimes presided over collaborative patriotism (646–647). By the mid-1980s, Kammen discusses, "orthodox Americanism was very much in vogue once again, prompted by President Reagan's rhetoric, catastrophic setbacks for U.S. marines in Beirut, splendid little wars in places like Grenada, and assorted other episodes foreign and domestic" (652). Keeping this context in mind, it would be erroneous to suggest that the patriotism of contemporary veterans is surprising or abnormal; what I do wish to point out, however, is the irony of remembering what may be an anomalous antipatriotic period in America's history through the lens of contemporary patriotism. While the erasure of the war's divisiveness and history of dissent certainly is problematic, I am most interested in examining the implications of this practice—rather than simply critiquing it—for the way the Vietnam War is remembered by veterans. How does memorializing a relatively unpatriotic period in American history through a lens of contemporary patriotic ideology affect the way the war in Vietnam is perceived by veterans and others today?

But what is the value of looking at the memorializing practices of replica walls that seem especially defined by their peripherality in terms of impact and importance? Most replicas are produced by individual veterans who have made it their lives' works to build and run these sites. Jim Schueckler, Ted Sampley, John Devitt, the Andersons (recently replaced by Barbara L. Smith and Judy Coleman): the central role these people play in their respective memorials may make their practices of narrow interest, just the efforts of a few individuals who cannot forget the war. But it is precisely the apparent peripherality of their actions that, en masse, constitutes the main features of contemporary vernacular memorializing practices—the vacillation between historical amnesia and obsession with the past; the symbiotic relationship between trauma, individual, and cultural memories; the individualization, materialization, and commodification of memory. If one of contemporary memorializing's most salient features is its availability and accessibility to all, then these individuals' memorializing practices are central to any study of memory today. Even though the memorials are created by just a few individuals, they have the ability to reach a wide audience as the traveling walls move across country and as people surf the internet from their home or office. The dialogic tensions between remembering and forgetting and between individual, cultural, and official memorializing practices, in the contexts of the materialization and democratization of memory, define the memory practices of these organizations and of society more generally.

PROTESTING ON THE MALL

The National Mall has always been considered a place of and for the people—a site of free speech, national commemoration, public gathering, and celebration. The majority of citizen activity and activism on the Mall can be described as temporary, lasting from a few hours to a couple of days, with one unusual exception: the Last Firebase, the makeshift vendor stands that sell various military-themed trinkets and that seem to be permanently ensconced

Figure 2. The Last Firebase, National Mall, Washington, D.C. Photograph by author.

in front of the Lincoln Memorial, just a few yards from the Vietnam Veterans Memorial. Despite the stands' original purpose to call attention to and demand governmental action regarding all U.S. soldiers missing or believed imprisoned abroad, the stands connect most directly to the Wall and to the issue of those missing from the Vietnam War not only because the POW/ MIA movement gained prominence during this conflict but also because the stands are owned, operated, and shaped ideologically by the Vietnam veteran Ted Sampley. Charles Griswold proposes that even through the stands are not "physically part of the architecture of [the Vietnam Veterans] Memorial" they are "nevertheless revealing of it" (706), suggesting that these stands could only be connected to the Wall, that only Vietnam War memorializing could foster this kind of impromptu action.

Although the two sites, the Wall and the Last Firebase, seem like entirely separate entities—one a place of contemplation and memory, the other of protest and commodification—they carry on a continuing dialogue about how the war and its veterans should be remembered and treated. The Last Firebase exists to protest the perceived governmental inertia over POW/ MIAs, but its presence implies that the issue is not being sufficiently addressed elsewhere and that it is not being adequately addressed at the Wall. The political stance of the Last Firebase is, I suggest, a legacy of the contentious history of the Wall, particularly the legacy of opposition to the Wall that emerged from patriotic veterans and conservative politicians who wanted a more traditional monument that they perceived would better honor the dead. The fact that the Wall and the Last Firebase coexist on the Mall, awkwardly yet in close proximity, reinforces the place as a site of democratic memorializing, as a place of and for the people, but it also calls attention to how, as alternative forms of memorializing evolve away from the Wall, memorializing becomes increasingly conservative.

When the Vietnam Veterans Memorial was in the planning stages in the late 1970s, some felt that its nontraditional design and lack of overt commentary on the war negatively complicated the master narrative of the nation's past that circulates at the National Mall. When the Vietnam Veterans Memorial Fund was trying to raise the money to build the Wall, it had difficulty securing both a location on the Mall and the funds to build it (see Scruggs and Swerdlow 1985). While these tasks were challenging enough, the biggest hurdle the organization faced was the controversy over the Wall's design. Opposition to the design, particularly from veterans, is best encapsulated in the comments of Tom Carhart and James Webb, both members of the Fund. Former infantry platoon leader Carhart dismissed the design as "a black gash of shame and sorrow, hacked into the national visage that is the

Mall;"⁴ and Webb, a prolific writer and a Marine, called it a "wailing wall
for future anti-draft and anti-nuclear demonstrators" (Scruggs and Swerdlow
84). Since those who opposed Maya Lin's design argued that it celebrated
U.S. failure in Vietnam, no one could have predicted the overwhelmingly
positive response the Wall received from veterans and civilians alike when it
opened to the public on 13 November 1982. Visitors welcomed the Wall's
commemoration of individual loss recorded in the chronological list of the
names of over 58,000 who died in Vietnam, and they appreciated how its
design provoked somber reflection without espousing a particular perspective on this contentious war. Today, the Wall is perceived by many as a truly
"living" memorial (Griswold 706; Mosse 224), "living" not in the sense of
living memorials built after World Wars I and II, such as community centers
and freeways, but in the way that the Wall inspires interaction, touch, protest, debate, and outpouring of emotion.

Yet, despite the Wall's immediate acceptance by most veterans, it faced
a vocal opposition backed financially by Texas businessman and future presidential candidate H. Ross Perot; ultimately, he garnered enough support to
force the commissioning of a second sculpture that was realistic in design,
and in 1984 Frederick Hart's "Three Servicemen" was erected. Nine years
later, after much lobbying by the Vietnam Women's Memorial Project, now
the Vietnam Women's Memorial Foundation, the role of women in the war
was recognized with the erection of Glenna Goodacre's Vietnam Women's
Memorial statue. Now, the Constitution Gardens area has become a memorial complex that includes the Wall, Hart's and Goodacre's statues, a large
U.S. flag at the entrance to the complex, and, most recently, a memorial
plaque located at the base of the flag to honor Vietnam's postwar casualties.⁵
Critical of this adding-on process, John Bodnar notes: "[t]he powerful and
dominant interests of patriots and nationalists could not let a text composed
only by and about ordinary people and ordinary emotions stand alone. The
profane was clearly a threat to the sacred" (6).

At the height of the controversy over whether to add a realist sculpture,
Frederick Hart suggested that Lin's design was "elitist" while his sculpture was
"populist;" he criticized her design saying, "I don't like blank canvases. Lin's art
is intentionally not meaningful," and asserted that his statuary monument is
"humanist" (Hess 124). This debate between elitism and populism was clearly
aesthetic as well as political. Hart's words reflect the feelings of many conservative veterans and politicians at the time who believed Lin's monument was
offensive precisely because of its minimalist design. But its design was not the
only concern; after all, the Washington Monument's "bare obelisk" form and
"indifferen[ce] to the perspective of the beholder" (Griswold 695) can also

be described as minimalist. The Wall was additionally offensive to conserva-
tives because despite its serenity and modesty, its "simple straight lines [and]
unobtrusive character" (Hess 122), the Wall cut a great gash into the earth.
Indeed, Marita Sturken reads this gash as symbolic of female genitals and
Maya Lin confirmed that the work has a female sensibility (Sturken 53; Hess
123). Unlike the Washington Monument, which is simply monumental and
phallic, the Wall is simply modest and feminine, and opposition to it reveals
anxiety about the demasculinization of war on the National Mall.

At the Wall, the practice of leaving objects, like the proliferation of
matericals, not only shows how the memorial invites citizens to make their
own meanings about the war and how it should be remembered, but—as
Bodnar's critique of the adding-on process implies—it also reveals anxiety
about the lack of patriotic narrative on the war at the Wall. Whatever the
reasons people leave objects, there is no doubt that they do so in large numbers: since 1982, the American public has left over 80,000 items at the Wall.[6]
Visitors leave objects at a steady rate all year round with a significant increase
during national holidays like Labor Day, Veterans Day, and Memorial Day.
All objects—ranging from common items like flags and flowers to the most
outlandish, like a brand new Harley-Davidson motorcycle—are collected by
the National Parks Service and delivered to the Museum and Archeological
Regional Storage Facility (MARS) in Maryland, where they are catalogued
and stored. By leaving objects at the Wall, individuals seek a way to honor
the dead, to construct their own understanding of the war, and also to reject
the Wall's perceived aestheticism in order to create a new "kind of culture fit
for their own consumption," to use Clement Greenberg's words. This new
culture, I have been suggesting, while increasingly democratic, individual,
and material, is also increasingly reactionary and patriotic.

Referencing funerary and war memorializing traditions in the United
States, Kristin Ann Hass in *Carried to the Wall* argues that the practice of
leaving objects contributes not only to a discussion of the meaning of the
war but to a renegotiation of U.S. patriotism. She suggests the "gifts" left at
the Wall reveal what she terms a "restless memory of war," that "the liminal,
contested place of the Vietnam War in American culture has disrupted the
expectation that dead soldiers can be retired to a stoic, martyred memory of
heroism and sacrifice and, in doing so, has disrupted American memorial
practices. I see the gifts Americans bring to the Wall as part of a continuing public negotiation about patriotism and nationalism" (3). In response to
Hass's argument, Edwin Martini argues that while "the memory being negotiated, or even contested at the . . . Wall, may be the result of a divisive and
devastating war, . . . the acts of memory performed at [t]he Wall offer little,

if any, public debate about the larger, public meaning of the war" (427). To read these acts of memory as contributing to a debate on patriotism and nationalism requires interpreting the motivations of the visitors who leave objects, a difficult, perhaps even impossible task, and something I discuss further in Chapter Four. Since the personal intent in leaving objects can never be known by outside observers, Martini correctly suggests that we cannot determine how this practice contributes to a debate over the war's meaning. But it is, in part, because the memory practices at the Wall do not try to assert one single meaning of the war that various individuals feel compelled to create their own meanings in other ways—through online and traveling walls as well as by leaving objects at the Wall.

While the Wall does not offer direction on the war's meaning, the same cannot be said of the Last Firebase. It is perhaps the most visible symbol of protest against U.S. government policies on an issue related to the Vietnam War, certainly on the Mall and perhaps even in the country, if only for its location: directly in front of the Lincoln Memorial on either side of the path around the Reflecting Pool. Founded by well-known veteran Ted Sampley (controversial for his conviction for assaulting John McCain's chief of staff, Mark Salter, and for his involvement in Vietnam Veterans Against John Kerry), the stands were built in 1986 initially to accommodate a Vietnam veteran, Gino Casanova, on hunger strike in protest against what he believed was the government's unwillingness to find those still missing in Southeast Asia. Sampley describes these stands as "the heartbeat of the [POW/ MIA] organization, providing activists with a powerful tool for educating the public on the POW/MIA issue, a resource for raising badly needed funds[,] and a rallying point for more protest demonstrations" (*U.S. Veteran Dispatch*). Now these stands publicize the POW/ MIA issue by displaying posters and newspaper clippings of those missing, as well as selling POW/MIA-themed and other military merchandise. The stands bring the memories and opinions of highly vocal individual veterans, and their groups, to the national stage in an effort to recentralize the memory of POW/MIAs and, through the stands and other forms of activism, to provoke the government into action. They confirm the significance of the Mall as monumental *lieux de mémoire*, but their conservative viewpoint challenges the historically pluralistic memorializing at the Wall, narrowing the meanings of the war produced there.

Despite the fact that the stands publicize those missing from all wars, they are most closely connected to the Vietnam War because the POW/MIA movement came to prominence during that era. The movement originated in 1970 with the National League of Families of American Prisoners and Missing in Southeast Asia, originally headed by Sybil Stockdale, the wife of the highest ranking officer held in the "Hanoi Hilton" at that time, Navy pilot James Stockdale. Through the League's work, the movement mobilized broad-ranging support for those "left behind." But after the war ended, opposition to the League developed along two fronts. First, the League's support for continued hostilities toward Vietnam led critics such as Bruce Franklin to suggest that the organization "has manipulated the legitimate concerns of those whose loved ones remain missing to orchestrate a right-wing chorus of support . . . for U.S. militarism" (Michalowski and Dubisch 100; Franklin 1992: 75–77). In addition, the League's willingness to work with the U.S. government provoked the radical right-wing elements of the movement, led by an organization formed in 1990 called the National Alliance of Families, to accuse "the League of being a willing collaborator in the U.S. government's efforts to hide the real truth" about American POW/MIAs in Southeast Asia. This radical wing, supported by "the Last Firebase [that] donated the original money used to organize the National Alliance of POW/MIA Families and was instrumental in aiding its formation,"[7] not only believes POWs still exist in Southeast Asia but that the government, from the Carter administration on, has systematically covered up its knowledge of existing POWs (see Keating; Franklin 1992 & 2000).

But discrepancies exist in the believed numbers of POW/ MIAs remaining in Vietnam after Operation Homecoming, when 591 POWs were released in the spring of 1973. Raymond Michalowski and Jill Dubisch suggest that most organizations working on behalf of POW/MIAs quote 2,265 as the number of soldiers missing or unaccounted for (100). They recognize this figure is widely disputed, and Susan Katz Keating, for example, presents differing numbers in her *Prisoners of Hope*. Keating suggests that after Operation Homecoming, the Pentagon's tally of MIA reflected the Defense Intelligence Agency's figure of 1,303; by the end of 1978, 224 MIAs were on the government's official list (27). Keating also suggests that in 1994, the date of her book's publication, 2,231 MIAs were on the government's official list. The number Michalowski and Dubisch quote originally included both MIAs (1,171) and MIA/KIAs (killed in action [1,094]), before the latter designation was changed to the less confusing KIA/BNR (body not returned). In 1976, the 1,171 soldiers originally termed MIAs were reclassified as KIA/ BNR, based on a presumptive finding of death. Some POW/ MIA families disputed the arbitrary nature of this redesignation: if after eight years, the family was unable to provide new evidence on the whereabouts of the missing, the MIA was presumptively found KIA (Keating 97–98). Whatever the discrepancy in numbers, it is more important to note, as Franklin does, that the conflation of POW with MIA for political ends ensures continued confusion about whether any of those still missing in Southeast Asia are prisoners (2000: 175). This confusion has allowed opportunists to exploit the grief of families, with POW hunters or scam artists such as Bo Gritz, Kambang Sibounheuang, and Jack Bailey fundraising millions of dollars to chase what have ultimately always been false or falsified sightings of American POWs (Keating).

The POW/ MIA stands on the Mall provide none of this factual information, but they do sell items to raise money for the movement. Although they have been on the Mall for almost 20 years, their status and future has at times been precarious. The stands—basically small, wooden merchandise booths—are temporary and unsightly counterpoints to the grandeur of their closest neighbors, the Lincoln Memorial and the Reflecting Pool. The tension between the stands and the more permanent sites, including the Vietnam Veterans Memorial, is illustrated in the years-long bitter dispute between Sampley and the Vietnam Veterans Memorial Fund's director, Jan Scruggs. According to Sampley, a disagreement over his reproduction on t-shirts of Hart's "Three Servicemen" statue burgeoned into Scruggs' criticism of the POW/ MIA issue, which Scruggs argued was a "lost cause" and a hindrance to reconciliation efforts between the United States and Vietnam. In addition, Scruggs felt, again according to Sampley, that the stands "were destroying the 'integrity' and 'heritage' of the Vietnam Veteran and Lincoln Memorials."[8]

But the stands have endured. T-shirts are no longer on sale, but I did observe on my two most recent visits to the Mall in 2002 and 2005 that the stands sold a range of Vietnam War-themed merchandise such as badges and buttons representing various military divisions and units, stickers, postcards, a few books, and, of course, POW/ MIA bracelets, each with a name of someone still missing in action imprinted on it. In 2002, there were two stands; on my more recent visit, that number had increased to four. The stands' military merchandise and laminated newspaper clippings of soldiers currently missing promotes—or at least does not question—the idea that the U.S.'s purpose in Vietnam was valid and that the military should still be there looking for POW/MIAs. Somewhat ironically, the POW/MIA movement's rhetoric of remembering communicates "You Are Not Forgotten" to the missing, yet the stands seem to forget everything else about the war, from the government reports that no more soldiers are missing in Vietnam to, more generally, the heterogeneous perspectives on the war that include the divisive attitudes toward the war during it and the sizeable veteran-led opposition to war since. On my most recent visit, I was struck by the run-down state of the stands and the out of date materials for sale. I was even more struck by the lack of engagement with the current war in Iraq, with only one flyer depicting images from the World Trade Center attacks on 11 September

2001, declaring it the "darkest page in American history." This disengagement seemed all the more poignant because of the enormous protest against the war in Iraq occurring less than one mile away on the day of my visit.[9]

Situated closer to the Lincoln Memorial than to any of the war memorials, the stands connect the POW/ MIA issue with the Mall's master narrative of war as honorable, promoting a view of the Vietnam era soldier as both hero and victim. In turn, through proximity and merchandising, this view of the war and its soldiers is brought to the Wall by way of $5 POW/ MIA bracelets, bought at the stands and, with more frequency than any other object, deposited at the foot of the Wall (Hass 121). If leaving these bracelets can be read as part of a "continuing public negotiation about patriotism and nationalism," the ready availability of the bracelets at the nearby POW/ MIA stands routinizes and commodifies this negotiation. Hass suggests that while most other objects are personal mementos, "the POW/MIA things are designed, produced, and sold as part of an organized effort to make and maintain a particular memory of the war" (105). This memory, Hass suggests, "rewrites the roles of the central characters in the war such that the Vietnamese become the victimizers and the Americans become the victims" (106). It positions veterans and the missing as victims of government inertia, a government that, in the rhetoric of the POW/MIA movement, does not care enough to find those missing in Southeast Asia and to bring them home.

The Last Firebase presents an extreme political perspective on the treatment of the missing after the war. The stands draw legitimacy from their general proximity to the permanent memorials and monuments and yet their temporality and shabby appearance seem to reject this legitimacy. Basically the stands are tolerated squatters, with their presence on the Mall symbolizing a difficult aspect of the war that the various responsible government agencies have not been able to resolve with the families of POW/MIAs and highlighting an awkward issue of free speech on the Mall that the National Parks Service and Vietnam Veterans Memorial Fund cannot resolve with the Last Firebase. Despite its marginal perspective, the Last Firebase's location— as well as Sampley's relentless campaigning on any number of issues directly or tangentially connected to the war and its veterans—provides it with a loud voice that resonates throughout the Mall. However, rather than thinking the Last Firebase speaks on behalf of the majority of veterans, I hope and indeed believe visitors to the Mall are simply made more aware that the Wall itself cannot accommodate all the competing opinions about the war and patriotism. Whether visitors think of the stands as an "ugly presence" as Scruggs calls them or "a powerful tool for educating the public" as Sampley describes them, they are one example of how the Wall is no longer the central place for memory making about the war. Indeed, the Last Firebase, along with Hart's sculpture, Goodacre's statue, the memorial plaque, the U.S. flag, and the Wall itself illustrate how sites of memory have proliferated on the Mall, even as the meanings have become more fixed.

It seems that the more sites there are to visit, the more routinized the memorializing practices at these sites become. Visitors now leave objects as part of a well-scripted routine that includes approaching the Wall from the left, touching the Wall, and taking pencil rubbings of the names. Those leaving objects expect curators to label, catalogue, and store them, so much so that some even attach directions on how to categorize the object or ask for it to be attributed to a particular name on the Wall. Today, the practice of leaving objects is part of a highly public ritual at the Memorial even though the practice derives from intensely private feelings and emotions. In my observations of visitor interaction at the Wall, I noticed that the majority of visitors follow the same route whether they are on their own, in family groups, or part

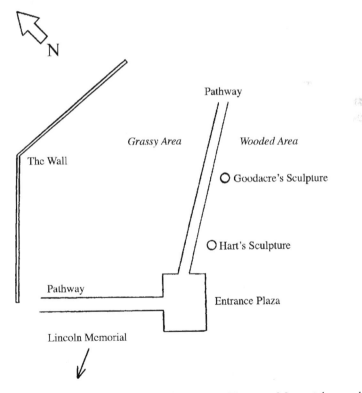

Figure 3. Diagram of layout of National Vietnam Veterans Memorial complex, Washington, D.C. Courtesy of Matthew Bryant.

of organized tours: they approach the Wall from the Lincoln Memorial area, stop for a photo opportunity at Hart's sculpture, progress downhill to the west side of the Wall itself, then finally exit the Wall's path at the east end. Some but not all of the visitors then visit the Women's Memorial, which requires heading back toward the entrance. Many visitors, as previously mentioned, buy a POW/MIA bracelet at the Last Firebase only to immediately carry it to the Wall and leave it there. When the Wall stood alone, visitors memorialized the war there in an infinite number of ways. Now, these practices have become more routinized precisely because of, not despite, the proliferation of sites of memory to the war. It seems that because there are so many sites to visit, the tour through them has become increasingly scripted.[10]

Like the POW/ MIA movement itself, the Last Firebase has constructed a story of the missing, of Vietnam veterans, and of itself as victimized by the war, the government, and even the Vietnam Veterans Memorial Fund. This rhetoric may help draw attention to the POW issue, but in doing so it shifts the focus from the other, and the real, victims of the war, including the Vietnamese. In this process, an uncomplicated patriotism emerges in which the most difficult aspects of the history and memory of the war are forgotten. The Last Firebase draws on the Mall's locational significance in order to bring the POW/ MIA issue to the attention of visitors to the Mall; in the process, it acknowledges the import of the Mall while simultaneously showing a certain lack of reverence for it. The other portable *lieux* I examine here—the traveling and virtual walls—more unambiguously reject the topographical significance of the Mall, offering alternative ways to memorialize at the Wall without going to Washington, D.C., and confirming how memorializing becomes physically, historically, and politically decentralized and decontextualized as it moves away from the Mall.

TRAVELING WALLS

Ted Sampley's character and commitment have fundamentally shaped the development of the Last Firebase and his other projects, such as the newsletter he distributes around Capitol Hill, *U.S. Veteran Dispatch*. The traveling walls also are shaped by the individuals who manage them, particularly so in the case of The Moving Wall, founded in 1984 by John Devitt, Norris Shears, Gerry Haver, and other Vietnam veterans on behalf of Vietnam Combat Veterans, Ltd., a private limited company based in San Jose, CA, and run by Devitt. Wall replicas are on the road year round, traveling to community and veterans groups willing to pay $3,000 for a week's visit by The Moving Wall and $4,500 for a four-day weekend visit from The Wall

That Heals, administered by the Vietnam Veterans Memorial Fund and managed by friends Barbara L. Smith and Judy Coleman. In effect, then, site managers must dedicate their lives to bringing the replica wall in their care to communities across the country.

During one week in the summer of 2003, both replicas toured the Midwest states—The Wall That Heals came to Waverly, Iowa, and The Moving Wall to the City of South Saint Paul, Minnesota. From my home at the time in Minneapolis, Minnesota, I traveled to both. Both organizations argue that their traveling walls provide a safe haven for mourning and contemplation that is lacking in the "epic proportions" of the National Mall. While promoting themselves as alternatives to national commemoration on the Mall, the replicas also function as alternative forms of the Wall by bringing to local communities an approximation of its experience. While surely some people are able to visit the replica wall simply because of its proximity to their homes, they visit it not because it is a replica but because to them it represents or offers the same experience as the Wall does. In other words, it is the Wall's efficacy and resonance that draws people to replicas, rather than their techniques of replication, for instance. Thus, while the virtual walls offer a form of memorializing that is a locational alternative to the Wall, the form strives to be experientially similar to that of the National Memorial; put differently, the location is different, but the site of memory is assumed by visitors to be the same.

THE WALL THAT HEALS

One Saturday in mid-July, I drove 200 miles south from Minneapolis to Waverly in the northeastern corner of Iowa. The small town was celebrating its annual Heritage Days, a weekend long cultural event that showcases the town "as a place to live, work and play."[11] In the afternoon I arrived at Harlington Cemetery, located on a hill overlooking the town where The Wall That Heals was set up. I observed as visitors walked first toward a truck converted into a Traveling Museum that presents information about both the Vietnam Veterans Memorial and its official traveling version, The Wall That Heals. Then, passing a children's cemetery, the visitors made their way toward the replica. Just a few hours after a street parade, the main event of Heritage Days, somewhere between fifteen and twenty people wandered around the memorial site, mostly younger families and older couples, a high percentage of them wearing hats, jackets, and t-shirts emblazoned with U.S. flags.

In addition to the replica, The Wall That Heals comprises an information center (a tent) and a Traveling Museum (eight display cases built into the sides of a fifty-three foot, fifth-wheel trailer truck, which also carries the replica across the country). The tent provides a wide range of materials pertinent to veterans and their families including books about the Wall, lists of those killed or missing in action organized by county, glossaries of weaponry used in Vietnam, and searchable computer databases to help visitors find names on the Wall. On the trailer, the first display case presents a chronology of the conflict; the other seven present a history of the war and the Wall that includes the controversy over the Wall's design, responses to the war at home, the practice of leaving objects, samples of U.S. and Vietnamese weaponry and military clothing, copies of letters left at the Wall, a photo gallery of prominent veterans, and finally a timeline of the Wall's construction with photographic representations of Hart's and Goodacre's additions to the Memorial complex. The Traveling Museum carries the Vietnam Veterans Memorial Fund's purpose from Washington to communities across the country in order to, as the Vietnam Veterans Memorial Fund states, "preserve the legacy of the Vietnam Veterans Memorial, to promote healing[,] and to educate about the impact of the Vietnam War."[12] In this display, the Fund emphasizes the difference between the Traveling Museum and The Wall That Heals: while the Traveling Museum educates visitors on how citizens have embraced the National Wall and on the apparently successful recovery and readjustment of veterans, The Wall That Heals, the Fund claims grandly, allows the souls of the dead to return home to their families and communities.

In one of the display cases, for example, two narratives are presented about veterans' experiences on their return to the U.S: one about veterans' physical and psychological wounds from Vietnam, the other about the isolation they felt on their return. This display features a large, distorted photograph of veterans and civilians at the Wall's dedication ceremony in 1982 with the by-line: "Vietnam veterans at last found a home in the hearts of Americans at the Vietnam Veterans Memorial." At another part of the display, veteran John Dibble is quoted as saying, "[e]verybody was wounded in Vietnam, everybody." The statements suggest that veterans returned hurt and alienated and that when the Wall was dedicated in 1982, it helped veterans to heal, emotionally and psychologically, by finally allowing them to feel "welcomed home." These two narratives are, in fact, part of a larger one concerning how those on the home front helped, or as the case may be did not help, veterans readjust when they returned to the United States. Although not stated explicitly, the display's juxtaposition of Dibble's quote with the by-line implies that veterans were not able to recover from their woundings in Vietnam because they had not been welcomed into "the hearts of Americans." The Wall, the Traveling Museum suggests, enabled a change of heart among Americans about how to treat returning veterans.

To convey the significance of the Wall, the museum discusses the practice of leaving objects both by reminding visitors of the ritual at various points in the display and by showing objects as they might look if they had been left at the Wall. In this staging, selected items are set in front of a reproduction of the Wall's panels. However, most of the items have not been left at the Wall but are, rather, war-era artifacts such as military supply bags and guns, items of clothing, antiwar buttons, and newspaper clippings. There are, however, a few items on display that were left at The Wall That Heals including, for example, a pair of welder's gloves and a set of brazing irons left in Dearborn, Michigan. While these items are sure to evoke a contemplative and perhaps emotional response from some visitors, most of the objects on display serve, rather, an instructional purpose: to inform visitors about the importance of the Wall and its historical context. The items instruct visitors in how individuals behave at the Wall, but the display is unable to reproduce or evoke the viscerality of the Wall itself. Like the "Personal Legacy" exhibit discussed in the next chapter, the inert displays—the sun-bleached backdrops, the glass cases that prevent direct engagement, and the unvarying information panels—tend to sterilize the objects, limiting interactions other than those of a visual or in some cases contemplative nature.

When I visited The Wall That Heals, I noted that almost without exception visitors would work their way around the truck-museum before moving to view the replica. With this background and context in mind, visitors would then file past the replica made of highly reflective black, powder-coated heavy aluminum attached to a tubing frame also made from aluminum, with the names laser etched in white. Because the wall is above ground and at its highest point only five feet—an exact half-size replica—it lacks the powerful experience of feeling surrounded and overwhelmed by the National Wall's height and length. But only visitors who have been to the Wall would notice the difference and, as the Fund suggests, the replica is not necessarily for them. An undated flyer about the replica obtained on site articulates its purpose thus:

> The Vietnam Veterans Memorial has helped all veterans find healing and a powerful connection with the military experience. Nonveterans, from school children to parents and grandparents, find in [t]he Wall a deeper appreciation of their sacrifice, service, and courage. . . . The Wall That Heals offers [a] powerful gift to the nation: an opportunity for the souls enshrined on the Memorial to journey back to the places they called home, to exist among friends and family once more, not in a monumental city, but in the comfort and peace of familiar surroundings.

In narrating a progression from the Wall to The Wall That Heals, the flyer suggests that the Wall is a custodian of the dead souls of soldiers, a common trope that suggests that real bodies (or at least their spiritual residues) reside behind the names engraved on the granite. If the Wall helps veterans find healing and provides visitors with an appreciation of those who sacrificed their lives, the replica completes this process by bringing the souls home. Yet the narrative undermines the National Mall by pitting the "monumental city" against the "comfort and peace" of the familiar. Might the Wall lose its efficacy if the souls enshrined there return to their homes? In its flyer, the Fund's rhetoric suggests that, ultimately, the souls enshrined in the Wall really belong at home with their friends and families, and that memorializing is best located at the local level.

THE MOVING WALL

If The Wall That Heals presents itself as an extension to memorializing on the National Mall, bringing its features to localities across the country, The Moving Wall sees itself, in contrast, as an alternative to it. Unlike The Wall That Heals, The Moving Wall does not have the official endorsement or affiliation with the National Wall that surely brings financial benefits, administrative support, and a high profile. Vietnam Combat Veterans, in a sense, is the underdog that has to work harder to prove its worth, first to community members who may want to host a replica wall and later to the townspeople who visit The Moving Wall. To suggest how the memorializing experience at The Moving Wall differs from the National Wall and from other traveling walls, Vietnam Combat Veterans stresses the importance of personal and local connections when visiting the replica, presents its founding as shaped by the efforts of a single veteran, and asserts that The Moving Wall is the original and authentic traveling wall.

Two days after I visited The Wall That Heals, I went to South Saint Paul High School, the temporary location for The Moving Wall. This time I had particular expectations, not only because I now had firsthand experience of traveling walls but also because for the past six weeks, during February and March 2003, I had been following the progress of the planning committee for The Moving Wall's visit via minutes sent to me by its coordinator, Dick Leighninger. Even though it was early on a Monday morning, between fifteen and twenty people were already moving around the school grounds and along the wall. Set up in the middle of the school's playing fields, the wall was surrounded by floodlights, a scoreboard, and bleachers. A local landscaper and florist had provided gravel and potted plants to construct a temporary pathway in order to direct human traffic along the wall. Like The Wall That Heals, The Moving Wall stands approximately five feet tall, a half-size replica of the Wall; with panels that are not sized proportionately, the replica slopes less dramatically than the original. Made of sheet metal panels attached to metal supports, the names are screen-printed in white on a highly reflective black surface.

Vietnam Combat Veterans (VCV) emphasizes local and personal connections, attempting to make The Moving Wall appealing for visitors and setting it apart from the Wall and other replica memorials. Opening and closing ceremonies at the replicas always include a roll call of the local dead. The deceased were often well known to members of the host committees because they lived in the same neighborhood, went to the same high school, or signed up and served together. While this, of course, also is true for The Wall That Heals, VCV makes localization a selling point: visitors can expect to experience this personal touch when they speak with a guide, who usually is an active member of the local Vietnam veteran community with knowledge of those from the locality who died. An example of the powerful interaction between guide and visitor appears in "I Came to See My Son's Name," an article by Jim Schueckler published at The Moving Wall's website about his guide work during the replica's visit to Batavia, New York:[13]

> A group of four people stood near one panel. I [Schueckler] offered to make a rubbing of a name. The man pointed to the name Paul D. Urquhart. I asked[,] "Is that Captain Paul Urquhart, the helicopter pilot?" The man nodded and said[,] "He's my brother." I explained that I flew with Paul on his first tour in Vietnam and read that he had been shot down during his second tour. Paul's brother said that he and his family came from Pennsylvania on the anniversary date of Paul's becoming Missing in Action. I made a rubbing of Paul's name and added a rubbing of the Army Aviator wings from my hat, a symbol we had both worn so proudly so long ago.

Immediately striking is the level of personal connection between the guide and visitor. Right away Schueckler establishes his credibility as a guide and a veteran by revealing that he knew the visitor's brother, Paul Urquhart. Schueckler emphasizes the connection by noting that he flew with Urquhart and subsequently heard about his death. While Schueckler does not record the brother's response, we can imagine the brother was moved to find someone at this place of memory who had a personal connection with Paul and was able to share details of his life. In contrast to the boundaries that exist between guide, visitor, and veteran in the traditional memorial setting, an unusual moment of intimacy, as well as a presumption of shared patriotism, occurs here when Schueckler adds a rubbing of the Army Aviator wings from his own hat to the rubbing of Urquhart's name.

Personal connection between guide and visitor occurs once again in an interaction between Schueckler and the relatives of Douglas Smith: "One man asked me to look up the name Douglas Smith. I asked back, "Do you mean Doug Smith, a Marine, from North Tonawanda High School?" The man introduced me to his wife, Doug's cousin. She was pleased to be able to talk about Doug with a classmate who remembered him. I showed her Doug's name on my own, personal, list." In this exchange, Schueckler again uses his personal knowledge of the deceased to establish connection and credibility with Smith's family. Unlike the interaction with Urquhart's brother, here we are told of the relative's response: Doug Smith's cousin is "pleased to be able to talk" with someone who "remembered him." The VCV's localizing and personalizing techniques protect this particular Doug Smith from anonymity (there are in fact nine Doug Smiths on the Wall) and make the experience at the replica more personally significant for family members. Of course personal connections occur at the National Wall, and when they do—between loved one and guide, between two veterans—they are more dramatic because they are less expected. But VCV does more than suggest personal connection as happy serendipity; by making the replica part of a community for a week, it promotes the increased likelihood of personal recognition and connection as a positive feature of a visit to The Moving Wall.

VCV presents its guides as authentic veterans in order to establish the authenticity of The Moving Wall. In Schueckler's article, he positions himself not just as a veteran with personal knowledge of the deceased but also a mourner himself with his own list of names to find on the wall. The blurring between guide and bereaved cannot be underestimated when considering the appeal of the replica for visitors who themselves have experienced grief. Schueckler and other bereaved guides can claim that their own loss is a testament to their authentic experience in Vietnam and a qualification for their roles as guides, which helps them connect to grieving visitors in powerful ways.

The idea of authenticity extends to The Moving Wall's founder, who is presented as a "suffering" veteran of the war. Newspaper articles posted on VCV's website present the replica as a labor of love for John Devitt. During the building of the replica, describes one article, Devitt felt at times like he "wanted to just get into [his] truck and leave." But, he adds, "I never left. I just said, 'Let's go for it.' And that meant stop when you finish or die trying."[14] In another article, journalist Karen Sandstrom quotes Devitt's friends who say The Moving Wall has helped him deal with his own emotional pain.[15] She portrays Devitt's obsession with the replica by quoting Jan Scruggs: "I would say this has taken over his life in a pretty serious way." She even uses a physical description of Devitt—"[he] carries no extra weight on his lanky frame, wears faded jeans and pulls his dark hair back into a ponytail that stretches halfway down his back"—that draws on physical stereotypes of the contemporary Vietnam veteran and links his physical appearance with his single-mindedness.

Yet, presenting The Moving Wall as the obsession of one veteran has the potential to undermine its national significance, making the replica of limited interest. The figure of a lone veteran spending all his time traveling from town to town setting up and taking down the replica could be read not as the VCV's attempt to share the healing powers of the National Wall with others but as Devitt's attempt to rid himself of his own demons. However, just as Schueckler blurs the lines between guide and mourner and makes the experience for bereaved visitors that much more personal, so perhaps part of The Moving Wall's appeal to veterans and families of those who died in Vietnam is the very fact that its founder not only went through the same suffering that they or their loved ones did but also wears this suffering on his sleeve. The humble persona of Devitt, the antithesis of official commemoration encapsulated in the prominent and well-groomed figure of Jan Scruggs, must surely be appealing to veterans and the families of the dead who do not care to visit the city of federal government and who wish to localize their memorializing. Despite the distance Scruggs puts between himself (as a well-adjusted veteran) and Devitt (still dealing with his problems) with his comments on Devitt's obsession, the Vietnam Veterans Memorial Fund finds the story of one man's struggles to "bring the wall home" compelling, so much so that The Wall That Heals' traveling museum displays Scruggs' hand-written version of his impassioned first speech that called for a national memorial to honor those who died in combat in Vietnam. Even national memorials, the display suggests, are shaped by the motivations and passions of individuals.

VCV also repeatedly emphasizes that The Moving Wall is the original replica. Displaying a disclaimer denying any connection to the Vietnam Veterans Memorial, VCV warns its website visitors to "beware of copies." Explaining that The Moving Wall was the first of its kind, the warning continues:

> Over the past several years, some organizations and profit-making enterprises—with no relationship to us—have made similar models of [t]he Wall. One organization markets theirs as "The Moving Wall" in spite of letters from us and the confusion and pain it causes their "customers."

Yes, it is ironic that someone would claim to "honor" war casualties by
using trademark infringement.

Uneasily positioned between the Wall and other traveling replicas, VCV
makes the claim that The Moving Wall is the original traveling wall by denying any kind of relationship with the Wall and the rights of other organizations to use The Moving Wall name, a denial that, of course, keeps The
Moving Wall in dialogue with the Wall and other organizations. At the same
time, the concern with trademark infringement seems misplaced: using The
Moving Wall name does not fail to honor war casualties (as what is the connection between honoring trademarks and honoring the dead?), but it may
show dishonor to Vietnam Combat Veterans, as the organization sees it. The
organization's concern about copyright is also somewhat supercilious when
it suggests that the renegade "Moving Wall" causes its visitors confusion and
pain, implying that they are being cheated out of a genuine Moving Wall
experience. Yet, in the era of localized memorializing and the proliferation of
representations of the war and the Wall, one replica wall may be pretty much
like any other, each providing a comparable experience. The fact the VCV
feels compelled to copyright its name at all bespeaks its mistrust of other veterans' organizations and its anxiety about competition within the replica wall
industry. What seems most ironic about VCV's copyright concerns is not
that another traveling wall claiming to honor war casualties actually dishon-
ors The Moving Wall by infringing on its trademark but that The Moving
Wall, itself a copy, claims to be an original.

VCV's discussion of customers and copyright infringement reinforces
the commodification of memorializing. In this case, unlike the purchasable item of the POW/ MIA bracelet, the commodity is the memorial itself,
which customers pay to bring to their hometown for a week. The organization's concern with its customers (masked as concern for the customers of
the other moving wall) coupled with its emphasis on the individual guides
and founder, threaten to overshadow The Moving Wall's original purpose—
to enable the living to memorialize the dead. Ultimately, by focusing on its
marketability, promoting the work of individual veterans, and localizing
memorializing, The Moving Wall rejects the Wall's national significance and
embraces the commodification, privatization, and competitiveness of localized commemoration.

Every week, both traveling replicas move to a new location somewhere
in the United States. Local host committees decide where best to house the
visiting replica, a decision based both on pragmatic reasoning and symbolic
significance. For instance, when the planning committee discussed where to

house The Moving Wall in South Saint Paul, the replica was at first going to be based at Commemorative Air Force, a small World War II museum in a converted Quonset hut located in the Twin Cities' third and smallest airport, Fleming Field. However, the committee decided to shift The Moving Wall to nearby South Saint Paul High School because the grounds would be secure at night, better illuminated, and easier to find than the museum at the labyrinthine Fleming Field. Perhaps also for pragmatic reasons, the Heritage Days committee in Waverly decided to house The Wall That Heals within the town's cemetery because of the large open areas in the grounds.

However, while hosting the replica on the grounds of a high school might make it more publicly accessible, the location draws poignant attention to the young soldiers who died in Vietnam, many of them just out of high school. If visitors notice the location at which the replica is based, and it would be difficult not to notice the bleachers and flood lights, they will surely be reminded of life cut short, of young men drafted right out of high school whose names are now on the wall. The National Wall's descent into the earth begs for a comparison to a tomb; however, the traveling walls are placed above ground and thus bear closer resemblance to gravestones. This is especially true with the juxtaposition of The Wall That Heals beside the children's cemetery named Babyland, where it becomes difficult not to draw connections between the two kinds of memorializing. Visually, the two sites differ: the light pinks and blues of the flower arrangements and toys beside the small graves arranged in a circle contrast with the stark black angles of the replica. However, enshrined in both are young people who died too soon. At both locations in South Saint Paul and Waverly, unintended narratives emerge of the soldiers' premature deaths rather than their heroic lives. At The Moving Wall, this narrative contrasts with another one of future promise, as any high school location might imply; in the case of The Wall That Heals, the narrative competes with the celebration of small-town heritage and heroic pride of which the replica is temporarily a part.

To survive and to carve out their own space in the increasingly commodified arena of Vietnam War memorializing, The Wall That Heals and The Moving Wall describe respectively their purpose and achievements in comparison with and in opposition to the National Wall. But remove the various ceremonies, information tents, and other educational aspects, and the same basic object remains: a half-sized replica of the Vietnam Veterans Memorial. Because of this elemental fact, rituals first established at the Wall are reenacted at these places: visitors file past the Wall starting at the left end; they notice their reflections as they walk past; they behave with quiet respect and reverence; and they leave flowers, flags, and other tokens of remembrance. Of the behaviors that have become routinized, the most common is the practice of making a name rubbing. Since the Wall's dedication, visitors there have felt compelled to touch its shiny surface and feel the textured engraving of names. Running fingers across the names of loved ones is one way to connect with the dead, and people make rubbings of these engraved names as a memento of their trip to the Wall. The practice is now so widespread that the National Parks Service provides visitors sheets of paper to place over a name and pencils to take rubbings. And the practice highlights two of the Memorial's most praised features: the overwhelming yet intensely private list of names and the tactile surface that seems to call out for interaction.

At the replicas, this ritual is also enacted but with a difference. Publicity materials from The Wall That Heals and The Moving Wall promote taking name rubbings as an important custom that can be performed at the replicas. Yet, practically, it is difficult to take real rubbings because names are not engraved as deeply into the surfaces and are only half the size of those at the Wall. I am sure that my observation in South Saint Paul was typical as I watched frustrated children whose rubbings didn't turn out. These children, I would argue, typify visitors to the traveling walls in another way, in that they have been taught how to behave at the Wall without fully understanding what they are doing or why—without knowing, in other words, the significance of touching a name etched onto the granite. While The Moving Wall encourages visitors to take rubbings, The Wall That Heals offers visitors a "virtual rubbing," a printout of a full-sized name. Visitors are well aware that they take home a computer-generated simulation that lacks the visceral action of making a rubbing. The fact that everyone participates nonetheless indicates the similar routinization of memorializing at both the National Wall and the replicas.

While traveling walls are locational alternatives to the Wall, in terms of shaping visitor practices they are very much the same. The organizations promote their replicas as extensions or alternatives to the National Vietnam Veterans Memorial, and practices first enacted at the Wall are routinely performed at the replicas. In contrast, virtual walls offer a different experience: visitors do not have to travel to get there, guides to help or direct them, or material or spatial cues to orient them. Because virtual walls are both physically and practically detached from the National Mall, visitors could potentially feel free to reach their own understanding of the war as they interact with them. However, for various reasons, the meanings of the war that circulate at the virtual walls are often, again, aligned with the dominant contemporary discourses of uncritical patriotism.

VIRTUAL WALLS

Scholarship on cyberspace has focused on its "range of new social spaces in which [people] meet and interact with one another," Peter Kollock and Marc Smith suggest (3). These authors point out that the scholarship tends toward utopian or dystopian views: the former "highlights the positive effects of networks and their benefits for democracy and prosperity," while the latter "see[s] a darker outcome in which individuals are trapped and ensnared in a 'net' that predominantly offers new opportunities for surveillance and social control" (4). In popular discourse, discussions of the World Wide Web generally fall into two camps: one that sees the web as exacerbating the loss of meaningful community, the other that believes it allows for the creation of new virtual communities. However oversimplified, the discussion importantly addresses a new definition of community, "now conceptualized not in terms of physical proximity but in terms of social networks" (17). (Of course the concept that a group of individuals may constitute a community even though the individuals do not personally know or physically interact with one other is nothing new, as Benedict Anderson's *Imagined Communities* reminds us in relation to the formation and shaping of national identity.)

By detaching community from its physical location, the web has the ability to transform the way the war is memorialized and alter how veterans and the families of those who died in Vietnam interact and communicate. But is this possibility realized? The number of virtual walls is increasing, but here I focus on three of the most well-established ones: The Vietnam Veterans Memorial Wall Page, also known as The Wall USA (founded in 1996); The Virtual Wall (founded in March 1997); and the Virtual Wall of the Vietnam Veterans Memorial Fund (launched on Veterans Day, 1998). At each of these websites, visitors post messages to or about soldiers who died in Vietnam. Potentially, a nationwide network of people can express grief or offer condolences and in doing so can establish or join communities from the comfort of their home or office. In this way, memorializing becomes relocated from locally or nationally specific places to the sites of everyday life (see Gillis for a discussion on the movement to make memorializing a part of ordinary life [17]). But while the web does provide opportunities for new social networks and communication that may be absent from the Wall and the traveling walls, based on the online postings I surveyed, the community constituted at virtual wall websites is a metaphoric construct only, truly virtual and imaginary. This imaginary community, however, is not like the "deep, horizontal comradeship" of nations, which Anderson notes creates a willingness to die for one's country (7); it is, instead, a virtual community that lacks commitment from its members, who are prevented by the limitations of technology from communicating with each other or who are otherwise not motivated or interested in doing so; it is a virtual community that's dispersed geographically and politically. However, because the community is not fixed, it does have the potential, albeit as yet unrealized, to grow and develop in deeper as well as more diverse ways.[16]

On 11 November 1998, then Vice President Al Gore officially launched the Vietnam Veterans Memorial Fund's Virtual Wall with these words:

> For 15 years, people have come to the Vietnam Wall to run their hands across the names and remember those who never came home. Now, anybody who can run their hands across a computer keyboard will be able to make contact with those names and learn even more—that these names belong to people who were brothers and sons, husbands and wives, mothers and daughters, and that their courage helped make our freedom possible.[17]

Describing the concept of the virtual wall as experientially similar to the Wall, Gore suggests visitors can touch and then connect to the names on the wall/screen, and at the virtual wall visitors can learn more about those who died. He further implies that the Vietnam Veterans Memorial Fund is making this online experience (which I will call The Fund's Virtual Wall) available for the first time, when in fact at the time Gore was speaking at least two other virtual walls existed: The Vietnam Veterans Memorial Wall Page (The Wall USA) and The Virtual Wall (founded by Jim Schueckler among others).

All online replicas share one basic feature: they are places where visitors post remembrances to someone whose name is on the Vietnam Veterans Memorial; rather than leaving a physical object, they leave a message or a photo. At all three online sites, no two-way dialogue between visitors is possible because the sites do not sponsor chat rooms or threaded discussions; Edwin Martini mentions that The Fund's Virtual Wall formerly supported a discussion room that closed in 2001 due to lack of interest.[18] Since the three walls can become easily confused, I start with a brief description of the visual features of each website and how visitors can search and post messages.

The Vietnam Veterans Memorial Wall (The Wall USA) home page has an ominous black background with a large POW/ MIA insignia to the left and, to the right, the text of "Save a Place," a poem by Major Michael David O'Donnell, who went missing in action on 24 March 1970 and eventually was listed as killed in action on 7 February 1978. An audio track of "Taps," the military bugle call for the dead, starts when the home page loads. The page tells us that "The Vietnam Veterans Memorial Wall Page is a nonprofit endeavor maintained by veterans of the 4th Battalion 9th Infantry Regiment for the benefit of all." At the bottom are links to various parts of the site and beneath these links are additional search options where visitors can look through the official database of names for a particular individual by using one or more of a variety of criteria (name, date of birth, casualty date, hometown, and so on). Initially, they can access some basic information about the serviceman; for more details, they can click on "Info Page," which contains information about an individual's record of service, including cause of death. From there, visitors navigate to "Personal Comments or Pictures" where they can read all postings to this particular person, one after the other on the same page. Postings are divided by a thick line in the pattern of an American flag, while another flag in soft focus provides a backdrop. At this page, they have the opportunity to add their own information and photos. Instead of accessing personal comments directly from the home page, visitors must go through a series of links in order to navigate through the comments.

The Virtual Wall's home page also uses a black background and features the following disclaimer: "The Virtual Wall ® Vietnam Veterans Memorial contains personal remembrances of letters, photographs, poetry, and citations honoring those women and men named on the Vietnam Veterans Memorial in Washington, DC. maintains the real Wall. The phrase 'The Virtual Wall' is a registered trademark of www.VirtualWall.org, Ltd, open since March, 1997." The website's home page is cluttered with photographs, busy graphics, and hyperlinks to other parts of the site. Visitors can also access "Faces of Freedom" from this page to browse through all the postings that include photographs. Unlike the other two virtual walls that use the entire list of names from the National Wall, visitors can only search The Virtual Wall for names that have already been posted, or they can add another name from the official list of those who died in Vietnam. Visitors can also go directly to a letter of the alphabet and read through the postings for names beginning with that letter, or they can browse the "100 most recent Virtual Wall names." Once in a serviceman's memorial page, visitors will see either a "basic" or a "custom" memorial; the latter often includes elaborate frames with military insignia background, photographs of the deceased, and graphics of his or her medals. As with The Wall USA, each person's memorial is on one page.

Like The Virtual Wall, The Fund's Virtual Wall home page looks busy with several banners at the top and bottom and frames to the right, but its light background color, clear font, and well-organized layout all signal a professionally designed and maintained site. Three main components comprise the Fund's Virtual Wall: visitors can make a virtual rubbing, post remembrances, or interact with a Flash-powered re-creation of the Wall. Click on "Experience the Wall" and a photographic image of the Memorial fades into view with words like "Sacrifice" and "Honor" moving slowly across the screen. These words are then replaced with the following statement: "58,220 gave their lives. Millions Remember. The Virtual Wall." When this statement fades, a computer-generated reproduction of the Wall appears. Visitors can scroll around the Wall and click on any panel; when selected, the panel enlarges for easier viewing. They can search directly for a name from the home page or can click on "Remembrances" in order to choose options such as search, view, or post remembrances; create a name rubbing; or read remembrances for those who died on the date (the day and month) the visitor accesses the site. One key difference between this site and the other two is that remembrances can only be read one at a time, though visitors can read the subject headings listed for all the postings (as we do for electronic mail) and can immediately see the number if not the content of remembrances.

Because the full list of names is available to browse on the Fund's Virtual Wall and The Wall USA, many of the names have no postings, a fact alone that compels some to leave multiple messages to them. Out of the fifty two names I surveyed on the Fund's Virtual Wall, ten had postings by a retired naval radio operator (whom I shall call L.D.); on The Wall USA, a former marine (H.R.) had posted six times. All sites have repeat posters, individuals who return again and again, often over the span of years to post messages about or to the dead. Some posters are Vietnam veterans or claim to wear the POW/ MIA bracelet of the person to whom they write. Others post because of their work, such as Candace Lokey, the chair of the Adoption Committee for the National League of Families of Prisoners of War and Missing in Action in Southeast Asia, or Clay Marston, a military biographical researcher. Yet, all repeat posters have in common the fact that they are strangers to the person whose name is on the Wall.

L.D. uses a couple of scripts for his postings that vary slightly from each other. One speaks to the dead serviceman from several differing personas:

> As a fellow Buckeye, I say "THANK YOU"
> As a Veteran, I say "JOB WELL DONE, MAJOR"
> As an American, "YOUR DEATH WAS NOT IN VAIN"
> And as a believer, 'YOUR SPIRIT IS ALIVE—AND STRONG"
> Although we never met personally, I want to thank you Major . . . , for your courageous and valiant service, faithful contribution, and most holy sacrifice, given to this great country of ours! REST IN ETERNAL PEACE MY FRIEND. (19 March 2003)

Another contains a somewhat similar message that has been simplified:

> Although we never met personally, I want to thank you . . . for your courageous and valiant service, faithful contribution, and most holy sacrifice, given to this great country of ours!
>
> Your Spirit is alive—and strong, therefore Marine, you shall never be forgotten, nor has your death been in vain. Again, thank you . . . for a job well done! REST IN ETERNAL PEACE MY FRIEND. (26 July 2003)

When his posting is to an enlisted soldier or naval officer, L.D. changes the ending slightly to "FAIR WINDS, AND ETERNAL PEACE MY FRIEND." L.D.'s motivation certainly appears well intentioned. He seeks out those who seem to have been forgotten—for whom no message has been left—and leaves a posting for them. Once visitors spend any time at all browsing through postings, they will see L.D.'s and others' postings repeatedly and, despite the best intentions of the posters, the inevitable generic nature of the messages has the effect of undermining the personal and intimate aspects of the virtual memorial.

Even though L.D. is a stranger to the deceased and their loved ones, he speaks in the familiar second person and talks directly to the dead. By contrast, friends and family members often speak of their loved ones in the third person. For example, family members commonly use the virtual wall to ask for information: "Charles was one of my younger brothers. He quit college to get his tour of duty over with and never made it home alive. If you knew him, and served with him, would really like to hear from you. . . . I miss him!" (The Wall USA, 17 February 2003; wording amended in consultation with poster, 18 July 2005). Sometimes, friends or family members want to correct information from the military service record on their loved one:

> Corporal . . . was one of the most popular men in his platoon and company. . . . He was a kind, competent, and good man. He did not die in a vehicle accident. He was riding in his Amtrac (Amphibian Tractor) as crew chief and commanding a convoy to An Hoa. His vehicle was in the lead, as usual, and was hit by a command detonated box mine of approximately 40 lbs. [He] was thrown from the tractor and sustained a broken neck. It was a sunny, warm day. When we heard his "zap number" [the first initial of his last name and the last four digits of his service number] on the radio, we all cried. (The Wall USA, 30 May 1999; wording amended in consultation with poster, 5 October 2005).

Others use the cyber format to offer a belated eulogy of sorts:

> John was a free spirit guy, love[d] motorcycles [and] women and nobody
> messed with him. I grew up directly across the street from John, his two
> brothers, sister and mother and father—a real nice family. JOHN was at
> the end of his tour when he was killed leading his guys in combat. He
> won two bronze stars that day. I also went to [N]am and was wounded a
> couple months before John died. I helped with getting our street named
> after John it[']s now called "JOHN VINCENT [. . .]" SQ. his name
> will be there forever to remember a Real American Hero. (The Wall
> USA, 19 September 2003)

Some family members and friends do write directly to their loved ones to tell
them they miss them, how their family is doing, and so forth. But, perhaps
because they are acutely aware that their loved ones are no longer around,
many posters don't feel the need to speak directly to them, choosing therefore to write about rather than to them. Writing in the third person, visitors
use the virtual walls for practical purposes—to tell others about the deceased,
to announce a memorial built in his honor, to ask for information, or to find
people he served with. But this practicality masks underlying and unresolved
grief, and, in this way, conversing using the third person suggests an inability
to directly confront the dead as it might also suggest a discomfort with this
form of memorializing.

Of course, visitors do more than speak about or to the dead, and they
leave more than words at the virtual walls. As at the National Vietnam Veterans Memorial, "On The Virtual Wall, visitors may leave tributes, letters,
poems, photos, and other memorials to someone named on The Wall for
other visitors to view. The goal is to provide an environment like The Wall
itself, with the dignity and respect those named on The Wall have earned."[19]
The types of objects that can be left online are necessarily limited to those
that are transferable from one computer to another such as poems and
quotes; photographs of the deceased, family members, or groups of veterans;
and computer renditions of other images such as military insignia. Also, like
visitors to the Wall, visitors to the virtual wall participate in physical rituals
online: they sit at their desk, switch on the computer, and, as Gore says, "run
their hands across the computer keyboard." Despite the ephemeral aspect of
the online experience, interaction is made concrete and given material weight
as Gore equates the experience of running fingers across keyboards with running them across names on the Wall.

Perhaps the most significant difference between the virtual wall and its physical counterparts relates to what visitors can communicate and learn there. Posters can explain the specific meaning of any objects they leave; they can provide details of someone's life or post a photograph or poem, and they know that these postings will remain as long-lasting, though virtual, memorials to the dead. Visitors can, quite literally, put a face to a name; they can learn how a serviceman lived and how he died. In contrast, the objects left at the Wall are seldom accompanied with explanations; when they are, the explanations are collected and stored by the park service and are inaccessible to visitors. The online postings construct personal narratives about the dead and continue to communicate the meaning and significance of someone's life to whoever reads them.

Web mourners might visit a virtual wall and feel comforted to know that others have had similar experiences, but the virtual walls do not facilitate the kind of interaction that a chat room or discussion board might. Since they do not foster interaction between their visitors, the communication is one way. While visitors can return to a soldier's page as often as they like, answers to questions or responses to requests for information are rarely posted; thus, visitors unconnected to the posters never know if these calls for information are answered or not. Because the communication is one directional, Martini argues that,

> [w]hile the structure of the Virtual Walls provides the potential for a more public-oriented discourse, what we see are visitors using the space for personal communication. Although connections are sought out, these acts of memory remain focused on individual, localized stories. As such, they reflect the larger political and cultural environment of the Real Wall, which does not offer a public space for public debate about the war and its legacies, but rather a liminal space for personal, private acts of memory. (442–443)

Despite the new forms of community and social networks promised by the web, virtual walls miss an opportunity to foster meaningful conversations among web mourners that could potentially carve out a productive way of remembering the war and the dead. While I do not wish to diminish the powerful effects of posting a message on a virtual wall, generally web mourners participate in this online community in isolation. Unlike comprehensive online support networks for cancer survivors, for example, the benefit of posting a message on the virtual wall does not come from feeling part of a community but from the individual satisfaction of communicating memories or feelings. The term "community" is used in cyber scholarship to describe a social network not limited by physical proximity, but in the case of the virtual walls the term is simply metaphoric: the network created is technological, not social; the only community is an anthology of texts and images.

Beyond displaying personal narratives and memories, virtual walls attract much patriotic commentary, which, as Martini suggests, does not necessarily contribute to a public debate on the war but does facilitate the expression of personal attitudes about it. Some postings, not surprisingly, reflect a post-9/11 understanding of America at war; this one, part of a high school project, seems to suggests the U.S. got involved in Vietnam because it was under threat: "Thank you very much for any help you offered during our countrys time of trouble. You gave your life so I could be free. Thank you for your courage and selflessness. You are truly a great American. Thank You" (Fund's Virtual Wall, 10 April 2003). Other postings convey a youthful understanding of patriotism and heroism: "Our class is doing a project to honor all the American Heros who gave their lives fighting for our country and what it stands for. We will never forget the courageous sacrifice that you made so others could know the freedom you knew. . . . You will always be remembered as an American hero; courageous, brave, and free" (Fund's Virtual Wall, 10 April 2003). And, similarly to the National Mall, visitors use the forum to comment on current U.S. policy and political issues:

> Well it is Sunday afternoon, 13 April 2003 and everyone is so happy that the seven POWs have been found in Iraq! We rejoice with them and their families! My thoughts turn to all of the POWs who are not accounted for from Viet Nam. [John] was a NAVY pilot who was lost in the service to his country in Southeast Asia. Godspeed John, wherever you are! (Fund's Virtual Wall, 13 April 2003)

While the majority of online narratives express mainstream perceptions of patriotism, the virtual walls have the potential to encourage a diverse range of meanings and responses. Even considering the technology gap, the web is accessible to a large cross section of the population and, thus, could offer an alternative to the homogenous narratives that emerge through other memorializing practices, such as those at the Last Firebase. However, because the virtual walls do not provide a forum for discussion, visitors post messages that reinforce rather than question entrenched beliefs. Visitors who post messages are provided no sense of historical context or continuity and, thus, as is the case with other heterogeneous but unmoderated and unstructured discussion forums, entrenched ideologies proliferate in a political and historical vacuum.

Maya Lin's simple design was chosen because it met the Vietnam Veterans Memorial Fund's specific request that the monument be "without political content" (Hess 121). And yet dissenters like Frederick Hart saw this lack of content as an expression both of liberalism and, in turn, of subversion (Hess 123–4). Today, at the Memorial complex and at replicas of the Wall, narratives on the war have become increasingly homogenous and narrow; often they simply focus on the heroism and sacrifice of American veterans and ignore the history of dissent then and the heterogeneity of memory today. While the controversy over the National Wall's design epitomizes deep divisions about the meaning of the war, the replica walls and their visitors rewrite the war's meaning into homogenous and uncritical narratives of patriotism that frequently ignore those divisions.

While the proliferation of memorializing across the country shifts the centralized remembering of the Vietnam War away from the National Mall, the practices themselves are often as routinized as they are at the Wall. This homogeneous memorializing emerges from the reactionary narratives of the war that circulate around official and unofficial "add-ons" to the Wall but also, of course, from the democratization of memorializing, which enables particular narratives to emerge and circulate and others to be minimized or erased. With broadening accessibility and narrowing meanings, more people memorialize but in more homogeneous ways. More positively, although virtual walls currently confirm rather than challenge dominant narratives of patriotism, online memorializing may evolve to provide a forum for multiple voices and perspectives.

As an authentic place, much like battlefields both in the U.S. and Vietnam, the Vietnam Veterans Memorial has an aura that Carol Becker from the Art Institute of Chicago suggests wall replicas do not.[20] In discussing how mechanical reproduction, such as photography and film, changes the nature of art, Walter Benjamin attributes the aura of an original piece of art to its qualities of authenticity, uniqueness, and distance, no matter how physically close it is (222–224). The central paradox of the concept is that an object's aura can be recognized through people's desire to reproduce it, but in that reproduction the aura of the object is destroyed. In these terms, Becker is correct: replicas of the Wall—both material and virtual—confirm the Wall's aura as an original work of art that evokes powerful responses from visitors, but in trying to replicate the Wall's aura they lack their own; at the same time, they also undermine the aura of the Wall.

But Becker seems to miss another part of Benjamin's critique: mechanical reproduction, he suggests, does not undermine an artwork's aura but "emancipates the work . . . from its parasitical dependence on ritual" (224). But replicas of the National Wall, as I have argued, may undermine its auratic status by reinforcing the routinization of rituals first enacted at the Wall. While the displacement of memory from location, enabled through traveling and virtual walls, creates memorializing practices that are increasingly democratic, decentralized, and decontextualized (or put differently, while citizens throughout the country have more access to the Wall through replicas), in the end the experience citizens have at the replicas is prescriptive. Because the tactile and physical experiences at the National Wall are missing, the copies cannot replicate the truly visceral and effective experiences at the Wall.

In the next chapter, I continue my analysis of the routinization of memorializing at the Wall by examining how the practice of leaving objects is presented in a now-closed Smithsonian Institute's exhibition, "Personal Legacy: The Healing of a Nation." In this display, the practice becomes somewhat sterilized as the Wall's viscerality is translated into a visual and contemplative experience at the museum. The chapter offers another model for how memorializing moves away from the Mall as it compares the Smithsonian's exhibit with the National Vietnam Veterans Art Museum in Chicago. One official, the other veteran led, both museums illustrate the materiality and individualization of memorializing in their displays of objects—items left at the Wall, veterans' art, guns taken from the dead, dog tags, and so on. The items signify a multiplicity of attitudes toward and political perspectives on the war, which the museums organize into fixed narratives of it.

Chapter Four
Objects of War and Remembrance

They carried all they could bear, including a silent awe for the terrible
power of the things they carried.

—Tim O'Brien

O'Brien's story "The Things They Carried" highlights the physical and
psychological weight of the war and its memory. The story emphasizes the
relationships between the physical objects the grunts carried as they were
"humping the boonies" and the psychological, emotional, and visceral import
of those objects, both during the war and after. The powerful, awe-inspiring
things they carry are both objects of war and destruction and objects of memory, containing the ghostly residues of various events or experiences occurring
in the past. It is this relationship between object and memory—the materiality of memory—that I seek to explore here, by focusing on two museum
exhibits that construct narratives of the Vietnam War using artifacts of war
and memory: "Personal Legacy: The Healing of a Nation" at the Smithsonian Institute's National Museum of American History and the exhibits at the
National Vietnam Veterans Art Museum in Chicago. "Personal Legacy" (now
closed to make way for an ambitious new military history exhibit, "The Price
of Freedom: Americans at War," discussed in the endnotes section to this
chapter) displayed a selection of objects left at the National Vietnam Veterans Memorial in Washington, D.C., and the Veterans Art Museum in Chicago continues to show art beside weaponry and other war relics. Wishing to
describe visitors' experiences at these museums, I will speak of both exhibits
in the present tense. The display of these objects of war and remembrance
illustrates their significance to the process of memorializing the war: at the
Smithsonian, the exhibit stages the practice of leaving objects at the Wall,
while the veteran-led Veterans Art Museum is both a site of memory and
itself a memorial practice. I argue that through their displays, the museums

construct new meanings of the objects by neglecting historical details of the war and the era, foregrounding a dichotomy between history and aesthetics and reinforcing the significance of memory in contemporary understandings of the Vietnam War.

I focus on Vietnam War-themed exhibits within museums that have broader purposes, the Smithsonian and the Veterans Art Museum, because the United States has no national history museum devoted to the war in Vietnam, with one exception. National in name only, the National Vietnam War Museum in Orlando, FL, has a limited focus and appeal: it works to educate high school students about the war through its display of war relics, a mock Vietnamese village, and an online discussion board, which currently has just twenty nine members.[1] The United States lacks one cohesive national museum that narrates the history of America's participation in war at home and abroad, akin to Britain's Imperial War Museum. National museums to specific wars exist, such as the National Civil War Museum in Harrisburg, PA, which portrays the entire story of the American Civil War "without either union or confederate bias."[2] In addition, some regional museums claim to cover all wars, such as the Virginia War Museum, which offers an "interpret[ation of] American military history from 1775 to the present."[3] With the exception of the Pearl Harbor museum-ship, USS Battleship Missouri, no national museums in the U.S. record the histories of American involvement in the two world wars.

That no national war museum exists illustrates, in part, an ambivalent American identity. The "imperial" in Britain's Imperial War Museum speaks of that country's at times self-identification as a colonial power whose strength was formed through conquest and resistance. In contrast, the United States historically has vacillated between shying away from interventionism and proclaiming itself to be an international superpower. The U.S. has always justified its participation in foreign wars as a defensive response to threats from other countries. Britain celebrates its military history in the Imperial War Museum, but if a national museum to war existed in the United States, it may have to acknowledge its uneasiness with that part of its history. Thus, the United States has preferred to build monuments to war, at which the construction of a coherent narrative of the history of the war is not required. On the National Mall, the war monuments are isolated from the Smithsonian Institute, which allows the museums to both present and shape a more comprehensive narrative of the nation and the role of war but without the need to directly engage with the monuments.

Because, literally and symbolically, the National Mall is at the center of U.S. war memorializing, visitors can piece together a chronology of the

United States at war through a carefully choreographed tour of the monuments outside; that tour would include the Washington Monument, the Lincoln Memorial, The Hiker (commemorating the Spanish-American War), the Seabees and Marine Corps (Iwo Jima) Memorials, the World War II Memorial, the Korean War Memorial, and the Vietnam Veterans Memorial. Charles Griswold argues that these structures are a particular kind of "recollective architecture, a species whose symbolic and normative content is prominent." Because no one died on or is buried under the Mall, the "Mall's memorials connect . . . war and politics on a purely symbolic level" (Griswold 690). Thus while the chronology of war is available to those who participate in guided tours or who come to the Mall having first researched their route, without that preparation the historical context is missing.

But, of course, visitors to the Mall can learn more about the role of war in America's history at some of the Smithsonian museums. For example, the National Air and Space Museum includes "WWI: The Great War in the Air" and "WWII Aviation," and the National Museum of American History formerly presented the "Hall of Armed Forces History" and now exhibits "The Price of Freedom: Americans at War." At both museums, war histories are constructed through a combination of artifact display and written explanation. At the World Wars aviation exhibits, visitors gaze on a sampling of war-era planes; in the Armed Forces hall, before it was removed, visitors could read brief histories of the roles of soldiers in war from George Washington to the G.I. during World War II, illustrated with various artifacts that symbolize the era and animate the written narrative. The new exhibit, "The Price of Freedom," strives to present a comprehensive chronological history of wars that has hitherto been lacking in the museums, starting with the Wars of Independence and concluding, at least for the time being, with the current War in Iraq.

The Smithsonian "collects artifacts of all kinds—from gowns to locomotives—to preserve for the American people an enduring record of their past" through which it hopes to "inspire a broader understanding of our nation and its many peoples."[4] By telling American history through the display of objects, the museum suggests that history is made from the ground up, although, of course, as a national government-funded institution, the museum constructs and depicts history in the opposite direction, from the top down. In comparison with this institutional history, the National Vietnam Veterans Art Museum, located in Chicago, was founded and is run by veterans; in its purpose as well as its methods, it attempts to produce grassroots knowledge about the war. Despite its regional location, its unique scope, broad-based appeal, and substantial collection of veteran artwork make it nationally significant.

Unlike the majority of regional war museums that do the important work collecting war items from local veterans but display them in rather unimaginative ways, the Veterans Art Museum utilizes innovative display techniques in order to present the war in Vietnam experientially.

Veteran-led sites of memory that are informed by veterans' support for a conservative political ideology construct patriotic narratives of the war that tend to ignore the Vietnamese, the antiwar movement, and the political and social divisiveness the war produced. However, the Veterans Art Museum is an important veteran-led site of memory that constructs narratives of the war in a different way: while various art pieces on display represent the heterogeneity and divisiveness of the war and its memory, its construction of what I call a quagmire aesthetic creates an alternative to the history of the war. Simply put, rather than narrate the war's history, the museum evokes its experience. Similarly, "Personal Legacy" presents not the history of the war but rather the public's response to it in the resonant practice of leaving objects at the Wall. While the absence of historical context can be somewhat problematic for a museum, of course, the focus on experience and memory over history reinforces a mistrust of the official history of the war, mistrust that was paradigmatic of the war era. As many Vietnam veteran writers argue, memory's disjointed, messy, repetitive, and heterogeneous aspects more accurately represent the war than formal history. While continuing to focus on the ways the war is rewritten at veterans' sites of memory, this chapter also highlights the marked differences between official and veteran-led sites of memory and examines the Wall's significance in continuing to shape memorial practices, exploring how veterans construct memorials that simultaneously confirm and challenge that significance.

The particular features that make the two museums so disparate are, in part, what make a comparison of them so compelling. While the Smithsonian is in many ways the quintessential modern museum (or disciplinary museum, in Foucault's terms), the Veterans Art Museum exists on the margins of this disciplinary framework. In different ways, both places combine techniques of museum display with memorializing: at the Smithsonian, this merging happens through its display of the evolution of memorializing at the Vietnam Veterans Memorial, which the museum demonstrates by presenting developments in the practice of leaving objects there. At the Chicago space, museum and memorial practices merge in its "Above and Beyond" memorial made of dog tags and in its display of the individual memorializing of hundreds of veterans who create art about or through their war experiences. By using objects to construct narratives of the war and the nation, the museums face questions of responsibility: if the Smithsonian as a national museum has the purpose to reflect American identity, what are the consequences of omitting the history of the war from that identity? Does it have an obligation to portray the war accurately and completely? And as a veteran-led, grassroots institution, does the Veterans Art Museum have the same obligation?

At these museums and, in fact, at any museum that displays artifacts, the meanings and evidentiary potential of objects are constructed in particular ways.[5] The scholarship on this practice spans several fields and disciplines, including material culture, art history, and ethnography. Kristin Hass suggests that scholarly work in material culture, which has influenced the fields of American studies and art history, falls into two distinct camps: "one is interested primarily in theories of interpretation as they might apply to things, and the other is interested in details of the things themselves" (30). In the first approach, exemplified in Christopher Tilley's anthology *Reading Material Culture*, attention is given "to ideas of signs and systems of signs, but it is almost completely without mention of particular things" (Hass 31). In contrast, the second approach, in work such as Thomas Schlereth's *Material Culture Studies on America*, examines "details about the origins, production, and histories of things" but does not "explore the symbolic work of material things." Hass suggests that because "a tension [exists] between the context from which they come and the communicative work they do," both approaches together are needed to understand the practice of leaving objects at the Wall (32).

Art historians focus specifically on how museums construct and construe the meanings of objects through selection and arrangement. For example, in *Museums and the Shaping of Knowledge*, Eilean Hooper-Greenhill charts the "taxonomies used to explain the interrelationships of objects and species" in the disciplinary museum during three epistemes—Renaissance, classical, and modern.[6] Hooper-Greenhill suggests that in the classical episteme, objects were arranged in the museum according to "theme, material, or size," whereas in the modern museum they are organized by, for example, school or nation. In these new arrangements, "successive identities and differences began to replace the visual identities and differences of the classical age" (188). Attending to the display of art in the museum and developments in art history, Donald Preziosi examines the hybridity of the art object. He suggests the discipline of art history positions the object within an historical teleology, such as an art movement or school, but also reads it as a unique piece of art (1992, 1993, 1996). In the museum, art is most commonly arranged spatially, such as the period room, or temporally, according to school, style, or artist (1993: 226). The period room presents the objects within "a complex function of multiple relationships within its contextual milieu," while temporal arrangements "foreground the work's significance as an integral part of an aesthetic or historical development over time" (226).

Focusing on ethnographic displays in museums, Barbara Kirshenblatt-Gimblett examines what she terms the "the agency of display" in museums (as well as in folkloric performances and festivals), the idea that display "not only shows and speaks, it also *does*" (6). As she argues in *Destination Culture*, items become ethnographic objects not because of what they are intrinsically or where they are found but by their "detach[ment] from their original culture or environment" (18). Any object has a use value for an individual or a community, but this value does not make it ethnographic; only when it is "defined, segmented, detached, and carried away by ethnographers" (18) does it become so. Kirshenblatt-Gimblett highlights a paradox in ethnography when items with little visual interest that "were never meant to be displayed" are exhibited (2). This lack of visual appeal highlights how interest must be manufactured (2), and it also suggests that the meaning of the object is generated not at its point of origin but at its destination or place of display (12).

Shared across material culture, art history, and ethnography scholarship is the idea that an object's evidentiary potential is constructed rather than is intrinsic to it. Ernesto Laclau and Chantal Mouffe argue the object's meaning is shaped within a system of socially constructed rules they call discourse. To explain the concept, they offer a useful illustration:

> If I kick a spherical object in the street or if I kick a ball in a football match, the *physical* fact is the same, but its *meaning* is different. The object is a football only to the extent that it establishes a system of relations with other objects, and these relations are not given by the mere referential materiality of the objects but are, rather, socially constructed. . . . the discursive character of an object does not, by any means, imply putting its existence into question. The fact that a football is only a football as long as it is integrated within a system of socially constructed rules does not mean that it thereby ceases to be a physical object. (82)

In discussing the difference between a spherical object and a football, Laclau and Mouffe call attention to how the meaning of an object depends on its particular use within social or historical contexts (consider how a football is only a spherical object in certain contexts: in the United States, a football is oval, whereas in Europe or Mexico, for example, a football [soccer ball] is spherical). But they stress that just because meanings are always constructed within certain contexts this does not imply that objects cease to exist outside that context. The illustration shows the difference between the "being" or meaning of an object, which changes according to the discourse in which it is located, and the object's "entity" or materiality, which doesn't (85).

If objects with no aesthetic visual interest are on display, museums must have another reason for showing them: to this end, Hooper-Greenhill and Tony Bennett examine the educational purposes that inform the display of objects in the modern museum. In *The Birth of the Museum,* Bennett posits that toward the end of the nineteenth century the modern museum "allowed cultural artefacts to be refashioned in ways that would facilitate their deployment for new purposes as parts of governmental programmes aimed at reshaping general norms for social behaviour" (6). Hooper-Greenhill examines how museums became part of the state education system and "new practices emerged as the 'museum' attempted to fulfill its function of transforming the population into a useful resource for the state" (182).

In these readings, museums put objects on display in order to facilitate the construction of narratives of the nation, which in turn instruct and shape visitors' perceptions of and dedication to it. As the United States' official historical and educational institution, the Smithsonian is an exemplary modern museum. The Museum of American History, in which "Personal Legacy" is housed, continually reconceives displays by bringing together the objects in its existing collection in new ways. For example, in April 2004, the museum opened "Taking America to Lunch," which displays seventy-five lunch boxes from its collection. These boxes could easily be used in period exhibits such as "Within These Walls," the story of five families who lived in the same house over a period of two hundred years, or "More Work for Mother" in "Hands on History," one of the museum's interactive rooms. In addition, the museum's floor plan organizes objects thematically such as "the history of science and technology" and "technological and social issues." The architectural design (doorways, walls, and stairs directing the flow of human traffic) forces visitors to proceed through the museum in a particular direction and, at the same time, teaches them conventional behavior in the museum (even if they choose to ignore it, which many do). Through these apparatuses and techniques, the museum shapes as much as it displays American identity. In contrast, while the Veterans Art Museum also educates visitors about the experience of war, it does so without government funding and its concomitant constraints. Like the "Personal Legacy" exhibit, the art museum's displays and floor plans are used to stage narratives about the war. However, the building itself is a converted warehouse not specifically designed for display or visitors and has not been significantly altered to shepherd visitors along certain paths. If the Smithsonian constructs and represents American identity generally, the

Veterans Art Museum does the same with veteran identity more specifically. But their differences—in the display choices and the narratives of the war produced through these decisions—matter, as I show.

PERSONAL LEGACY: HEALING THE NATION BY OMITTING THE WAR

"Personal Legacy: The Healing of a Nation" was on display in the Smithsonian Institute's Museum of American History from 1991 until its permanent closure in September 2003. The exhibit consists of two elements: a selection of objects that were left at the National Vietnam Veterans Memorial, displayed in a large glass display case along the full length of one wall, and a free-standing structure in the center of the room that includes a model of the Memorial on one side and more objects encased in a small vitrine on the other. In both elements of the exhibit, jointly organized by the Smithsonian and the National Parks Service, information labels provide some history of and background to the practice of leaving objects at the Wall and summarize the difficulties faced by veterans on their return to the United States.

Figure 4. "Personal Legacy: The Healing of a Nation" exhibition. Courtesy of the Smithsonian's National Museum of American History.

On Veterans Day, 2004, a new military history exhibit replaced "Personal Legacy" and its adjacent "Hall of Armed Forces History;" the new exhibit, "The Price of Freedom: Americans at War," provides a coherent narrative of the history of American involvement in wars, emphasizing the perspective of ordinary Americans who fought in them.

Objects collected from the Wall and displayed in "Personal Legacy" are arranged and juxtaposed to construct a narrative of the war that calls attention to the cultural resonance of the Wall and the preponderance of memory over history. At the same time as the exhibit contextualizes the practice of leaving objects within what it deems a uniquely American cultural and historical milieu, it omits the larger historical background and political circumstances that would explain the existence of the Wall and why people leave objects there. The implications for these erasures are particularly significant for a museum that has as its primary goal the education of the American public.

As visitors make their way through the museum, they will see directions to a third-floor exhibit titled "Vietnam: Personal Legacy." If visitors follow the route suggested, they will walk through the Hall of Armed Forces History and into an area containing "Personal Legacy" along with other exhibits related to military history such as "West Point in The Making of America," "A More Perfect Union: Japanese Americans and the U.S. Constitution," and "Gunboat Philadelphia." Once past the hall, the exhibit's name changes from "Vietnam: Personal Legacy" to "Personal Legacy: The Healing of a Nation," losing direct reference to Vietnam and offering an interpretation and outcome for the exhibit's focus—the leaving of objects at the Wall.

"Personal Legacy" displays a selection of objects that were left at the Wall between its dedication in 13 November 1982 and the cutoff date for the exhibit, 31 October 1991. Twice a day, the National Parks Service (NPS) collects items that have been left there and transports them to a storage facility in Maryland, where they are catalogued and preserved. Edward Ezell of the Smithsonian and Duery Felton and Pamela Beth West of NPS selected items from storage for display in "Personal Legacy." In the display, the objects are grouped into the following four time periods: 1982–1985, 1986–1987, 1988–1989, and 1990–1991 (see Figure 4). In the narrative accompanying the exhibit, curator Ezell explains that the types of object left at the Wall have changed over time:

> The kinds and the nature of the objects left at the Memorial have evolved over the past decade. In the early years, remembrances generally were smaller, unsigned, spontaneous offerings. Today they tend to be personalized assemblages. Early messages were hastily scribbled and

left out in the open, but many now are framed, laminated, or covered in protective plastic. Among the first donors were family members, comrades, and loved ones of those who served and died in Southeast Asia. Later offerings reflect all segments of society—young and old, American and foreign. The Wall speaks to more than the Vietnam generation. It reminds all people of the ultimate cost of war. The only consistent data available for objects are the date they were left and the place or panel at which they were placed. Each object's story often remains known only to the donor. These items invite our contemplation, reflection, and our own conclusions.

To depict the evolution Ezell discusses, the exhibit organizes the objects temporally and spatially. The chronological format of the encased objects, most clearly suggested in the four date markers, makes it possible for visitors to perceive both an evolution in the types of objects left at the Wall and a progression from spontaneous offerings to personal assemblages. Paradoxically, the cutoff date, 31 October 1991, mitigates any possibility of further evolution. Perhaps the exhibition would have been updated had Ezell not passed away in 1993, but his death delimits the exhibit with the result that "Personal Legacy" memorializes the curator as much as the objects memorialize the war dead.[7]

Visitors also see in the large display case a spatial arrangement replicating how the Wall might look after many items have been left there. Despite Ezell's assertion that the types of objects left at the Wall have evolved over time, any significant progression is hard to identify in a display that generally appears cluttered with seemingly random items. Commonly left objects such as helmets, teddy bears, buttons, badges, and handwritten or typed notes appear at every stage of the display. Dotted between these common items are larger and more eye catching pieces, such as a nurse's uniform and a mock up of a tiger cage, used by America's south Vietnamese allies to imprison members of the Viet Cong. The exhibit clearly has been arranged for aesthetic appeal as well as to attempt an accurate portrayal of the practice of leaving objects. But this staging, mimicking how the Wall might look, is artificial because while some objects have been chosen for their ordinariness, others are on display for their unusual appeal. As the selection of objects mitigates an accurate re-creation of the Wall, so the number or range of items displayed in the exhibit is far greater and more varied than would be seen on an average day at the Wall.

In contrast to the loosely temporal yet randomly organized display, selected items dividing each of the four time periods are arranged in a highly structured fashion. A display of dog tags is set in between the first two time periods, 1982–85 and 1986–87, while a collection of military stripes appears between 1986–87 and 1988–89, and rows of Prisoner of War/ Missing in Action (POW/MIA) bracelets are set between the final two time periods, 1988–89 and 1990–91. So far I have suggested the exhibit arranges items in two ways—in a chronological trajectory that narrates the evolution of object leaving and in a spatial staging that simulates the leavings at the Wall. But these in-between sections present the objects in a third type of arrangement: not temporal or spatial but thematic. The dog tags, stripes, and bracelets demarcate each of the temporal periods and create a different kind of aesthetic interest. In the center display, a frame containing approximately one hundred neatly arranged military stripes reaches almost four feet high. Candles are placed beneath the frame with, at each side, desk flags depicting military and state insignia. Matching candle and flag arrangements are positioned beneath similarly organized dog tag and bracelet displays. These arrangements thus have the appearance of shrines, reminding visitors of those who died or are missing and referencing the grief of those who mourn at the Wall. Presented as sites of mourning, these thematic displays speak to the living, helping visitors understand the significance of the other objects on display. Although it is

Figure 5. Display of military stripes in "Personal Legacy: The Healing of a Nation" exhibition. Courtesy of the Smithsonian's National Museum of American History.

not clear if the candles and flags were collected from the Wall or provided by the museum, they also narrate the exhibition as a place of memory and ritual, like the Wall itself.

Because the dog tags, stripes, and bracelets are placed between each periodized section, the display implies their leaving occurred in a chronological order also. The arrangement implies that in the early years, visitors to the Wall would leave dog tags and that later military stripes were more common. By the end of the 1980s, according to the chronology, visitors favored leaving POW/ MIA bracelets. The time order produces a specific narrative about visitors' interactions with the Wall. Evolving over the ten-year period covered by the exhibition, changes in the types of objects suggest parallel changes in attitudes among the American public toward the war, veterans, and the role of the Wall in memorializing the war. The progression from dog tags to stripes narrates a shift from soldier to hero (all soldiers had tags, but only those who rose through the ranks of the military had stripes), while the move from stripes to bracelets narrates another shift from the dead to the missing and presumably alive soldiers (recall how the POW/ MIA movement's rationale is based on the firm belief that soldiers are still alive), as well as from the war era to the postwar era (soldiers were decorated during the war, but the POW/ MIA movement continues to the present day). But, like the spatial arrangement that stages the exhibition to look like the Wall, these themed sections also are artificial because the items were left at the Wall during the entire period represented by the museum's collection, not just within the specific time period within which they are displayed. So, the dog tags placed between 1982–1985 and 1986–1987 might have been left at the Wall during any time between 1982 and the exhibit's completion date in 1991; in other words, the narrated evolution in object leaving is as much constructed as it is observed.

In the museum, these offerings are presented as meaningful simply because they were left at the Wall. In *Carried to the Wall*, Kristin Hass argues that each object left at the Wall "is a response to the problem of patriotism in the wake of the war" and that "each object is caught up in the symbolic negotiations of the shape of the nation at the Wall" (89). But when she elaborates on the symbolic meaning of objects to leavers, this argument cannot be sustained because those meanings can never be known by outside observers. Let me use one example from Hass' generally very persuasive work to illustrate how her argument becomes undone at the point when she tries to read symbolic potential into the objects. Hass interprets a Slim Jim, a metal device for unlocking car doors that was left at the Wall in 1990, in several symbolic ways. She starts by suggesting it might symbolize a "memory about stolen life" or "a metaphor for unlocking the seamless listing of the memorial" and concludes that the Slim Jim "helps the living to unlock, to release, the dead" (100). While Hass acknowledges that the item might have been left at the Wall for a more mundane reason, in "reference to a habit of stealing cars," she does not draw a distinction between the meaning of the objects to its leavers and the meaning to her, the ethnographer at the Wall. But this distinction is a crucial one because the interpretations are Hass' and not the leaver's, and the meanings are only generated at the destination (at the Wall, with Hass observing) not at the source (with the person who left the Slim Jim at the Wall), to put it in Kirshenblatt-Gimblett's terms.

As Laclau and Mouffe suggest, the identity and meaning of an object is constituted by the discourse it enters. Thus, the Slim Jim will have significantly different meanings in everyday use, at the Wall, or on display in the Smithsonian. In the discourse of the everyday, a Slim Jim, as Hass correctly suggests, is a device for breaking into locked cars. Although Hass' reading implies its illegal use, Slim Jims are commonly and legally available. Because the Wall is a memorial site, when left there a Slim Jim becomes an offering for the dead, a way to connect the leaver to a name on the Wall. While we cannot know its specific significance, we can know that it has some significance to the person who left it. When the item moves into the museum, it takes on other meanings. If displayed in "Personal Legacy," a Slim Jim's everyday meaning would lessen and the item would convey instead an official recognition of the war, the dead, and the person who left it. The item would become meaningful as an object of memorialization (at the Wall) and of aestheticization (in the museum). Visitors would look at the item and see a Slim Jim, but its display would provoke speculation on its other meanings, as I have suggested above.

Items on display in the museum also become meaningful as ethnographic objects by being removed from the Wall. This removal decontextualizes the items from their relationships with leavers and with names on the Wall and recontextualizes them as cultural and historical artifacts. Culturally, they illustrate the American public's response to the Wall. Historically, they represent contemporary memorializing. In ways similar to the function of objects in the natural history or ethnographic museum, objects plucked from the Wall to be displayed in the museum are at once essentialized (becoming the quintessence of the objects left at the Wall) and totalizing (standing in for all objects left there), to reference Kirshenblatt-Gimblett's argument for a second time (55).

In the "Personal Legacy" exhibit, items are displayed temporally, spatially, and thematically, depicting the evolution in the kinds of items left at the wall, staging the Wall as it looks when people leave objects at it, and conveying the Wall's spiritual and symbolic resonance. In the spatial organization of the museum itself, "Personal Legacy" is located in a room immediately beyond the Hall of Armed Forces History. Visitors can pass through the hall into a room that contains "Personal Legacy" and several other war-themed exhibits. Because the Hall of Armed Forces History ends with "G.I.: World War II" and this hall leads into "Personal Legacy," visitors might assume that the museum chronologizes war and that "Personal Legacy" addresses the war in Vietnam the way that "G.I.: World War II" presents that war. However, two problems emerge with this chronology: first of all, the sequence only works if visitors ignore (as the museum did before the installation of the new exhibit, "The Price of Freedom") the intervening war in Korea. More importantly, the Armed Forces Hall and "Personal Legacy" are clearly separate exhibitions. Thus, to understand the chronology, visitors must themselves make the connection between the World War II exhibit at the end of the Hall and "Personal Legacy" in the adjacent room. However, visitors might have additional difficulty making this connection because "Personal Legacy," like the Hall of Armed Forces History, does not discuss the history of the war in Vietnam at all.

The war itself is mentioned twice in the exhibit's written explanations, both times in relation to its legacies on the home front. The label explaining the main section of the exhibit, quoted earlier, states: "[a]mong the first donors were family members, comrades, and loved ones of those who served and died in Southeast Asia. Later offerings reflect all segments of society—young and old, American and foreign. The Wall speaks to more than the Vietnam generation. It reminds all people of the ultimate cost of war." The narrative affixed to the model of the Wall declares: "[t]his selection of remembrances provides us an opportunity to ponder the continuing impact of the Vietnam Veterans Memorial on the generation that lived through that conflict." In both explanations, the focus is on the legacies of the war, not its history. In the first, the text suggests that the objects rather than any direct or specific details of the war remind people of the ultimate cost of war. The second label reinforces the exhibition's proposal that the Wall not the war has a continuing impact on the war-era generation. Because the exhibit's purpose is to display objects left at the Wall, it might not seem fair to criticize its omission of the war's history. However, the exhibition's placement beside the Hall of Armed Forces History implies that a history of the war is being presented, just as a history of World War II is presented through the figure of the G.I. In effect, the museum presents a history of America at war that omits the Vietnam War yet includes American citizens' responses to it.

While the labels fail to historicize the exhibit, other accompanying materials do provide some historical and cultural context to help shape visitors' perceptions about the Wall. In the printed brochure accompanying "Personal Legacy," the objects are described using a variety of carefully chosen expressions like "tokens of remembrance," "mementos," "keepsakes," "collections of messages and gifts from the heart," "outpourings," "gifts," "remembrances," "personalized assemblages," "messages," and "offerings." The museum describes leaving objects as personal and individualized gestures, emphasizing both the emotional reaction of the visitor and the connection between the donor (the person leaving the object) and the dead (the name on the Wall). The brochure tries to personalize the practice (Personal Legacy) as it also nationalizes the experience of recovery (The Healing of a Nation). Further serving to limit the meaning of national healing to personal grief, the cover of the brochure features a man wearing what looks like a military shirt with his arms dramatically outstretched above his head, his palms flat against the Wall touching several names, and his forehead resting on the granite. The fact that he touches several names at once suggests that he feels grief not just for one person but for several soldiers who died at the same time. Because the man's face cannot be seen, he functions as a symbolic griever at the Wall, and his anonymity allows both veterans and nonveterans to connect with his grief. The image does nothing to illustrate directly the practice of leaving objects, which is the exhibit's focus after all, but the portrait of an anonymous griever helps to connect the exhibit with the emotions evoked at the Wall.

This emotive image is one way the Smithsonian counteracts the potential sterilizing of the objects' meanings when it displays them behind glass in the museum. The photograph, like the text in the pamphlet and the labels in the exhibit, guides visitors to understand the significance of the exhibit. But unlike the exhibit, which lacks reference to the history of the war, the brochure includes a historical overview of the war in three short paragraphs. The first starts with one word—"Vietnam"—and provides some basic statistics about the war, including its duration; figures for the amount of Americans dead, wounded, and disabled; and number of those still missing. The second paragraph discusses the difficulties veterans faced trying to explain their war experiences to those at home, especially before the Wall was built. In the final paragraph, the brochure presents the America to which veterans returned, divided as it was by opinions about the war. According to the pamphlet and aligned with the narrative at The Wall That Heals, few veterans received a thank you, and few who died were publicly mourned—until the Wall was built.

In order to provide visitors with the context in which to understand the Wall, these materials need to be available at the exhibition. Yet while exhibition

Figure 6. Cover, "Personal Legacy: The Healing of a Nation" pamphlet.

pamphlets usually are available in abundance at the museum, in the spring of 1999, the museum had to photocopy one of the few remaining pamphlets for me. When I visited "Personal Legacy" in 2002, no printed literature was available. The absence of supplementary materials suggests that the exhibit had become neglected but also perhaps that the museum wished to separate the objects and the Wall's history it displays from the history of the war. Indeed, the lack of war history produces a specific narrative of memorializing in the postwar era. The museum's basic mission is "to inspire a broader understanding of our nation and its many peoples;" and Brent Glass, the museum's director, writes that "the Museum takes care of more than three million objects that preserve the memories and experiences of the American people.[8] The museum's large collection of objects and its interpretive activities make this "the place where history comes alive." But the history presented in "Personal Legacy" is partial and incomplete. It is a history not of the war but of the response of the American public to the war. Within that history, only one response is presented—grieving—and only one form of grieving is presented—leaving objects at the Wall. Even the pamphlet, which does address the war, provides barely enough information for the visitor/ reader to appreciate how personal grieving for the dead is aligned with healing the nation. In addition, the Wall's facilitation of national healing is presented as a given and no discussion occurs on whether or not the nation really has been healed after the war or even what exactly healing constitutes.

In the museum, objects become meaningful through their role in the construction of an official history of the nation's healing process after the war in Vietnam. The context in which visitors contemplate objects is carefully scripted by the museum, but the particular meaning of any object to its leaver can never be known by others. An object's significance will thus always be shaped through the context of its position on the Mall, either at the Wall or in the museum. And because observers can endlessly contemplate the meaning of an object and its significance to the person who left it, its source meaning remains elusive to them. The objects themselves not only resist the knowledge produced about them in the museum space; they also reinforce memory's dominance over history in the exhibit and in cultural discourse. The museum does not use the objects to narrate history, but they can be used to demonstrate memory.

In comparison with "Personal Legacy," objects displayed in the National Vietnam Veterans Art Museum omit history as much to foreground the viscerality of war as its memory. The exhibits produce knowledge about the war that is immediate and experiential—visitors are shocked or moved by the art works and memorial of dog tags, and veterans are reminded of their own experiences in combat. Through its chaotic and overwhelming displays and exhibits, the museum creates a sensory overload that I call aesthetics of the quagmire, an exhibitionary technique that serves to recreate the grunts' experiences of war.

THE NATIONAL VIETNAM VETERANS ART MUSEUM: AESTHETICS OF THE QUAGMIRE

The National Vietnam Veterans Art Museum in Chicago presents the brutal and confusing experience of war through its displays of objects of war and remembrance. In the museum, artworks produced by veterans are displayed alongside captured weapons. At the entrance to the museum, a memorial made of over 58,000 dog tags brings together art and military relics. If the Smithsonian's "Personal Legacy" exhibit puts citizens' memorializing practices on display, the Veterans Art Museum shows how visiting the museum and creating art for display are themselves memorializing acts. At every level of the museum's display, from individual artworks to the arrangement of items on the floor or wall, to the juxtaposition of artworks with war relics, a narrative of the war as quagmire is presented. This aesthetic attempts to simulate a visceral experience for the viewer, comparable to Michael Herr's simulation of the viscerality of war in *Dispatches*. In addition, this narrative, like in "Personal Legacy," erases important aspects of the war but at the same time allows visitors to experience some of what veterans experienced in Vietnam.

The seed was sown for the National Vietnam Veterans Art Museum in the late 1970s when a group of three veterans put together a show of veterans' artwork at N.A.M.E. gallery in Chicago. Calling themselves the Vietnam Veterans Art Group, the three soon joined with Vietnam veteran artist Joseph Clarence Fornelli and Sondra Varco, who would later become the museum's Executive Director, to open an exhibit titled "Vietnam: Reflexes and Reflections" in October 1981 (Varco 9–13), a title that foregrounds the museum's choice to focus on experience and memory over history. By the end of the 1980s, the art group had grown from its original five members to over one hundred. Between 1983 and 1992, the group brought its exhibition to over thirty galleries and display sites across the U.S. and attracted new members at each place. After being housed free of charge for two years in a temporary gallery space, it purchased a warehouse from the City of Chicago on the corner of 18th Street and Indiana Avenue South in the Grant Park neighborhood for a token payment of $1; the City also donated over $1,000,000 to renovate the premises. In August 1996, the National Vietnam

Veterans Art Museum opened to the public. On its opening, the museum owned over 500 works of art and accepted everything donated by veterans; now it must jury the acquisition of new pieces. Today the museum owns over 1,000 pieces of art by over 130 artists, the overwhelming majority of whom are American, though some are Australian, Cambodian, Thai, and Vietnamese, including former members of the National Liberation Front and North Vietnamese Army.

The museum's history and mission statement focus proudly on its refusal to offer political commentary on the war or to modify the collection in any way. On its website, the museum asserts that it is "adamantly apolitical and without bias," a claim that, however admirable, seems somewhat implausible for a museum based on war. In the museum's only full length publication named for its first exhibition, "Vietnam: Reflexes and Reflections," Vietnam veteran and art historian Anthony Janson explains the museum's apolitical claim, noting that in its collection "[t]here is remarkably little direct commentary for or against the war in the art of Vietnam veterans" (202) and that most veterans are "deeply offended by the use of their art as a vehicle for someone else's political opinions." Yet he concludes that to treat this art neutrally is "hardly possible" (199). In her brief history of the Vietnam Veteran Art Group, Varco points out the group's refusal to censor or edit works that may be offensive to individual viewers or corporate sponsors because of their graphic nature, for example. Her assertion that in the early days veterans brought their wives and children to see the exhibit in order to "show them what Vietnam was really like" (11) indicates how the museum's emphasis on the perceived truth of the war and on artistic authenticity were and continue to be a significant lens through which visitors appreciate its art and understand its general mission. Put differently, the museum puts the representation of the war in the control of those who experienced it first hand—the veterans—refusing to discriminate among the artworks and at the same time privileging their perspectives.[9]

The museum's commitment to apoliticism and veteran authenticity translates into a general lack of curatorial practice as it is usually conducted at a traditional museum. In many places, paintings and photographs are displayed salon style, covering some walls almost to capacity, while sculptures are spread all over the floor space. Praising the lack of spatial organization at the museum in her article, "The Blank Space on the Gallery Wall: The Art of Vietnam Veterans in Context," Eve Sinaiko argues that the museum "has always resisted the rhetoric of pristine museum walls and sought to undermine the aesthetic hierarchies of gallery practice" (230). Her comment implies that the museum deliberately challenges the conventions of display in the traditional museum as described by Hooper-Greenhill, Preziosi, Kirshenblatt-Gimblett, and Bennett, among others.

The organization of space and objects at the Veterans Art Museum, or more appropriately the lack of organization, is as much a challenge to the prevailing conventions of display as it is the creation of an aesthetic of the quagmire in representing the war. This aesthetic enables the construction of a specific experience for its visitors and also produces a particular meaning of the war. For veterans, the word "quagmire" reminds them of immediate, confusing, and overwhelming experiences during their time in Vietnam. The museum tries to teach visitors what Vietnam "was really like," which for many veterans was a combination of physical and mental exhaustion, sensory overload, increasing frustration, and hopelessness. The term also functions as a political metaphor, which, along with "imperialist" and "noble cause," constitutes three competing descriptions of the war that continue to circulate, as Bruce Franklin argues in *Vietnam and Other American Fantasies*.[10] Franklin suggests that while the noble cause theory depicts the U.S. government during the war era as "a coward and a weakling," and the imperialism critique reads the government as "a ruthless agent of power and domination," the quagmire paradigm positions it as "a well-intentioned but self-deceived incompetent" (43). The idea that the war was a quagmire, proposed originally by David Halberstam in his 1965 work *The Making of a Quagmire*, provides an account of war that was appealing to many soldiers and veterans who came to question or oppose the conflict but still desired to have their role in it honored. Halberstam describes how the U.S. government found itself "caught in a limited, ineffective[,] and almost certainly doomed holding action" (38, 322) that was followed, according to Franklin, by "years of errors, misunderstandings, and confusion as America lurche[d] and wallow[ed] deeper and deeper into the mire of Vietnam" (42). The quagmire theory highlights the confusion and frustration felt by those stationed in Vietnam and primarily evokes the first-hand experience of veterans without addressing the larger political agenda. The theory is political but focuses on government incompetence rather than deliberate imperialism and affirms the individual nobility of soldiers without claiming the war was a noble cause. As a metaphor, "quagmire" refers to not only the confusion of battle but also the idea that Vietnam's landscape contributed to that confusion, thus emphasizing an experience only the grunts— on the ground, in the jungle, in the quagmire—could have knowledge of. While the imperialism theory implies forward planning and the future conquest of nations, and the noble cause theory retrospectively rewrites the war as a history of American military success, the quagmire theory captures the immediacy of the war experience in Vietnam. By representing the war as quagmire, the museum suggests the war can be understood as aesthetic experience rather than historical event. It also suggests that the veterans' experiences can be accepted as a type of authentic history without discussions of the political aspects of the war (the causes, purposes, and outcomes other than those directly affecting veterans).

At the Veterans Art Museum, the lack of attention to the larger political agenda that precipitated and prolonged U.S. involvement in Vietnam, the foregrounding of experience over history, and the privileging of veterans' perspectives on the war all contribute to the construction of a quagmire aesthetic. These elements appear in individual works of art, in the juxtapositions of items, and in the display of art with war relics. The quagmire aesthetic, however, should not be considered the result of carefully constructed curatorial practice. Curation, in the form of the systematic ordering of relations between objects, appears lacking at this museum for the most part, but individual works of art function as they do at the modern museum: each piece has its place in the taxonomy of Vietnam veterans art and, at the same time, represents an element of what can be termed, albeit somewhat problematically, the Vietnam experience. The artwork on display also functions ethnographically: whether purposely or not, many of the works do not meet standards that have developed through traditional forms of art connoisseurship or observe the styles of particular art schools. Thus, the artworks are more likely to be contemplated for what they convey about the veteran artists' war or postwar experiences. But the absence of modern curatorial practice becomes its own form of curatorial practice; the absence of the history of the war in the museum's aesthetics of the quagmire produces another way of knowing and understanding the war; and the museum's professed apoliticism becomes itself a political stance.

The authenticity of the veteran-artist is central to the quagmire aesthetic and to the museum's ideology as a whole, but this authenticity is particularly important for photographs, the only medium on display created during the war and in the battlefields (with the exception of Joe Fornelli's works: watercolors constructed using C-ration coffee and river water and sculptures like "Dressed to Kill," made in the field and shipped back to the U.S.)[11] Photographs confirm the quagmire aesthetic in more immediate ways than other artistic media. Despite the artistic subjectivity in their composition, developing, printing, selection, and framing, photographs represent the experience of war as it was happening, not afterwards when the veteran returned to the U.S. John Tagg argues that institutions give photography "its status as a unified something," which conveys the belief that "photographs picture the real" (63). While Tagg is writing of disciplinary institutions, such as the police force, the prison, the asylum, and the like, I would argue photographs function in a similar way at the Veterans Art Museum: they authenticate the other art on display, provide the context through which to understand some of the most abstract pieces and, as a result, are used to constitute a particular truth about the war. Because the quagmire functions on at least three levels in the museum—in the content of individual art, the arrangement of items, and the display of art with war relics—my analysis also proceeds through each of these layers. The museum's visceral effect works on all levels, from the overwhelming power of a single image to the questions and confusions provoked by the layout of the museum as a whole.

Art Dockter's photograph, "Real Dead Dead," depicts a hideously mutilated body lying in an unidentified field in Vietnam. The body is so deformed it is difficult to tell immediately whether it is American or Vietnamese, although the uniform rags around the body's ankles and upper thighs tell us this was a soldier not a civilian; the size and shape of thighs indicate, additionally, the body was male. (On closer inspection, it is possible to determine he was Vietnamese.) The legs and torso are cut in sections, the left knee is severed, the head is completely detached, and the face appears to have been ripped off, turned inside out, and flung away from the rest of the body. Despite its destruction, the body lies in an odd, silent state of repose—the

Figure 7. Art Dockter, "Real Dead Dead" (1970). Courtesy of artist.

left arm, severed at the elbow, gestures upwards, the feet point towards each other, and the body lies slightly to one side as if in a sleeping position. And yet, it has been violently torn apart; muscles and tissue are exposed and the upper part of the torso is charred black. The absence of blood suggests, mercifully, that this young soldier was killed on impact.

In many ways, the graphic photograph is the most recognizable and influential documentary medium of war. (Graphic depictions such as "Real Dead Dead" recall the long history of photographing the war dead beginning with Timothy Sullivan's shocking Civil War photograph, "A Harvest of Death, Gettysburg," which by depicting dead bodies strewn all over the battlefield illustrates how dying in war lacked gallantry.[12]) Photographic and televisual images of Vietnam—including firefights, the wounded, Vietnamese landscapes, and GIs arriving, leaving, and sitting around—saturated televisions, newspapers, and magazines across the U.S. from the mid 1960s on. Iconic images from the era, like Eddie Adams' 1968 portrait of General Loan shooting a Viet Cong prisoner in the head and Nick Ut's 1972 image of nine years old Kim Phuc and other children fleeing a napalm attack, are frequently accorded the distinction of shifting public opinion in the U.S. against the war.[13] This kind of photography shaped public perceptions of the Vietnam War to a greater extent than photography has done in any war before or since. While Joe Rosenthal's photograph of soldiers raising the flag atop Mount Suribachi in Iwo Jima has become the single most widely known photograph of war, photographic images captured during the Vietnam War do more than signify patriotism and victory, like Rosenthal's does, but have the power to effect change. By strongly influencing public opinion about U.S. involvement in Vietnam at the time they were released by Associated Press and distributed across the world, Adams' and Ut's images seem to challenge Roland Barthes' and Susan Sontag's arguments that photographs only confirm political or moral positions but do not change them (Barthes 1978; Sontag 1973). Today, the war continues to be defined and remembered by a handful of still images taken in Vietnam, from General Loan pulling the trigger at the height of the war to Huey helicopters lifting the last evacuees from the U.S. Embassy in Saigon on 29 April 1975.

In this context, Dockter's photographs are understandable as part of the history of Vietnam War photography. Photographs taken in Vietnam and displayed in the art museum function both as documentary, reproducing a moment of the war, and as artwork, creative renderings of that moment. Their display in the art museum affirms this duality, which promotes the photograph as both a part of history and a piece of art. In turn, the duality confirms the museum's belief in the veteran-artist's bona fide experience in

Vietnam, permitting the photograph to convey both the immediacy of the war and the authentic role of the veteran in it.

In "Real Dead Dead," the mutilated body fills the whole frame except for the hint of another dead body in the top left hand corner. The image's gruesome content surely evokes an immediate visceral response of horror, revulsion, or disgust from all but the most hardened viewer. But the viewer's visceral response may be tempered by the sterilizing aspects of the photograph—the distinct lack of blood as well as the lack of context, such as might be provided by the depiction of other soldiers, weaponry, or scenery. The fact that the soldier's face has been torn off and thrown away from the body adds to this tempering, complicating what Susan Sontag calls the "powerful interdiction against showing the naked face" in war photography (2003: 70). "The more remote or exotic the place, the more likely we are to have full frontal views of the dead and dying," Sontag suggests (70). Images of starving or mutilated children in, for example, Biafra or Rwanda, "show a suffering that is outrageous, unjust, and should be repaired. They confirm that this is the sort of thing which happens in that place" (71). In contrast, by World War II, American casualties were always photographed "prone or shrouded or with their face turned away[,] . . ."a dignity not thought necessary to accord to others" (70). Because the Vietnamese soldier's face is missing, viewers should not assume the photograph necessarily affirms American opposition to the display of full frontal suffering, or that this image challenges the war photograph's willingness to portray the suffering of the "Other." Rather, the image is doubly confrontational, showing a view of suffering (the torn apart body) that is full frontal (the camera looks directly at the dead) and is even more "Othered" by the face being absent from the body yet still visible in the image.

The first time I came across this photograph, in December 1999, it was on display in a special area of the exhibition space labeled with a warning about its "potentially disturbing" content. The image was displayed beside other gruesome photos by Dockter in a multi-artist collection of particularly graphic works depicting violent deaths. By August 2002, the photograph had been moved into the first floor gallery and set below another of Dockter's images titled "Living Dead Contemplating the Dead Dead," a photo depicting several GIs looking at the bodies of dead Vietnamese. (By June 2004, my most recent visit to the museum, both images had been removed by Dockter. See endnotes to this chapter for a discussion on other changes to the museum.) This image shows the full figures of five soldiers standing with their backs to the camera and gazing down on several mutilated bodies (the exact number is unclear). As we look closely, we see that

Figure 8. Art Dockter, "Living Dead Contemplating the Dead Dead" (1970). Courtesy of artist.

one of the dead bodies to the right of the soldiers is the same one that fills the frame in "Real Dead Dead."

The placement of "Living Dead" above "Real Dead Dead" invites us to view the image of the mutilated body in the same way that the group of five soldiers is depicted as viewing it in "Living Dead." Because "Real Dead Dead" is a close up of the most mutilated of the bodies in the wider shot of "Living Dead," its arrangement on the wall suggests Dockter has moved forward to gaze on the dead body in the same way the soldiers did, gathering closer to get a better look. And as visitors to the museum, we voyeuristically gaze over the shoulders of the GIs to see what they see.

If immediate shock at "Real Dead Dead" is somehow tempered by the photograph's unemotional representation of the dead body, the display of the photographs together is likely to provoke a new visceral response to the images. Displayed on its own, "Read Dead Dead" coolly documents the human cost of technological warfare in Vietnam. But when "Real Dead Dead" is placed beside "Living Dead," the photographic arrangement shifts the viewers' focus to the American soldiers' perspective and constructs an American narrative of Vietnamese death. Looking at these images, viewers will consider what it means for this kind of gruesome death to become

Figure 9. Art Dockter, "Living Dead Contemplating the Dead Dead" and "Real Dead Dead," on display at the National Vietnam Veterans Art Museum. Photograph by author.

commonplace, and what it means for the photograph to represent only the grunts' response to the dead body and not, for example, the response of local Vietnamese observers.

These images, individually and in juxtaposition, depict the war as quagmire: no one knows exactly who killed these Vietnamese soldiers, and the GIs' casual stance appears to suggest that coming across these bodies is unremarkable. Whether or not they were horrified when they first came across these bodies, in Dockter's photograph, the GIs' body language—their legs apart, one of them lighting a cigarette, all of them standing rather than kneeling—speaks of resignation not shock. In *Vietnam: Reflexes and Reflections*, Dockter explains that the GIs were not nonchalant, as the photograph might suggest, but "seemed exhausted and dazed" (54). Ultimately, the GIs' stance tells us that this scene, while gruesome in its extremity, is not at all unusual in its occurrence. When the museum rejects overt political commentary and yet depicts gruesome violence as common practice, how can visitors read the aesthetics of the quagmire but as primarily experiential? In this way, the museum displays graphic photographs, such as Dockter's, to narrate the war experientially rather than historically.

And yet the juxtaposition of military relics beside artwork helps put the quagmire aesthetic in historical context. The collection includes small and medium sized arms brought back from Vietnam—mostly Russian, Chinese, and Czech weaponry used by the National Liberation Front or North Vietnamese Army. These relics provide the material, or more precisely the military matériel, to convey the technological details of the U.S.'s foray into Southeast Asia. Placed beside artistic renderings of veterans' war experiences, the military relics add empirical knowledge of the war to the meanings conveyed by the artwork, and they complicate visitors' understandings of this place as an art museum. These war relics are randomly scattered around the gallery space. Their apparent lack of organization, like the art displays, stages the museum as representative of the quagmire of the war, coded as confusing, lacking in planning, and ultimately without clear meaning or order. No obvious attempts to juxtapose a particular relic with a specific art piece are apparent, but the very presence of the war relics contextualizes the art: if the lack of curatorial practice with regard to the artwork does not make painfully clear to visitors the milieu in which these artworks were created, the war relics remove any uncertainty.

Because the weapons were found or captured by U.S. soldiers, they both illustrate the soldiers' experiences in Vietnam and confirm the museum's self-presentation as an authentic site of veterans' memory. Some items are common: both the U.S. military's standard issue M-16 rifle and the Russian-made RPG-2 and RPG-7 rocket launchers used by the North Vietnamese Army would be instantly recognizable to anyone who was stationed in Vietnam, is interested in military history, or has watched at least a couple of Vietnam War movies. Other weapons are more obscure: for example, a Pattern 1912 Maxim machine gun, not widely used by Vietnamese, and a Czech VK light machine gun to which someone has attached a Japanese magazine are likely to be rare curiosities for even the Vietnam War veteran. Each weapon could suggest two narratives: one of the U.S. veteran who donated it to the museum and another of the Vietnamese soldier to whom it initially belonged.

But the museum is not interested in telling the story of Vietnamese soldiers; rather, it situates the weapons among the artwork of U.S. veterans in order to narrate their versions of the Vietnam War experience only.

By creating a techno-military context by which to view the art, artistic critique becomes more difficult. Thus, the art juxtaposed with war relics collected from Vietnamese can be read more as ethnographic objects, giving visitors insight into guerrilla warfare but again always from an American perspective. Because these guns and rocket launchers could only be brought back to the U.S. discreetly and illegally, in pieces, and hidden in a soldier's luggage, their display in the museum space feels like a private collection on show. This impression is strengthened by the fact that the museum has not edited the collection for display or arranged the weapons in any particular order. The displays of weapons donated to the museum and their function as ethnographic objects produce two specific narratives: that the war can be known through the individual experiences of veterans and that it was an American experience. In addition, because the weapons contextualize the artwork yet make critique of it difficult, veterans' artistic representations are allowed to stand without scrutiny or analysis, and the absence of labels directing visitors to read the artwork in particular ways compounds this lack of critique. Ultimately, then, the juxtaposition of war relics with art reinforces the quagmire aesthetic, providing a visceral encounter with the American veterans' war experience that avoids addressing the historical and political social causes and consequences of the war.

In fact, weapons authenticate the veterans' artwork through not only their placement beside art but also their incorporation within it, making a clear distinction between art and war relic sometimes impossible. For example, Ned Broderick's sculpture, "Le Duc Tho Goes to Paris to Discuss the Shape of a Table," includes a submachine gun barrel protruding from a face constructed of polyurethane resin embedded in a suitcase. Joe Fornelli's "Dressed to Kill" comprises a teak head with spiked hair made from brass 50-caliber shell casings. Several sculptures include helmets and combat boots while other works are constructed from pieces of metal, prosthetics, and other material residues of war and injury. But the most impressive piece that brings art and war relics together is "Above and Beyond," a memorial made of 58,226 dog tags, each imprinted with the name of someone who died in Vietnam. The dog tags of "Above and Beyond" hang from the ceiling twenty-four feet above the atrium entrance to the museum and are arranged in chronological order according to the date of death, just as they are on the Wall. The large mobile, if you will, is ten by forty feet, each tag spaced exactly one inch apart, with the whole structure perpetually in motion. When the

Figures 10 & 11. "Above and Beyond" dog tag memorial, National Vietnam Veterans Art Museum, Chicago. Photographs by author.

door opens into the museum or when a breeze blows through the atrium, the dog tags knock against each other, ringing gently like a massive wind chime and constantly reminding visitors and staff of their presence. A staff member told me she did not imagine the memorial would shiver and chime in this way, but stressed all staff members feel this unexpected consequence of its position above the atrium is one of its most moving features.[14]

The efficacy of "Above and Beyond" memorial as art emerges from its composition, its location in the museum, and its symbolic potential. The overall design, a basic rectangle, is so simple that the shape does not detract from the tags themselves; in fact, it is the tags that shape the memorial (perhaps, as a large rectangle, the shape mirrors that of a tag itself). All tags hang on wires of exactly the same length and are made of the same thin and shiny silver metal, with one exception—at one corner, a plain black tag hangs to represent those still missing in action. The overall result is uniformity and simplicity. The memorial hangs from the atrium ceiling and is surrounded by a pre-existing narrow mezzanine walkway. Visitors can walk along the mezzanine floor, getting closer to the tags and even reading some of the information stamped on the closest ones. Because the tags appear to be uniform from a distance and yet on closer inspection are unique, the memorial has the capacity to invite interpretive and affective responses.

The memorial's power emerges also from its ability to incorporate elements of ethnography and history. As ethnographic objects, the dog tags offer basic information about the lives of soldiers—their name, service number and branch of service, blood type, and religion if the soldier wished it. As documents, they provide some historical information about the military—the number who died and the technology of soldier identification. As a memorial, "Above and Beyond" is the only material structure in addition to the Wall to include the names of the more than 58,000 soldiers and nurses who died in Vietnam. The dog tag is an ingenious choice for a memorial because it is perhaps the most personal and democratic icon of war. Every soldier and nurse stationed in Vietnam was issued two dog tags in order to identify his or her body in the event of death. And the sight of all these tags gathered together is overwhelming both in its entirety and in the uniqueness of each tag. Dog tags serve as authentic artifacts from the war: the living bring them back from Vietnam as souvenirs, or the military gives them to parents as part proof of their child's death. In the museum space, the artwork and war relics donated by living veterans narrate the stories of their lives after the war, while the dog tags narrate the stories of deaths during it.

Because "Above and Beyond" is both ethnographic object and historical document, it differs from the Wall in one important aspect: it addresses head-on the connection between the names of the dead and the fact that they died in war. While no one denies the power of the Vietnam Veterans Memorial, its efficacy depends upon the viewer's willingness to imagine the individual lives behind the names. But with "Above and Beyond," each name is inscribed on a dog tag that is unavoidably recognized as an accessory of war. The irony of the memorial is that to preserve and memorialize the identities of these soldiers, it uses dog tags, the military symbol for uniformity and anonymity, which suggests that the only time the soldier actually needs an identity is when he dies.

Of course, the other important way "Above and Beyond" differs from the Wall is the fact that it makes noise. As wind catches the thin metal tags, they knock against each other and chime gently. The sound serves as background noise for visitors as they peruse the artwork and for staff as they go about their work days. In the quiet museum, which often has only a couple of visitors at a time, the sound of the dog tags can have a powerful effect. The chiming does not evoke or create the sounds of war; rather, referencing a wind chime, the sculpture is more likely to evoke a western domestic space—the familiar comfort of a suburban front porch, for instance. Yet this gentle sound, peeling for those who died, contrasts starkly with the graphic images of war in the exhibits. Like other memorial spaces of contemplation, for example the Hall of Remembrance at the U.S. Holocaust Memorial Museum in Washington, D.C., the sound of "Above and Beyond" offers an opportunity for visitors to reflect and gain composure. The memorial, it seems, evokes not the viscerality of war but the viscerality of mourning.

Richard Steibock, the museum's volunteer director of travel and relations and the main architect of the memorial, offers a way to understand its music. One day, as he says, "I bumped into a model we were making of the sculpture, and all of a sudden I heard music. It started to come alive. It had a spirit." Steibock continues, "I believe that, with this memorial, we are going to bring together all the spirits of those who fought and died."[15] He and others read this sculpture built of military accessories as a site that collects the spirits of dead soldiers. Indeed, one visitor to the memorial observed that it "sounds like angels,"[16] and the museum's website talks of the memorial moving "like a living thing."[17] As the name of the memorial implies, the tags naming the dead are located above the heads of visitors, while the dead, who gave their lives "above and beyond the call of duty," are placed symbolically and literally beyond visitors, beyond the museum, and beyond life itself.

The fact that the dog tags were made for the memorial rather than obtained from the families or estates of the dead could potentially undermine the authenticity the museum strives so hard to achieve. However, I believe their lack of originality does not diminish the memorial's efficacy. The act of making each tag, repeated more than 58,000 times—a process that took Steibock and others months to complete—becomes powerful in its own way. During the construction of the memorial, visitors could watch volunteers making the tags on a Vietnam-era embossing machine that is now exhibited to remind them of the labor of the volunteers and the accurate reconstruction of the dog tags. Even though the tags are not original to the war, as volunteers spent months imprinting each individual tag with the name of someone who died, the construction process became a form of memorializing for those volunteers.

The artwork, weapons, and dog tag memorial make a visit to the Vietnam Veterans Art Museum a multi-sensory experience. No single element within the space has this impact; rather, the visceral experience at the museum is created through the ways that all elements work together. The aesthetics of the quagmire in place at the museum is a political paradigm even though it attempts to explain the war by shifting the focus from the war's history to the veterans' experiences. By describing the war as quagmire, the museum may ignore competing histories of the war, but its art pieces, collection of war relics, and dog tag memorial are material reminders of combat. In this way, the museum, on the margins of the discourse of the traditional museum, resists the forgetting of the war. Thus, the museum's lack of political commentary, rather than contributing to the erasure of national memory about the war, forces visitors to recognize that erasure. The visceral experience helps visitors to memorialize the war in their own ways while they are there and after they leave.

VISITING OBJECTS, ACTING SUBJECTS

This discussion has so far focused primarily on how the meanings of objects are constructed and construed through curatorial practices, or lack thereof, and other forms of museum display. As Art Dockter's provocative images demonstrate, the meanings and evidentiary potential of objects cannot be divorced from visitor responses to them. It is clear, however, that meanings and significances can alter visitor interaction. When the visitor moves around the space according to or in spite of direct or implicit instructions in the layout, narrative, chronology, or other prompts, she makes connections between objects and interprets them based on the information given. Focusing on how both museums shape visitors' perceptions of the war, I argue that while the primarily visual experience at "Personal Legacy" might prevent visitors from understanding the war emotionally, the visceral experience at the Veterans Art Museum has the potential to teach visitors about combat.

The "Personal Legacy" exhibit is certainly not the biggest attraction at the American History Museum and, housed in a room that dead-ends on the third floor, it may be missed by many. If visitors walk through the Hall of Armed Forces History toward the room that houses "Personal Legacy," they will first confront the model of the Wall, positioned in the center of the room. A large display case containing objects left at the Wall is located to the right (the west), and the museum's Archives Center is housed on the left (east) side of the room (see Figure 4). Continuing from the Hall of Armed Forces History into "Personal Legacy," visitors will view the exhibit in chronological order, from 1985 to 1991, but will move from right to left, a nonconventional way to view an exhibit. The large display cases filled with objects may attempt to recreate the experience of being at the Wall through the practice of object leaving, but the visitor's own sense of the appropriate way to view an exhibit, cued through curatorial practices in the rest of the museum, may prompt them to move to the other side of the room in order to start their examination of the exhibit from the left. When chronology and perceived appropriate behavior conflict, visitors ultimately can make up their own minds about how to view the displays.

With the objects enclosed behind glass and physically out of reach and with no interactive features, visitors' experiences are visual. Because the display is small and contained mostly along one wall, visitors' movement through the exhibit is minimal, although they might turn around to examine the model of the Wall in the center of the room. While the experience of the exhibit is visual and stationary, the contents of the exhibit—the objects left at the Wall by the bereaved—demand contemplation that works on two levels. Because the majority of objects on display are recognizable as quotidian items—such as cigarette packets, shoes, and buttons—visitors' contemplation of them is based on existing popular knowledge or their own personal experiences of these items. Visitors recognize these objects and make whatever meaning they want to about why they were left at the Wall. In addition, even if they have not been to the Wall, visitors know of it and of the practice of leaving objects there. They know, to a greater or lesser extent, how to contemplate these objects not only because of the written directions at the exhibit itself but also because of the popular discourse that circulates about the Wall. This contemplation is not based on their experiences but on their prior knowledge of the significance of the Wall in memorializing the war. These two forms of contemplation make the visitors' experiences at "Personal Legacy" visual and interpretive, experiences undeniably shaped by the curatorial practices in the museum as well as by popular discourse on the war.

At the Veterans Art Museum visitors are bombarded with a cacophony of colors and shapes seemingly displayed in no particular order but with the power to create an overwhelming effect. Trying to make sense of the museum, visitors move through the entire space, upstairs and down, looking at artwork and war relics, maybe doubling back to find a piece that was of interest to them the first time around and making their own connections among the artists, the genres, or the artworks and relics. In other words, because the museum does not direct them to follow any particular path, visitors may cover more ground than in a traditional museum space. Added to this experience is the "Above and Beyond" sculpture, gently chiming in the background, announcing the entrance or exit of a visitor. The experience at this museum, then, is multi-sensory: it is kinesthetic, visual, and auditory.

The museum's quagmire aesthetic helps visitors know the war experientially. The lack of curatorial techniques replicates the experience of war, particularly its lack of order and coherence. Visitors to the museum may feel a sense of discomfort at not knowing where to begin, which items are especially significant, or how to understand or respond to specific images. This sense replicates, to a certain extent, the experience of soldiers arriving in Vietnam. In addition, the aesthetic promises a kind of immediate experience, a rush of senses without time for contemplation. As one visitor wrote in the guest book: "The museum is moving, shocking, enlightening, and confounding all at once. In short, it has shown the immediacy of war and its many horrors better than I ever imagined could be done."[18] I understand the visitor's idea of the war as immediate as a sort of "allatonce-ness," to use Marshall McLuhan's expression, both in terms of the soldier's experience in Vietnam and of the visitor's experience in the museum; this "allatonceness" is conveyed by the simultaneity of artworks that depict moments of combat in all their detailed vividness, the juxtaposition of art-works and weaponry in the museum, and the sound of the dog tags jin-gling overhead.

Both museums display objects with no aesthetic interest of a formal artistic nature: the items—quotidian objects, artwork powerful though sometimes lacking formal skill, weaponry, etc.—become particularly mean-ingful at their destination. These items are displayed for their ethnographic significance in order to educate their audience: again, the American History Museum, as noted in the director's welcoming comments on its website, attempts to bring history alive and is committed to "inspiring a broader understanding of our nation and its many peoples." The Veterans Art Muse-um's educational purpose is "to show [visitors] what Vietnam was really like." In the mission statement of both museums, education is experiential—to bring the past into the present in order to show visitors the real Vietnam. But, I suggest, while both museums educate about the dominance of mem-ory and experience over history in recording and representing the war, only the veterans museum successfully educates about the war experientially. The difference in success between the two museums relates to their focus: the Veterans Art Museum recreates the experience and memory of war, while "Personal Legacy" represents the experience at the memory of the Wall. To present these aspects, both museums use objects (artwork, weapons, dog tags at the Veterans Museum; items left at the Wall in the traditional museum). So while the Veterans Museum asks visitors to imagine what Vietnam was really like, the Smithsonian asks visitors to imagine what the Wall is like. However, because visitors can easily travel from the museum down the Mall to see the Wall for themselves, this exhibit can never as effectively evoke the multi-sensory experience that visitors can have there.

Together, the museums attempt to educate about the experiences of war and about how the war and the dead are remembered and memorialized, but they do not educate about the war itself—its causes or its larger politi-cal and social legacies beyond the personal consequences of war for Ameri-can veterans and their families. But, perhaps these limitations are acceptable. At the veterans museum and "Personal Legacy" exhibit, visitors gaze on the memorializing practices of veterans and their loved ones. These personal ren-derings of the war are honest even if the knowledge of the war produced is partial, skewed, or incomplete. We cannot expect these museums to do more than what they already do, nor can we ask them to speak for those whom they do not represent such as politicians, military leaders, academic historians, and antiwar protestors. The limitations of memory must be considered as an important feature of these places; in the words of James Young: "I would rather preserve the complex texture of memory—its many inconsistencies, faces, and shapes—that sustains the difficulty of our memory work, not its easy resolution" (1993: xi). If we were to demand a fuller history of the war from these museums, we might undermine the accurate presentation of memory's inconsistencies and might also seek totality where none exists.

Thus, if education about the war does not include its history, what do visitors really learn? By looking at artwork aside weaponry at the Veterans Art Museum, visitors learn about the experience of combat not the history of the war. Its presentation of the quagmire personalizes the war and shifts the focus from the politicians and military decision makers to the veterans themselves. But the museum's lack of political commentary, I would argue, forces visitors to recognize how a similar erasure has occurred in dominant cultural discourses of the war. By shifting the focus away from the history of the war at "Personal Legacy," the Smithsonian calls attention to how memory practices have supplanted the war's history. The exhibit offers visitors the opportunity to consider that the most important or lasting aspect of the war has been how Americans at home choose to memorialize it.

ENDNOTES: CHANGES AT THE MUSEUMS

While meanings constructed within exhibits may be static or fixed, the exhibits themselves are not. The Veterans Art Museum has edited the collection on display that I discuss here and added new exhibits to its space. "Personal Legacy" and the Hall of Armed Forces History at the Museum of American History have been replaced with a new exhibit, "The Price of Freedom: Americans at War." Initially I considered that the changes may render this chapter obsolete, but ultimately I decided on the value of presenting this discussion and on updating it; in doing so, the chapter shows how curatorial practice both reflects and shapes contemporary discourse: in the case of the Veterans Museum, this means reflecting the evolving memories and experiences of veterans; in the case of the Smithsonian, it means meeting visitor expectations and both reflecting and shaping cultural understandings of war and the military.

I returned to the Veterans Art Museum in June 2004 and found changes to the displays that in many exciting ways challenge the line of argument I make here. In addition to the removal both of Dockter's photographs and weaponry from the display areas, the permanent collection on the second floor has been replaced with a temporary exhibit titled "Trauma and Metamorphosis." This exhibit presents a new, updated authenticity, not of war experience but of post-traumatic stress disorder. Ron Mann's work dominates the floor; his black and white paintings detail his complex and extended struggle with PTSD. As I stood examining these paintings, my immediate response was embarrassment—I felt that I was looking at the excruciatingly private products of the tortured mind of a trauma survivor. I felt at first that these paintings did not need to be on display because they held value only for the artist, who used the painting process to work through his private struggles with the illness. Mann's images are not deliberately contrived representations of trauma, as are Tim O'Brien's trauma writings; rather, the images *are* Mann's trauma, rendered in black and white paint. But, on further consideration, I realized that because Mann's paintings are so personal, their efficacy lies in their ability to evoke strong visceral responses in other survivors of post-traumatic stress disorder, as well as provoke similarly strong feelings of empathy among visitors.

The exhibit is just one example of how the museum is evolving to address and reflect the contemporary experiences of veterans. While graphic images of war continue to have the power to narrate veterans' visceral experiences and to provoke comparable experiences in viewers, the museum also recognizes that for many, veterans and nonveterans alike, the war is over—it is in the past. Thus, more important than representing the events of the war is recognizing the memory of it that continues to exist in the present. If the museum's permanent collection tries to construct the experience of war, "Trauma and Metamorphosis" narrates the structure of veterans' war memory, which is both intensely personal and socially constructed. By constructing the viscerality of trauma as well as the visceral experience of war, the museum's visual and kinesthetic appeal reaches beyond Vietnam veterans to the postmemory, using Marianne Hirsch's term, of the postwar generation.

In September 2005, I visited the new military history exhibit at the Smithsonian's Museum of American History, "The Price of Freedom: Americans at War." The new exhibit replaces the somewhat stale and disjointed Hall of Armed Forces History, which contained "Personal Legacy: The Healing of a Nation," with a highly interactive and visually and aurally stimulating exhibit that narrates the history of America at war, beginning with the Wars of Independence and ending with "New Roles," a room that includes the Persian-Gulf War, the World Trade Center attacks on 11 September 2001, the War in Afghanistan, and the current War in Iraq. The Vietnam War section has been greatly expanded, while only a small section of the "Personal

Legacy" display has been preserved. After reading about the Cold War and Cuban Missile Crisis, visitors' first introduction to the Vietnam War is a mock-up of an early 1960s American home, complete with patterned wallpaper and comfortable chair and couch. "A Television War" emblazoned on the wall explains the reason for the display of televisions in the replica home. Playing repeatedly on the televisions is a five-minute narrative of carefully edited newsreels covering American involvement in Vietnam from 1954, when the United States agreed to support the French, to the withdrawal of the last troops and American citizens in 1975. The next room in the exhibit contains a Prisoners of War display as well as glass cases showing grunts' and enemy soldiers' clothing and various accoutrements of war. A Huey helicopter dominates this room, the largest artifact in the exhibit; from its open side door, a flat screen monitor projects short videos of veterans describing their specific experiences during the war.

"Remembering the Lost" preserves just a small section of the now gone "Personal Legacy" exhibit. One small display case holds a selection of objects also seen in "Personal Legacy," such as a teddy bear, a cross handmade with wood and barbed wire, and a six pack of Budweiser. The framed dog tags, military insignia, and POW/ MIA bracelets are now gone, as are the chronological markers, and the accompanying text also has changed. While "remembering" remains part of the new display's title and theme, the rhetoric of "healing" has been replaced with one that "honors" the dead. The narrative informs visitors that "many who visit the Vietnam Veterans Memorial make a rubbing of the name of a cherished family member or friend who died in the war," then asks: "What do these impromptu mementoes recognize?" This question promotes visitor contemplation, but it is not purely rhetorical as the exhibit provides its own answer: beneath the question is a replica of a section of the Wall's surface. Instead of the names of the dead are the words "sacrifice," "memory," "service," and "honor." "Regardless of the differences over how the war should be understood" claims more text nearby, at the Wall Americans "could join in honoring those who served." In this updated rhetoric is the presumption that the healing process has ended and the divisiveness of the war's memory has been overcome by the need to remember honorably the war and its lost. The exhibit not only presents its perception of contemporary culture's evolving attitudes toward the war, but it also frames the war in terms of current, that is to say post-9/11, discourse on the military and war more generally, drawing on the contemporary popular vernacular of honor, sacrifice, and heroism. This framing, of course, is not limited to the Vietnam War section: the name change to "The Price of Freedom" draws on the rhetoric used by the current presidential administration to contextualize and justify current foreign and military policies.

If the Hall of Armed Forces History can be described, as I do earlier, as somewhat lacking in coherence—with, for example, the omission of the Korean War—"The Price of Freedom" swings in the opposite direction, providing a somewhat overly coherent narrative of America's history of war. Every war in the exhibit has a linear progression—a clear beginning, middle, and end—and one war progresses rather neatly into another, as the exhibition space presents it. The representation of coherence is somewhat problematic, particularly in the case of the Vietnam War, which dragged on for many years without seeming purpose and which many commentators describe as singularly lacking coherence both during the war and after as veterans sought to memorialize it. To construct the consistent narrative, "The Price of Freedom" ignores debates over whether the war's purpose was indeed to defend freedom when the United States was under no threat from Vietnam and when the Domino Theory, the concern that communism would spread throughout Southeast Asia and beyond, was found later to be misguided. And by shifting the rhetoric in the Vietnam War section from healing to honoring, the exhibit suggests this event no longer needs to be debated, that it has been resolved in America's memory and history. The shift functions the same way as does the location of the National World War II Memorial between the Washington Monument and the Lincoln Memorial, asserting the prominence of that "honorable" war as central to the shaping of twentieth-century America and relegating the "Asian wars" (Korean and Vietnam) to the margins of history.

The update and removal of exhibits reflect internal changes in the museums (new leadership in the case of the Veterans Museum; new curators and curatorial practices in the case of the Smithsonian), and these changes attempt to mirror contemporary discourse on the Vietnam War and on war more generally. The Veterans Art Museum has incorporated more of the postwar experience in its exhibitions (in particular, veterans' experience of trauma and recovery), whereas the Smithsonian's changes reflect current social and official discourses on war. In both cases, updated narratives do more that present changing perspectives—they have the ability to shape them. As visitors seek understanding and knowledge of the Vietnam War at these museums in a cultural context that lacks an ongoing dialogue on it, they are presented— particularly so in the case of "The Price of Freedom"—with a narrative that minimizes the history of dissent and foregrounds the idea that those who died in Vietnam made an honorable sacrifice, even though many veterans during the war and after it rejected that rhetoric. While most representations of history and memory mirror not the historical moment being represented but the contemporary period in which the remembering occurs, one responsibility museums must accept, I suggest, is to acknowledge and foreground the complicated practices of remembering and representing that are at work in curatorial practice. Without that acknowledgement, societal and official understandings of the war are presented within exhibits as ahistorical, without influence or change across space and time.

Museums in the United States influence visitors' perceptions on the history of and attitudes toward the war, and the same occurs for visitors to museums in Vietnam, including the many American veterans who go there. As veterans move through various sites of memory in Vietnam, including museums and memorials, their own memory becomes increasingly affected by how Vietnam remembers the war. At the same time, veterans will note that signs of their war experience have been replaced by exaggerated narratives of American involvement. Veterans' return journeys are a continuation of the memorializing practices they started in the United States, for some the last stage in their healing and recovery process, but in seeking the place where the war happened to and for them, they find instead that the "Nam" has been erased in Vietnam.

Chapter Five

Returning to Vietnam

In the physical, chronological, and psychological progression of Vietnam veterans' memorializing, memory practices become increasingly democratic and
individual, moving away from the national site of memory—the Wall—to
small towns across the country and to the internet.[1] In this progression, veterans and families of the dead search for the war's meaning and for ways to
keep its memory active. Veterans' search for a perceived authentic memorializing brings them, ultimately, back to Vietnam. This returning, for many, is
the final and most important step toward recovery from the traumas of the
war. Unlike the other forms of memorializing—when narratives of the war
can be endlessly edited to suit individual rememberings, cultural reimagin-
ings, and varying political agendas—returning to Vietnam butts veterans'
memories of the war up against the reality of contemporary Vietnam. When
veterans return to Vietnam, they encounter many physical, social, and political changes there that challenge their perceptions and memories of the war,
and they must come to terms with the difference between the country of
Vietnam today and the one they knew as Nam during the war. At one level,
the distinction between Vietnam and Nam is clear: Vietnam is a country
with a long history of culture and war that existed before American involvement and continues to exist after it. Nam, on the other hand, describes the
site and experience of war for Americans; it is a term that has become syn-
onymous with platitudes about the war itself—the confusion, the lack of
purpose, the death and destruction. Nam signifies the physical place where
the war happened and the psychological place where veterans return to visit
their memories. When veterans return to Vietnam, they often find the distinction between Nam and Vietnam blurred; they notice, for example, signs
of the American war on the contemporary Vietnamese landscape (as well as
indications that these signs have been erased), they learn about the history of
Vietnam as a country that has endured over a thousand years of war, and they

interact with Vietnamese veterans and civilians. By returning to Vietnam, veterans reconcile Nam with Vietnam, but they also recognize the difference between the two—some, like Balaban and Weigl, embrace this realization, others struggle to accept it.

With veterans shuttling back and forth between Vietnam and the United States, the blurring between Nam and Vietnam also complicates the distinction between memory and place. For veterans, memories are not just created during the war or in postwar America but in the physical and psychological journeys between the two countries and time periods. Tim O'Brien's aphorism "you don't have to be in Nam to be in Nam" ("The Vietnam in Me" 55) offers a useful way to think of how the relationship between memory and place is problematized by the returnee experience. The phrase complicates the notion of authentic experience as it relates to place by locating the memory of Nam in physical places during and after the war, as well as in psychological spaces then and now. In other words, O'Brien suggests that psychological space is as significant as physical place and that place is a psychological construct.

Vietnam's program of economic renovation known as *doi moi*, which started in 1987, makes possible individual veterans' return journeys. Although some veterans were able to return to Vietnam prior to 1987 and others go there to work on humanitarian projects, the majority of American veterans return to Vietnam because the country now encourages western tourism. Current veteran travel to Vietnam must therefore be understood as enabled and produced by Vietnam's promotion of tourism. While often setting themselves apart from mass tourists because of their prior experiences in and emotional connections to Vietnam, veterans nevertheless behave like mass tourists—wanting to purchase commodities, to stay in hotels that boast international standards and good value, and to have the usual touristic experiences. The veteran writers I examine throughout this chapter all returned to Vietnam early in *doi moi*, establishing precedence and context for the return trips of other veterans; widely disseminated when first published, narratives such as Broyles' "The Road to Hill 10" and O'Brien's "The Vietnam in Me" shape and reflect the cultural memories of other returnee veterans.

As veterans negotiate their ways through Vietnam, they visit at least three different types of sites that serve to memorialize the war: the specific places where they experienced the war, sites that have been developed for tourism, and museums that store and display U.S. war artifacts. I call these sites, in turn, authentic places, organized sites, and museum spaces. When veterans first arrive in Vietnam, they desire to visit locations where they engaged in war, such as battlefields and battalion headquarters. At these authentic places, veterans wish to revisit their experiences but often find the signs of American presence are erased—battlefields have been returned to farm land, bomb craters are now ponds, barracks are reduced to rubble. These places, then, are authentic only for Americans (and also, of course, for Australian veterans, who unfortunately are beyond the scope of this project) and, with the exception of their tourist potential, have been forgotten, neglected, or reclaimed by Vietnamese. Veterans also visit organized sites of war. The Hoa Lo Prison, which housed Vietnamese revolutionaries during the French colonial area and U.S. prisoners of war during the American War, and the Cu Chi tunnels, the underground location of the North Vietnamese Army and National Liberation Front, are important sites of memory for Vietnamese veterans because they symbolize Vietnamese resistance to the imperialists. But they also are significant for U.S. veterans because they symbolize to them cruel or elusive Vietnamese military tactics during the war. Finally, veterans are able to visit artifacts of the war at the third type of memorial space in Vietnam: the museum. One of the most important places in this category is the War Remnants Museum in Ho Chi Minh City, where veterans can view military materials they will likely recognize from their own war experience. Through the organization and display of artifacts in this museum, a narrative is constructed that perhaps many U.S. veterans are reluctant to face—a story about atrocities committed by the U.S. in Vietnam.

By classifying memorializing sites as authentic, organized, and museological—as experiential, symbolic, and material—I risk imposing U.S. perspectives on the war and on contemporary Vietnam. To a certain extent, this perspective is unavoidable: I focus, after all, on American veterans' responses to Vietnamese memory of the war and on how Americans impose western memorializing practices on Vietnam. Yet all the sites of memory I examine here are, in fact, memorials of Vietnamese resistance to colonialist and imperialist presence. Generally, Vietnam does not preserve battle sites that are, in Nora's terms, topographical sites of memory for U.S. veterans, as these places are now needed for everyday use. In addition, the Vietnamese political perspective communicated at organized sites and museum spaces is informed by the current communist government's agenda, not by any motivation to memorialize U.S. involvement. Thus, when U.S. veterans return to Vietnam they find that signs of the war, as they remembered them, are either absent or minimized. And instead, visitors discover at every turn other narratives about U.S. imperialism and the presence of a burgeoning capitalist economy that is, ultimately, a result of that imperialism. During the years of American occupation, U.S. troops promoted consumer capitalism, particularly in the form of supply and demand for western consumables, drugs, and prostitutes. There to defend the western values of freedom and democracy and a free market economy against the centralized planning and communality of communist ideology, Americans maintained the capitalist-based economy introduced to Vietnam by France during its years of colonial rule. Ultimately, while the sites of memory counter the history of the war as American veterans who return there perceive it, the sites force a new consideration of the history that insists on the inclusion of Vietnamese perspectives on the war.

I start this chapter with U.S. veterans' narratives about their returnee experiences in order to examine how their memories of and attitudes toward Vietnam are shaped and challenged by returning there. In the United States, as argued throughout, memorializing practices are increasingly decentralized and democratic and yet, conversely, the meaning of the war produced through these practices is homogenized: so much of the history of the war has been erased and replaced with a simplistic understanding of Vietnam (that "another one" must be avoided at all costs) and its veterans (who unquestioningly are seen as both heroes and victims). In Vietnam, despite the erasure of American presence at many of the memorial sites, U.S. veterans are forced to confront the war and their participation in it in ways that potentially are avoidable in the United States. As significantly, they must also face one of the legacies of the war—the commodification of Vietnam—and their responsibility for it both as soldiers then and as tourists today.

RETURNING TO NAM

Under the program of *doi moi*, Vietnam approved the Law on Trade and Foreign Investment and opened its doors to foreign companies and independent travelers of most nationalities (Weeks). In 1993, the Vietnam National Administration of Tourism began to encourage western tourism,[2] and a year later, after President Clinton lifted the trade embargo, U.S. companies started to promote tourism to Vietnam. Another year later, diplomatic relations were restored;[3] by 1996, the U.S. Embassy in Hanoi had reopened with former prisoner of war Pete Peterson as its first ambassador. In the early years of *doi moi*, American veterans made up the second largest group traveling to Vietnam after *viet kieu*, Vietnamese emigrants. Current statistics regarding the percentage of all tourists who are veterans are unavailable, although generally Vietnam's tourist industry has burgeoned significantly since 1987, becoming the destination for a broader range of travelers. Thus, it is likely that while the number of veteran returnees from the U.S. as well as Australia has increased, the percentage of veterans among all tourists has decreased, as

Vietnam attracts more backpackers and civilian adventure and luxury travelers seeking cooking, cycling, hiking, surfing, or golfing vacations.

Today dozens of travel agencies in both the U.S. and Vietnam specialize in trips for veterans; many of the U.S.-based agencies are operated by American war veterans, while many of the companies based in Vietnam are run by Vietnamese veterans or by returning *viet kieu*, who moved to the U.S. or elsewhere after the war and returned home after *doi moi*. U.S. travel agencies with veterans' tours include Nine Dragons Travel and Tours, which promotes "Semper Fi, I Corps" and "Revisiting the Vietnam War" packages, and MilSpec Tours, which offers a range of trips to Vietnam for specific battalions such as III Corps Tour and 82nd Airborne Tour."[4] These agencies offer veterans groups customized tours to former unit bases as well as trips to the key war sites in Vietnam, at Cu Chi, Mekong Delta, Central Highlands, the former DMZ, Hue, and Hanoi. Other agencies promote educational or humanitarian tours for veterans and their families. As well as offering opportunities for veterans to participate in these special programs in Vietnam, Tours of Peace runs a Personal Effects Program to find and return to veterans and their families personal items such as dog tags and clothing.[5] Sage College's Vietnam Learning and Reconciliation Study Tours combine visits to many of the most popular war sites with nightly lectures and discussions on the war and Vietnam's readjustment.[6] Many of these American-based agencies promote the healing benefits of returning to Vietnam, but only one agency, Tours of Peace, offers formal emotional support on their tours.[7] Even if it is not always specified how returning to Vietnam aids veterans' recovery, the tours are presented in these terms. Richard Schonberger, director of veterans programs at Global Spectrum travel agency, for example, suggests veterans "get a feeling of closure" when they return to Vietnam because they "left [so] suddenly." Courteney Frobenius, director, Vietnam-Indochina Tours, doesn't "have an exact answer" to the question "why would anybody return?" because he believes that "maybe there is no answer," or that everyone has "different reasons or a mixture of reasons for going."[8]

Perhaps more importantly, veteran writers themselves see the return trip in terms of healing and closure; for example, as he discusses in *Going Back*, W.D. Ehrhart "wanted . . . a great catharsis, a personal healing that would finally allow me to put the demons to bed and get on with my life" (5). Some veterans describe returning to Vietnam as if they have finally "come home," while others suggest that on their return trip they are collecting a piece of themselves they left behind the first time. Ehrhart feels that "a small piece of my heart got left behind, suspended in the air above the clouds" (14), and Frederick Downs discusses how visiting a particular street "closed a little gap on our past experiences in this part of the world" (27). Believing that returning to Vietnam will provide closure is a phenomenon peculiar to American veterans: not only does it ignore the suffering of Vietnamese people, often at the hands of these veterans, but it also presumes that Vietnam is there to facilitate the healing processes of U.S. veterans. As mentioned previously, as many as 38% of veterans were diagnosed with post-traumatic stress disorder, and this fact combined with the proliferation of pop psychology and self-help mantras have together fostered a climate that encourages veterans to believe returning to Vietnam will provide meaning and closure to their war experiences. However, if professional support is absent, the promotion of psychological recovery seems more of a marketing ploy than anything else. Nevertheless, returning to Vietnam has been beneficial at least for those veterans who write about it. And Michalowksi and Dubisch's discussion of a veterans' biker group that rides to the National Vietnam Veterans Memorial every year provides one possible explanation: Run for the Wall provides healing for veterans because it is a ritual, "built around a set of American cultural symbols with powerful, positive meaning for many of the vets" and is "able to sustain a sense of brotherhood and community among many of its participants beyond the pilgrimage" (176). Similarly, on the return pilgrimage to Vietnam, veterans perform rituals, confront powerful cultural symbols of the war, and, by traveling in a group, build community.

In addition to U.S.-based tour agencies, almost all travel agencies operating from offices in Southeast Asia and especially Vietnam offer at least one package tour for American (and Australian) veterans. These tours have evolved as the agencies learn more about western tourist expectations; for example, in 1995 the Vietnam Administration of Tourism began promoting a tour awkwardly translated as "Areas of Heritage of the Standing Up to USA." Now its package tours are called simply "War Veteran Tours." To target western tourists, Vietnamese or *viet kieu*-operated agencies promote what it calls historical vestiges, sites that include ancient ruins, architectural wonders, and war sites as well as Vietnam's cultural heritage and natural beauty more generally. Even though not focused solely on the war, this touristic combination is particularly important for veterans because it draws on competing aspects of their previous experience in Vietnam—their overwhelming immersion in war, glimpses of the country's natural beauty, and often limited knowledge of the country's history and culture. When veterans return to Vietnam they wish to visit places where they were stationed or where battles were fought, where buddies died or where they were wounded. Yet, Vietnam was the first country outside the U.S. many had ever visited and certainly for many the most distant and exotic country they'd ever been to. On one level, U.S. soldiers were astounded by Vietnam's natural beauty and sometimes horrified by the U.S. military's defoliation practices, and because of this they developed a substantial respect for the country. On another level, to cope with the immediate horror of the fighting, soldiers sometimes constructed an image of a picturesque and peaceful landscape; this imaginary space served to exoticize Vietnam, an "Othering" that Hollywood continued to perpetuate after the war ended. Either way, soldiers usually did not have the chance or the inclination to learn about Vietnam's rich cultural history; thus, for many, a return trip affords the opportunity to learn firsthand about aspects of Vietnam's past that, perhaps, if they'd known them during the war, might have altered their behaviors and attitudes then.

In heritage tourism to Vietnam, the past is promoted to western tourists, in the words of L.P. Hartley, as a foreign country.[9] As Barbara Kirshenblatt-Gimblett puts it, heritage, as a marketing term, "convert[s] locations into destinations, making them economically viable as exhibits of themselves" (151). The heritage industry developed by the postwar government in Vietnam is motivated by two primary and interconnecting agendas: one socio-cultural, the other financial. As stated in its Master Plan for Tourism Development 1995–2010, the Vietnam National Administration of Tourism's socio-cultural purpose is to align tourism "with the preservation and promotion of cultural tradition [and] human dignity of the Vietnamese people. Contemporaneously [tourism] has to exploit valuable cultural heritage with plentiful specific characters of Vietnamese people, places of historical interest, [and] famous cultural architectures."[10] During *doi moi*, the communist government shaped by Ho Chi Minh's legacy of nationalistic communism recognized that the country's historical relics conveyed specific aspects of Vietnam's unique history and culture, important to developing a sense of Vietnamese identity among nationals as well as for attracting foreign visitors. No longer ruled or dominated by the Chinese, the French, or the Americans, Vietnam could showcase its cultural heritage, which as it turns out is comprised mainly of religious, architectural, and cultural elements of its previous colonizers. The Master Plan blends socio-cultural purposes with economic ones when it notes how tourism might bring economic improvement for inland communities, particularly those in "hamlet areas and areas [where] ethnic minority groups [live]," communities such as the Tay, Muong, Thai, Hmong, Dao, and Khmer. The administration recognizes that tourism is vital for the country's sustainability and that Vietnam needs foreign investment—through tourism or otherwise—to protect its historical vestiges and to improve the living conditions of its poorest and most isolated inhabitants.

When U.S. veterans return to Vietnam, they first visit sites of cultural heritage to discover what the sites might reveal about their own past. In this way, the sites work similarly for U.S. veterans as they do for Vietnamese. David Lowenthal makes it clear that heritage and history are distinct: unlike history, which in its written form is available to all who are literate, "[t]he heritage of others is little known. We are necessarily as ignorant of other peoples' heritage as they are of ours. . . . To serve as a collective symbol heritage must be widely accepted by insiders, yet inaccessible to outsiders" (49). When veterans visit memorial sites on their return trips to Vietnam, then, they visit their own heritage—memories from their previous time in Vietnam, or experiences shared with other veterans. Their goal is not to retreat into the past but to reimagine it in the present and reconstruct it for the future; the healing and closure elements of veterans' return journeys imply progression not regression. In this way, heritage, as Kirshenblatt-Gimblett defines it, is a "new mode of cultural production in the present that has recourse to the past" (149). Just as Vietnamese learn something about their Vietnamese identity at heritage sites, so U.S. veterans learn about their former identities as soldiers and their younger selves.

When visiting heritage sites, veterans do not literally visit the past, nor, strictly, do they visit a re-creation of the past; they do, however, visit a site that existed in some form in the past that has now been renovated and interpreted for contemporary visitors. The heritage industry, by preserving and developing these sites, "exploits our collective nostalgia for real places and historic roots" (Goss 36; see also Hewison). Increasingly, Tim Edensor suggests, memory is presented as heritage, creating the danger of "'fix[ing]' history and potentially limit[ing] the interpretative and performative scope of tourists" (133). While sites of memory may fix versions of history—as can be seen, for example, in the way American involvement in Vietnam is narrated at the Hoa Lo Prison and the War Remnants Museum—divergent interpretations of that history may occur because the sites have significance for different individuals and groups of people and for different reasons. For example, some sites important to Americans, such as former military bases, are not as important to Vietnamese, while others, like Ho's mausoleum and museum, are far more significant to Vietnamese than to Americans. Still other sites—such as the Cu Chi tunnels or Hoa Lo Prison—are symbolically important for both Vietnamese and Americans but, as I explain, for fundamentally different reasons.

Put in context, U.S. veterans' tours comprise only a small percentage of Vietnam's tourism industry. Mainstream tourism—as embodied in the tourist experience promised by the biggest selling travel guide, *Lonely Planet:*

Vietnam—seems, for the most part, to ignore or distort the history of American involvement in the war or at most minimize its significance in the context of Vietnam's long, rich, and troubled history. (In *Witnessing the Past*, Scott Laderman discusses how various tour guides present inaccuracies and misinformation about events during the war, which in turn shape visitors perceptions of the war, the history, and the country.) A significant proportion of western travelers to Vietnam are young adults, a generation at the age of the children of veterans. Some of this second generation experience what Marianne Hirsch calls post-memory or what James Young calls received memory, the passing down by survivors of the memories of traumatic experiences from one generation to the next. While the terms referred first to Holocaust memories, they can describe the passing on of any traumatic narrative from one generation to another. Other travelers, perhaps the majority of second-generation tourists, seem to have no post-memory or knowledge of the war and are startlingly ignorant about the country's history save what they are familiar with from popular culture; sadly, these people can easily avoid learning much about it while in Vietnam.

If the second generation of trauma survivors experience post-memory, today's travelers, generally speaking, may more accurately be described as post-tourists, a term that broadens our understanding of the different kinds of experiences sought by contemporary travelers, including veterans. As scholars beginning with Maxine Feifer have shown, the post-tourist "finds it less necessary to leave home," has a "pastiche of different interests," and "recognize[s] there is no 'authentic' tourist experience" (Ritzer and Liska 102; Feifer 257–271; see also MacCannell). To the extent that they are as much veterans as they are consumers, then, returnees would seem to fit the definition of post-tourist. Just as their expectations about how the war will be remembered in Vietnam are challenged on their return there, altering their ability to have an authentic experience as they perceive it, so also are their expectations regarding the quality of accommodations and services. Until very recently, hotels did not meet expectations regarding international standards of quality, food tasted "too Vietnamese" as Frederick Downs puts it,[11] roads and cars were treacherous, and—the greatest let down for consumers—there was nothing to buy, at least in the north. In Ho Chi Minh City, as William Broyles points out, the opposite is the case—everything is for sale: "Buddhas plundered from Cambodia, rare Chinese antiques, gold jewelry, sex with male and female prostitutes, heroin and—my favorite—a stamp collection (which, in fact, I bought)" (115).

U.S. returnees, then, are both veterans and consumers and, for them, Vietnam is both a place of memory and a tourist destination. At many memorial sites that mark the Vietnam War, the United States is presented as an imperialist power, but many U.S. veterans are only able to visit these sites because Vietnam has now embraced a capitalist economic model. Veterans' identities as returnees are thus constructed by these two discourses: as traumatized veterans of an imperialist war and as tourists in a capitalist economy. Even though veterans expect to visit the Nam of their youth and demand international tourism standards, they also understand, as post-tourists, that these expectations might not be met in contemporary Vietnam.

AUTHENTIC PLACES

In the veterans' writings examined here, healing and closure are tied to specific places—places where veterans were stationed during the war that have specific meaning to them. Veterans seek out these personally meaningful sites of memory when they first arrive in Vietnam; later, as they travel through Vietnam, they visit war sites that have been developed for tourism, places like the Hoa Lo Prison, the Cu Chi tunnels, and the War Remnants Museum. At these personal sites of memory, perceived by veterans as authentic, veterans seek the Nam they experienced as soldiers but find it has been erased by the new Vietnam. Produced by three of the most prominent veteran writers in the United States—William Broyles, former editor of the *Atlantic Monthly* and screenwriter for many television shows and films including *China Beach, Apollo 13,* and *Cast Away*; Tim O'Brien, prolific writer of fiction and, perhaps, "America's most celebrated writer of Vietnam War fiction" (Heberle 2); and W.D. Ehrhart, often lauded as America's premier Vietnam War poet— these narratives describe but also complicate the typical desires of American veterans on their return trips to Vietnam.

In "The Road to Hill 10: A Veteran's Return to Vietnam," William Broyles Jr. recounts a trip he made to Vietnam during the fall of 1984, three years before *doi moi* enabled international tourism. In the opening paragraph, Broyles describes how Hill 10, the site where his old battalion was based, has changed:

> On the north bank, where our bunkers had been, there was now a brick kiln. On the south bank, where I'd had my command post, two men dressed only in shorts were sitting in a shed, patiently sawing logs. Across the road, near where we had set up our recoilless rifle, was a small roadside stand selling tea, cigarettes, and drinks. It had all changed. But the bend in the river was still the same, and so were the mountains beyond. . . . [T]hose paddies had once meant booby traps and mines

and being caught in the open, and that tree line had meant ambush and death. Now the scene was a peaceful Asian landscape, a nice place to have a picnic. (91–92)

Impressively, Broyles remembers the exact location of the bunkers, his command post, and his squad's recoilless rifles. The curtness of "It had all changed" promises, in the progression of the paragraph, that Broyles will now leave the past behind and begin speaking of the present, but he follows this brief sentence with commentary on what remains the same—the bend in the river and the mountains beyond. His description of this scene as a "peaceful Asian landscape" flattens out the geographical difference between countries in that region and replaces them with a generic Asian ideal. Even though he admits that the paddies and tree line no longer signify war but peacefulness, Broyles still connects them to ambush and death, implying that he does not yet realize the limitations of his perception when he first was in Vietnam: as a soldier, he perceived Vietnam solely in terms of war.

Broyles begins and ends his essay with Hill 10. Not only does he return physically to this most significant site, but, in terms of the relationship between the narrative's progression and the author's changing attitude, revisiting Hill 10 at the end of the essay also marks Broyles' psychological return to the place that was central to his experience as a soldier:

> As we approached Hill 10, we came upon a ditch cut through the road. Beyond the ditch, where the base had been, was only a red scar on the hilltop. . . . I could remember perfectly how it had been: where everyone had lived and worked, where everything in that little world had happened. . . . This hill had been a little piece of America, our connection to the world, to reality. Now there were only the paddies, the mountains beyond, and the silence. . . . I could imagine a line of Marines making their way across the paddies, bound for the hill. The images were from a dream I still have, fifteen years later. (118)

With the exception of the scar on the hill, Broyles sees that signs of American presence during the war are now erased here. Imagining his Marine buddies walking to the hill implies both desire and acceptance: the image of Broyles standing on the hill envisioning his fellow Marines appears more revisionary than nostalgic, more about the desire to see these soldiers walk to the hill again than longing to return to the late 1960s to march with them. And yet, admitting that the Marines are part of a dream shows Broyles' willingness to acknowledge Vietnam has changed and that the Marines are no longer present on the Vietnamese landscape. At the same time, the dream indicates that he continues to struggle with unresolved memory. Whatever his imaginings, the reality is that the Marines are no longer there, and this "little piece of America" is now a "peaceful Asian landscape." While American involvement in the war has been erased, the legacy of their presence has not been: the scar on the hill bears the heavy weight of symbolism, marking both the absence of Broyles' grunt community and the damage done by the U.S. to Vietnam's landscape.

In his story about traveling to Vietnam, "The Vietnam in Me," Tim O'Brien also wishes to return to the specific site of his war experience. He hopes that visiting a particular place near Danang, called LZ Gator during the war, will make his dream come true: his girlfriend Kate will finally understand him by experiencing the same feelings as he does in this place. O'Brien expresses this wish with a certain sense of desperation with the story occurring in two locations: the Quang Ngai province, during a trip O'Brien and Kate made together in February 1994, and Cambridge, Massachusetts, where O'Brien is writing the essay two months later after Kate has left him for someone else. As the story begins, the author's experience in Vietnam seems remarkably similar to Broyles: "Now I stand in this patch of weeds, looking down on what used to be the old Alpha barracks. Amazing, really, what time can do. You'd think there would be something left, some faint imprint, but LZ (Landing Zone) Gator has been utterly and forever erased from the earth. Nothing here but ghosts and wind" (50). Like Broyles, O'Brien is more interested in seeing the place of his memories than the contemporary reality of Vietnam. Whatever the location looks like today, O'Brien can only see the absence of LZ Gator there, haunted as it is by the ghosts of Nam.

Yet he does accept that contemporary Vietnam influences how he remembers the war. His goal "to show Kate one of the prettiest spots on earth . . . a lagoon, a little fishing village, an impossibly white beach along the South China Sea" (56) is thwarted by their guide Mr. Ngu Duc Tan. On a tour of the Batangan Peninsula, Mr. Tan detours O'Brien and Kate from their quaint fishing village destination into a small hamlet. Mr. Tan, a former captain in the 48th Viet Cong Battalion, barks out some commands to the villagers; then, "[n]o time wasted, [the villagers] come out fast, carrying what's left of a man named Nguyen Van Ngu. They balance this wreckage on a low chair. Both legs are gone at the upper-upper thigh. . . . Mr. Tan does not smile. He nods to himself—maybe to me. But I get the point anyway. Here is your paradise. Here is your pretty little fishing village by the sea" (56). The real Vietnam, here symbolized in Nguyen's mutilated body, upsets O'Brien's desire to gaze on his idealized postwar Vietnam. As it turns out, O'Brien's exoticized ideal of contemporary Vietnam is not shared by Mr. Tan, who forces O'Brien to confront the disabled Vietnamese man as a physical symbol of the terrible legacy of the war.

The climatic visit to O'Brien's authentic site of memory forces a change in his perceptions of his memories of the war and his future with Kate:

> My Khe, Quang Ngai Province, February 1994—There is one piece of ground I wish to revisit above all others in this country. I've come prepared with a compass, a military map, grid coordinates, a stack of afteraction reports recovered from a dusty box in the National Archives. . . . At one point I hear myself talking about what happened here so long ago, motioning out at the rice, describing chaos and horror beyond anything I would experience until a few months later. . . . I doubt Kate remembers a word. Maybe she shouldn't. But I do hope she remembers the sunlight striking that field of rice. I hope she remembers the feel of our fingers. I hope she remembers how I fell silent after a time, just looking out at the golds and yellows, joining the peace. (56–57)

O'Brien starts this passage busying himself with compass, map, grid coordinates, and archival materials, the memorialist's tools he needs, he believes, to lead him to the exact site where Alpha barracks was located during the war. But, in part because his relationship with Kate takes a turn for the worse on this trip, O'Brien realizes that remembering how they both felt at this site is most important; he wishes, as she stands with O'Brien gazing upon the absence of war, that Kate will understand him by feeling what he feels. Before visiting the site of his authentic memory, Kate and O'Brien visit the site of the My Lai massacre, of which O'Brien has no direct experience. As they talk to survivors, Kate is overcome with emotion and O'Brien is consumed with guilt. When they leave they do not speak, but speaking is not necessary because, in the silence, Kate "leads me into a future that I know will hold misery for both of us. Different hemispheres, different scales of atrocity" (53). He doesn't want this separation to happen; instead, he wants to "tell her things and be understood and live happily ever after," but O'Brien realizes this is impossible; he realizes that because he has seen and done terrible things that she will never understand, the divide between them is too great. His desire to have her remember the feeling of being there even if she forgets the history discloses a dual anxiety on O'Brien's part: one related to their relationship and its inevitable disintegration, the other about the importance of story truth (the visceral experience of the event) over happening truth (the facts).

This kind of remembering—not the facts but the experience—occurs in his other works. In "How to Tell a True War Story," O'Brien describes his true memory of his buddy Curt Lemon's death through the images of light and song rather than graphic details of bodily injury. In both "The Vietnam in Me" and "War Story," the author links a traumatic experience with another one, the "feel of our fingers" or the "step from the shade into the bright sunlight." In this way, O'Brien realizes that the truth about the war, a physical and psychological sensation O'Brien wants Kate to experience while in Vietnam, is more important than its factual reality. The recollection of the touch of fingers or sunlight are screen memories for O'Brien, memories that relate to and displace other more painful memories that have been suppressed (Freud 1899). But they are not screen memories for Kate, who, of course, did not experience trauma in Vietnam. Ultimately, Kate's ignorance of the history of the war and her emotional response to Vietnamese narratives of the My Lai atrocity alter O'Brien's returnee experience: "In any other circumstances, I would have returned to this country almost purely as a veteran, caught up in memory, but Kate's presence has made me pay attention to the details of the here and now, a Vietnam that exists outside the old perimeter of war" (50–51).

O'Brien's understanding of himself as both a veteran of Nam and a guest in Vietnam, as someone both caught up in memory and acutely aware of his current surroundings, strikes me as an especially sophisticated articulation of the multiple perspectives and practices of the contemporary returnee. Even so, while O'Brien recognizes that he cannot return to Vietnam as it was during the war, he believes an authentic reexperiencing of it is possible. In this reexperiencing, new memories that screen painful older ones are produced. For Kate, in contrast, visiting sites of atrocity and experiencing postmemory passed on to her from O'Brien, ultimately, are more effective than being shown the "prettiest spot on earth." O'Brien drags her into his traumatic and guilt-ridden memory, and she has to flee from it.

Of the three narratives examined here, W.D. Ehrhart's *Going Back: A Poet Who Was Once a Marine Returns to Vietnam*, the second of his memoir trilogy, goes furthest in its acceptance of the absence of America in contemporary Vietnam. At first, Ehrhart discusses the difficulties of being a returnee in the early days of *doi moi*. Recounting his travel through Vietnam in 1987, Ehrhart details the frustration he felt at not having the experiences he wanted:

> That first night, alone in my room in the Unification Hotel (the Metropole in the days of the French), the enormity of the news [that he would

not be able to visit the Hue area, where he had been stationed during
the war] sank in. What did Hanoi matter to me? Or Saigon (now called
Ho Chi Minh City)? My friends had died in places called Hieu Nhon
and Dien Ban. I had lost my youth in places called Ai Tu and Phuoc
Trac. I had needed to see those places again, to see children playing and
old men tending water buffalo on the once-bloody soil upon which I'd
nearly died. I had dreamed of those places for years, and I had come a
long way physically and emotionally to see them. (7)

Ehrhart believes visiting particular sites where the war happened for him
is absolutely necessary so he can continue the psychological and emotional
recovery he started many years earlier in the United States. His own healing, as he understands it, is intrinsically linked to witnessing peace in the
specific places where he was stationed or fought. While Broyles continues to imagine signs of war at Hill 10 and O'Brien initially is amazed at
how LZ Gator has changed, Ehrhart seeks the absence of war—the signs
of peace—at the sites that are important to him. But a tension exists for
Ehrhart between wanting to see Vietnam at peace and continuing to imagine the country as a string of war sites with names like Hieu Nhon, Dien
Ban, Ai Tu, and Phuoc Trac.

It is a tension Ehrhart tries to resolve while he is in Vietnam. He admits
to "feeling a bit ashamed of myself: after all, here was a poor nation struggling against enormous odds—and I had been pouting because I couldn't
play out my private little fantasy" (14), and as the memoir progresses, his
attitude changes:

> As we drive along the roads of Cu Chi, I begin to feel a strangely sat-
> isfying sense of déjà vu. . . . This is the Vietnam I remember; rural,
> simple, almost eternal. . . . What's different is the absence of war, the
> absence of . . . the whop-whop of chopperblades and the whine of jet
> fighters. This is what I came for. Nevermind ideology or right or wrong.
> Half my life I have longed to witness peace in this land I have never
> been able to see in my mind's eye except in the midst of war. So what
> if it's Cu Chi instead of Hieu Nhon? Look at it, boy, I think to myself,
> and take it all in. Remember this. . . . There are winners and there are
> losers, but the war is over. (21)

In this passage, Ehrhart sees the Vietnam he imagined his first time in-country: not the Nam but a rural, simple, somewhat idealized landscape. The
idyllic memory is an illusion of déjà vu, however; the image of Vietnam

imprinted in his mind is the country "in the midst of war." Unlike Broyles and O'Brien, whose memories preserve images of Vietnam as microcosms of America, Ehrhart's memories put images of Vietnam at war and at peace in tension. While Broyles is forced to confront Vietnam at peace, he continues to map signs of the war onto it, as if he can't quite let go of the link between Vietnam and the war. For O'Brien, memories created by gazing on the contemporary peaceful landscape screen older, more painful ones. But by revealing the tension in his memories of Vietnam at war and at peace, Ehrhart is able to embrace the absence of signs of American military presence on the contemporary landscape. All three writers imagined the war on the Vietnamese landscape before they returned to their authentic sites of memory, but the key difference between them is while Broyles maps the past onto Hill 10 and O'Brien masks the past with the present, Ehrhart ultimately embraces the peaceful present.

Broyles, Ehrhart, and O'Brien returned to Vietnam in the early years of *doi moi*, their trips made possible by the Vietnamese government and, particularly so for Broyles and Ehrhart, before the burgeoning tourist industry of the subsequent years. The confusion and frustration, even disappointment, Broyles felt at Hill 10, the scuppering of O'Brien's plans by Kate and Mr. Tan, and the difficulties Ehrhart faced in trying to visit the specific places of his war experience all suggest these sites are important for American veterans only. The sites themselves, and in particular the absence of signs of American presence, force veterans to reconceive their memories of the war; the lack of the preservation of memory forces veterans to look elsewhere for reminders of the war—to organized and museum sites, where the narrative of American presence is distorted to portray the Americans as "crazy bunches of devils" and Vietnamese soldiers and civilians as heroes.

Although the memory of the war is not available to them through the Vietnamese landscape, the land still bears the many scars and traces of American involvement. Visiting places where the war is now physically absent, veterans realize Nam can only be visited psychologically, and that viewing the sites of war is less important than remembering them. If the absence of signs of American presence during the war is caused by Vietnamese-style capitalism, the scar on this hill troubles Vietnam's burgeoning consumer society. American veterans pay thousands of dollars to return to Vietnam looking for their own private Nam only to find that the war has been forgotten and the land reclaimed by local Vietnamese communities. Yet, if they look hard enough, they will note the scar on the hill is America's absent presence, a reminder to both Americans and Vietnamese of the suffering on both sides that cannot ever be completely healed, erased, or commodified.

ORGANIZED SITES

Authentic American war sites have been returned to nature or farming, cleared of U.S. weaponry by villagers who break them up for scrap or by the government to put on display. Yet, mass gravesites of and statuary monuments to Vietnamese "heroes" who fought or were victims of the French and American "oppressors" exist all over the country. In addition to these memorials, places that were significant in different ways to Vietnamese and Americans during the war are now being promoted as historical vestiges of interest to western tourists. I combine veterans' narratives with ethnography in order to discuss two of these sites—the Hoa Lo Prison and the Cu Chi tunnels—that are particularly prominent in American popular discourse of the war. Most westerners with passable knowledge of the war are familiar with the prison nicknamed the "Hanoi Hilton" and with the ingenious underground tunnel system that housed Vietnamese fighters and civilians; presentations of these sites in films and fictionalized accounts, for example, help shape popular conceptions of war-era Vietnam. Veterans visit these sites, in part, because of their prominence in popular discourse of the war even if they had no personal experience of them during their own time in-country. And because they had no personal experience, they are less likely to write about them except to address how the sites play into a larger discussion of the commercialization of the war's memory. (Veterans, it should be noted, who do have personal experience of these sites such as John McCain, who spent five and a half years in Hoa Lo, sometimes are reluctant to write in their memoirs about the full extent of the psychological impact of incarceration and torture.)

HOA LO PRISON

The Hoa Lo Prison, built in 1896 by the French, initially held Vietnamese dissidents and communist leaders, but from 1964 to 1973 it housed U.S. prisoners of war (POWs). Dubbed the "Hanoi Hilton" by American prisoners, the nickname ensured its notoriety in the annals of popular U.S. culture and history. Today, one third of the original prison site remains and has been converted into, as the museum's brochure declares, a "memorial to the revolutionaries incarcerated here who gave their lives for their country." Clearly, the museum's goal is not to remember American POWs but to create and memorialize Vietnamese martyrs.

Between 1964 and 1973 the prison was filled with U.S. pilots who had flown in bombing raids over Hanoi and were captured when their planes

went down. Because the majority of U.S. military personnel was stationed in
the south (where, of course, other POW camps existed), most of them would
not have experienced the Hoa Lo Prison firsthand during their tour of duty.
But for most veterans today, the Hoa Lo Prison was the most well-known
prison of the war, serving as the single most important symbol of prisoner
mistreatment at the hands of Vietnamese during the war. The Hanoi Hilton has become such an important aspect of U.S. cultural memory of the
war that after visiting the prison one commentator reported how he had to
"shake away memories that I never actually experienced."[12] The prison had
a significant impact on veteran Frederick Downs when he visited it in 1987;
it was, for him, "the one permanent symbol of the cruel victimization of our
prisoners by the spiteful Vietnamese" (72).

Downs' 1991 memoir *No Longer Enemies Not Yet Friends* is an ordinary
veteran's memoir about returning to Vietnam (unlike Broyles, Ehrhart, and
O'Brien, Downs is representative of many dozens of veteran writers whose
primary income does not come from writing). He is director of the Veterans Administration's Prosthetic and Sensory Aids Service and is himself a
disabled veteran who lost an arm when he stepped on a landmine near Chu
Lai in south Vietnam. The memoir details his five trips to Vietnam between
1987 and 1989 as part of a humanitarian team researching the prosthetic
needs of Vietnamese amputees. During one of his early research missions,
Downs visits many sites important to veterans and popular with tourists and,
in his memoir, reflects often on his feelings as a returning veteran.

The picture he constructs of late 1980s Vietnam under the control of
communists reveals as much about his own attitudes toward Vietnam and
its people as it does about the country itself. Although he is surprised to find
that his movements around Hanoi are not restricted, he jokes with his colleagues that their hotel rooms have bugs hidden in the walls (56). He still
has a "low opinion of Orientals" because they do "not have a high regard for
human life" and "they worship things, not God" (24). He suspects that anything he hears from these people is a communist trick (39). When he finally
talks with a Vietnamese person, Mr. Le Bang from the Ministry of Foreign
Affairs, he notes that "[i]t was interesting to talk to a real [c]ommunist, even
if he was probably lying" (39).

Downs is quick to deny personal responsibility for his naïve and clichéd attitude toward communism and Vietnamese people by suggesting he
had been "programmed" by the U.S. military and, to be fair, his memoir
does chart his change of attitude toward Vietnamese as he spends more
time in Vietnam. Yet he cannot let go of the notion that the Hoa Lo Prison
epitomizes cruel Vietnamese behavior. Hoa Lo, which at the time Downs

was writing was still in use as a prison and was therefore closed to the public, is not only "a focus point . . . of the despicable manner in which the Vietnamese treated prisoners" during the war but of "their continued meanness on the subject of POW/MIAs" (77). The prison, in Downs' mind, also signifies the late 1980s debate between the U.S. government and Vietnamese authorities regarding the number of POWs still remaining in Vietnam, a debate I discuss in more detail in Chapter Three. Indeed, Downs opens his book with this controversy, and he regards the difficulties previous U.S. teams have had in negotiating with Vietnamese authorities as proof of the troubles his prosthetics team will face. The bottom line, according to Downs, is that Vietnamese are not to be trusted.

Because Downs could not enter the prison, he stood outside and imagined the horrors within, but the prison has since opened to the public. When I visited in 2003, I first noted how the original entrance to the prison, with "Maison Centrale" over the doorway, has been restored, and the remaining structure, only a third of the original prison complex, has been converted into a museum concerned primarily with French mistreatment of Vietnamese during its years of colonial rule. On the land that formerly housed the other two thirds of the prison, "Somerset Grand Hanoi," a multi-use high-rise complex has been built that includes shopping, apartments, and offices. Inside the remaining prison structure, cells, detention camps, and interrogation rooms seem frozen in time, preserved as they were when the prison was in use. However, the space has been altered for visitor comprehension: walls have been cut away to afford a better view of the cramped and filthy conditions inside cells; wax models of Vietnamese prisoners in various contortions and states of agony illustrate the brutality of the French; objects symbolizing enemy crimes—a guillotine (what it calls the "head cutting machine"), shackles, electric wire, and handcuffs, among other items—are gathered in one room; and a narrative about the "struggle movement by patriots and revolutionaries" conveys the martyrdom of Vietnamese.

Two small rooms that appear to be former offices are used to display the "Detained American Pilots Exhibition." At the entrance to one of these rooms, the museum has posted this explanation, which I quote here exactly as written:

> From August 5, 1964 to January 24, 1973, US government carried out two destruction wars by air and navy against North Vietnam. The Northern Army and people had brought down thousands of aircraft, captured hundreds of American pilots. Part of these pilots were detained at Hoa Lo Prison by our Ministry of Interior. Though having committed untold

crimes on our people, but American pilots suffered no revenge once they were captured and detained. Instead, they were well treated with adequate food, clothing and shelter according to the provisions of Paris agreement, Our government has in March 1973, returned all captured pilots to the US government. Pictures in this exhibition room show how American pilots had their life in Hoa Lo Prison.[13]

In the rooms, visitors can view photographs of prisoners playing guitars, "[singing] a song of one's hometown in prison," at church, or receiving presents. They can also look into glass cases containing artifacts that demonstrate prisoner "leisure time"—a volleyball net, billiard balls, tennis shoes, and a French phrase book. The largest item on display is the pilot suit once belonging to John McCain. Its prominence, coupled with mention of McCain's subsequent distinguished political career, suggests this exhibit is geared towards the interest of U.S. visitors.

Figure 12. John McCain's flight suit and parachute in glass display case, Hoa Lo Prison, Hanoi, Vietnam. Photograph by author.

But it would surely be an understatement to suggest visitors, American or otherwise, get a distorted view of the treatment of POWs at this prison. Visitors like Downs, who expect to be misled by Vietnamese communists, would not be surprised by this distortion of truth or by the museum's focus on French colonial oppression. Perhaps what is more alarming, however, is how little the museum (or the regional committee of the Communist Party that runs it) believes its visitors know about American POWs. In addition, the response the museum expects from visitors is unclear: does it wish for visitors to be so horrified by this misrepresentation that they will complain or walk out in disgust? If so, how will this revulsion promote future tourism at the site? Or does it hope visitors will be transformed by the claims presented here? While the latter explanation seems the likelier, it would be more accurate to suggest that the American era in the prison's history is simply not given significant consideration because it is no more important to Vietnamese than the French colonial years. The purpose of the Hoa Lo Prison as an historic vestige is to foster Vietnamese national identity and pride by portraying the martyrdom of Vietnamese revolutionaries. The history of U.S. POWs at the prison does not contribute to this narrative and thus their mistreatment is minimized, the facts distorted. Museums like this one illustrate how the years of American involvement are only a spot in Vietnam's long history of war.

When parts of the original Hoa Lo Prison site were demolished, an international conglomerate led by the Hilton Group in partnership with Vivendi of France and the Vietnamese Dong Loi Tourism Company initially considered locating its new Hanoi hotel on this available piece of land. But recognizing the potential insensitivity of building on this site, the Hilton Group chose a location a mile or so away, close to the Hanoi Opera House. But these facts seem to have eluded Brian Cogan in his article, "Hilton in Hanoi: Irony or Apathy," which he begins with this criticism:

> Apparently it matters little to the Hilton management that the new hotel will be mere blocks away from the site of the former American P.O.W. camp jokingly dubbed "the Hanoi Hilton" by its unwilling American guests. While Hilton executives were presumably informed of this, they decided to go ahead with the construction of the hotel, despite the ghoulish connotations of the name "Hanoi Hilton."[14]

Cogan argues that this hotel symbolizes more than the encroachment of "American cultural imperialism in an emerging Third World culture;" it also shows that in American culture "we have experienced a seismological shift in which the line between the sacred and the profane has been nearly obliterated." As a result, "what once evoked the horrors that humanity can perpetuate upon itself in the name of ideology is transformed into a haven for weary travelers, unsure of what the fuss was all about in the first place." By suggesting that American culture has shifted from the sacred to the profane, Cogan seems to be suggesting not merely that the Hoa Lo Prison should be preserved as a memorial shrine to Americans who were held there, but that commercialization, exemplified in the building of Hanoi Hilton Hotel "mere blocks" from the Hoa Lo Prison, makes the sacred site profane. But his argument is flawed on at least two counts. First, Cogan fails to recognize that the prison has been maintained as a sacred site of memory but for Vietnamese rather than Americans. Second, as we know, the Hilton Group chose to locate its Hanoi Hilton at least a mile from the Hoa Lo Prison. While my desire is not to defend the encroaching capitalism of multinational companies, it could be argued, in this instance, that because it chose to locate away from the prison, the Hilton Group actually helped redraw the line between the profane and the sacred, the obliteration of which Cogan is so concerned.

Cogan misses an opportunity to offer a critique of the origins of American economic and cultural imperialism in Vietnam. He suggests American capitalist culture is indirectly responsible for undermining a sacred space, but he does not realize this process was already in place during the war when American military personnel sought to purchase commodities. Nor does he acknowledge the extent to which the presence of Americans in Vietnam was a result of consumer-oriented capitalism, motivated by a desire to protect the free world (and free market economy) from the influence of communism. In an effort to recover from the devastating economic effects of the war waged against it, Vietnam adopted the capitalistic practices introduced by the Americans during the years of occupation. Thus, the move from the Hanoi Hilton prison to the Hanoi Hilton Opera Hotel reflects a shift not from the sacred to the profane but from U.S. military imperialism to U.S.-style capitalism.

Part of the anxiety expressed by Cogan, Downs, and others is justified. If tourists only know the Hanoi Hilton as a north Vietnamese branch of an international hotel chain, the memory of a significant aspect of the war has then been lost. But the only memory lost is American memory: Vietnam has reclaimed the significance of the Hanoi Hilton, wrestling it away from its connection with American POWs in American cultural memory in order to re-present it as both a site of Vietnamese memory, in the case of the Hoa Lo Prison-Museum, and as a symbol of the success of tourism, in the case of the luxury hotel.

CU CHI TUNNELS

In comparison to the total number of military personnel stationed in Vietnam, only a very small percentage of American soldiers were held in the Hanoi Hilton. Its significance both during and after the war, therefore, derives in large part from its symbolic power, representing, as many veterans would have it, the brutality of Vietnamese and the concomitant bravery of American POWs. Instead, the site as it is today memorializes Vietnamese heroism, selflessness, and suffering at the hands of the French in particular. In contrast, no one expects the tunnels of Cu Chi to memorialize U.S. presence in Vietnam, as they symbolize, more than anything else, Vietnamese guerrilla tactics and endurance during the long war with America. When veterans and others visit the Cu Chi tunnels, they experience a carefully scripted celebration of guerrilla warfare that leaves little room for remembering the American experience there during the war.

The Cu Chi tunnels are located about 75 kilometers northwest of Ho Chi Minh City. During American involvement in Vietnam, the land above the tunnels was home to the United States 25th Infantry division while below ground were located the 7th National Liberation Front regiment and other National Liberation Front and North Vietnamese Army units. The tunnels are estimated to be seventy-five miles long and built over three levels. During the war they housed everything from military headquarters and air-raid shelters to schools and hospitals. U.S. military intelligence was never able to fully determine the extent of the tunnels, a fact that made them effectively unconquered. In popular discourse during and after the war, the tunnels often symbolize the incomprehensibility of the war and particularly the difficulty of waging conventional warfare against the NLF's and NVA's guerrilla tactics. During his foray into the tunnels, Broyles cannot fathom how the Vietnamese could live there: "I went down into one of their tunnels at Cu Chi, in the Iron Triangle, northwest of Saigon. It was cramped and claustrophobic and wet; furry creatures ran over my hands. After half an hour I was desperate to get out. They lived in such tunnels for years, under intense bombing, coming out only at night" (27).

Ehrhart, too, goes into the tunnels and describes his experience in particularly effective terms:

> It is hot, dark and close inside, the tunnel twisting and turning, rising and descending, pitch black and horribly confining. I'm frightened but Miss Bich keeps urging me forward. I grope along on hands and knees, my head scraping the ceiling. I follow the sound of her voice,

desperately searching for the light at the end of the tunnel. How could people actually live down here year in and year out, I wonder, let alone wage war so effectively? No wonder they beat us. . . . Finally I reach the end and climb out through a narrow trapdoor. I'm sweating heavily, breathing hard, and quite cha[g]rined to discover that I've traveled all of fifty yards. Miss Bich reaches down to offer me a hand up. Her red Communist Youth League pin catches the sun as she smiles and takes my hand. (23–4)

While Broyles expresses only distaste for the dark and damp surroundings underground, Ehrhart conveys admiration for the perseverance of the Vietnamese soldiers who lived there for so many years. The irony of being helped out of the tunnels by a woman who, ten years earlier, was his enemy is not lost on Ehrhart: he recognizes that he is only in Vietnam with the permission and under the control of Vietnamese.

Since western tourists have been able to travel freely within Vietnam since 1994, they have shared Ehrhart's claustrophobic and disconcerting experience by the thousands. They have also discovered the tunnels have been adapted for tourism. Today, along with the War Remnants Museum, the tunnels are the most popular tourist destination related to the war in south Vietnam. All travel agents in the touristy Pham Ngu Lao area of Ho Chi Minh City, and there are dozens, run day trips to the tunnels. I'm sure my own trip there was typical: our guide for the day was Mr. Bins, a former Viet Cong fighter who promised to "tell us the real story, not like in *Lonely Planet*," which, in fact, he encouraged us to throw away because we would no longer need it. We were told, "once you visit Cu Chi, you will know the real Vietnam."[15]

On arrival, our group was ushered into a meeting room for a presentation on guerrilla warfare and a video on how the peaceful life in Cu Chi village was destroyed by the Americans who, "like a crazy bunch of devils . . . fired into women [and] into pots and pans." After this talk, we walked a short distance to a jungle area where a small section of the tunnels has been preserved. While clearly we were in a tourist area, with many tour groups being shuttled around, the disconcerting sound of gunfire could be heard in the near distance. After we were shown how to get into and out of a tunnel and how to make poisoned punji sticks and other weapons, we made our way toward the sound of the gunfire: a shooting gallery where, for $1 per bullet, visitors can try out an M-16, AK-47, or pistol. The climax of the tour was, of course, the tunnels themselves. The first tunnel has been widened to accommodate the larger western girth, while the second tunnel

Figure 13. Billboard advertising the shooting gallery at the Cu Chi Tunnels, Cu Chi, Vietnam. Photograph by author.

has been preserved in its original state. All tourists are encouraged to climb through the first one and, if they dare, climb down into the second one. The final part of the tour provides the chance to drink tea and eat tapioca in an underground meeting room. After a quick photo opportunity with two wax models of Viet Cong fighters by which visitors can pose, we walked back to the minibus via the souvenir store.

Not surprisingly, U.S. visitors have described the tunnel site with an American sensibility, calling it a theme park or an amusement arcade. One U.S. newspaper suggests: "[t]he Vietnamese, who suffered much heavier casualties than the Americans, take a more practical approach [to agonizing over the meaning of the war]. They are intent on turning [the tunnels] into a tourist attraction."[16] On first observing the tunnels, former Vietnam War correspondent Peter Arnett stated: "[s]urvival . . . requires a knack for entrepreneurship. The Vietnamese are succeeding in marrying the two to a degree I have never before seen. Call it 'war as a theme park' if you will."[17] These comments suggest the Vietnamese tourist industry would rather make money from the tunnels than remember the American casualties who perished there. But Broyles offers another reason for this turn to capitalism: "Although we lost the war, our culture is clearly winning. . . . America is going to be much more difficult to defeat in this battle than we were in the

others; our clothes, our language, our movies, our music—our way of life—
are far more powerful than our bombs" (99). Broyles suggests gleefully and
rather disturbingly that while the U.S. lost the military war against communism in Vietnam, it is now winning this war by making Vietnam a capitalist
nation. But in addition, Broyles celebrates the very spread of American-style
consumerism in Vietnam that in effect ensures the American dead are forgotten at the tunnels and other war sites.

     Yet it is not hard to read the blatant commercialism above the tunnels
as an ironic commentary on the economic impact of the U.S. occupation of
Vietnam. The commercialization replaces the memorializing practices with
amusement activities. By playing with guns at the shooting gallery, crawling
through tunnels, and eating lumps of tapioca, visitors experience a simulation of the guerrilla experience during the war. For veterans, this experience
is at once unfamiliar as they shoot the favored weapons of the Viet Cong
and yet is as familiar as any amusement arcade or country fair in small town
U.S.A. For Arnett and others, the experience is disconcerting because Americans travel to the tunnels to learn about an authentic Vietnamese experience
and end up participating in a Vietnamese version of an American leisure
experience. Courtesy of the Vietnamese government, Americans see a reflection of themselves as seen through Vietnamese eyes: as consumers who desire
tacky simulations of the past for their own entertainment.

     The tunnels are included in all package tours for U.S. veterans and I
would argue one reason they are so appealing for veterans today is their very
inaccessibility during the war. With the exception of tunnel rats, specially
trained soldiers with small builds and little fear, few Americans actually went
into the tunnels during the war and those who did were likely to have been
maimed or killed by waiting Vietnamese soldiers or booby traps. By crawling
underground at this tourist site, veterans finally get a chance to invade the
tunnels. As they simulate an authentic war experience within entirely safe
surroundings, Vietnamese, not Americans, control the experience.

     Perhaps more importantly, when veterans travel to the tunnels for a
meaningful experience, they discover that while the place of Vietnamese
memory—the tunnels—remains intact, the place of American memory—
the military base—has been erased and replaced by a Vietnamese version of
an Americanized tourist park. Visitors on a tour of the Cu Chi tunnels, then,
will learn about peasant resistance, Viet Cong bravery, and guerrilla tactics,
and will listen intently while being told about the inability of U.S. intelligence to infiltrate the tunnels. The tunnel complex is an important memorial
to Vietnamese resistance, and its commercialization ensures western visitors.
If tourists desire an experience acknowledging what the U.S. was fighting for,

what they get instead is a memorial not to American loss but to Viet Cong resistance and American consumerism.

At the Hoa Lo Prison and the Cu Chi tunnels, veterans expect to experience Vietnam as they remember it, not because they believe Vietnam has stayed the same but because they cannot imagine how it has changed; the war is their central frame of reference for the country. Their expectations about these places are informed by their own experiences and memories and also by the prevalence of both sites in American cultural memory of the war. As veterans visit actual war sites that were formerly important to them—like Ai Tu, Hill 10, or LZ Gator—only to discover the American presence erased, they turn to organized sites of memory to the war. Here the veterans find that while the Vietnamese experience of war is remembered, their own involvement has been replaced by a new form of consumerism, which reveals more effectively than any memorial can the (commercial) legacy of U.S. involvement in Vietnam during the war.

VIETNAM MUSEUM SPACE: THE WAR REMNANTS MUSEUM

The War Remnants Museum, in the words of the *Lonely Planet* guide, was "[o]nce known as the Museum of Chinese and American War Crimes, [but] the museum's name was changed to avoid offending Chinese and American tourists. . . . it is now the most popular museum in [Ho Chi Minh City] with Western tourists" (438). Despite the name change to appease visitors, the War Remnants Museum relentlessly presents atrocities committed against Vietnamese people. Here U.S. veterans and other tourists will encounter both the American and Vietnamese perspectives, but they might find the narratives that emerge in their juxtaposition jarring and unpalatable.

The museum consists of six buildings or sections with an additional courtyard housing large U.S. military vehicles and weapons. Building one, "Historical Truths," ends with a plaque quoting war-era Secretary of Defense Robert McNamara's memoir *In Retrospect*: the simple "we were wrong" speaks volumes about the perspective on the war displayed in this museum. "Historical Truths" presents the eras from French rule to the end of American and Cambodian involvement, while building two contains "Requiem: The Vietnam Collection," a comprehensive exhibition of war photographs by American, European, and Vietnamese journalists who died during the Indochina War. Outside in the area numbered section three is a "perfect copy" of tiger cages used by the French on Vietnamese revolutionaries and then used by the south Vietnamese government on the Viet Cong. Beside this section, also in the courtyard, is "War Through Children's Eyes," paintings rendered within the last few years by Vietnamese children. "War Remnants" in building four is without a doubt the most disturbing part of the exhibit. It contains many photographs of Vietnamese with hideous mutilations caused either by direct contact with phosphorous, napalm, and orange bombs, or through birth defects due to parental exposure to dioxins. The exhibit includes a narrative about the massacre at My Lai; statistics on land defoliation, the chemical composition of Agent Orange, and war deaths; and, perhaps most unsettling, two jars containing deformed stillborns. Building five houses two more photographic exhibits: "War and Peace" by Bunyo Ishikawa narrates the Vietnamese experience during and after the American war, and "Agent Orange in Vietnam War" by Goro Nakamura charts the lives of children affected by chemical warfare. The final building, "The World Supports Vietnam in its Resistance," displays a collection of flyers and photographs pertaining to antiwar protests around the world.

If veterans desire to visit, as Broyles puts it, "a little piece of America" in Vietnam, they can do so at the War Remnants Museum: not only is the U.S. involvement in the war well documented at this site, but on display is an extensive collection of U.S. military artifacts left behind when the war ended. The courtyard is packed with, among other items, a D7 bulldozer, a U.17B observation aircraft, an A-1 Douglas Skyraider, and large guns like the 105mm, 115mm, and 106 caliber recoilless. This collection gathers in one place, in the center of Ho Chi Minh City, the residues of American war experience and displays with simultaneous awe and disgust both the might and the waste of the U.S. military.

The American and Vietnamese perspectives are, however, portrayed in ways that may be difficult for American visitors to confront. At the museum, U.S. military weapons are displayed close to images of the remnants of children's bodies. Both sets of items illustrate the brutality of war, but their juxtaposition provides a causal explanation: the display of huge U.S. weapons beside images of war-damaged bodies or birth defects clearly means to imply that the weaponry caused the injuries and deformities. This narrative exemplifies the museum's larger agenda: to present the atrocities against Vietnamese people committed by French and American powers regardless of the offense it may cause western visitors.

In the museum's brochure, which functions as a souvenir of American atrocities, two images most clearly present the museum's agenda: a propaganda flyer used by the National Liberation Front or the North Vietnamese Army against the Americans, and on the cover of the brochure (and also on display in the museum) a photograph of the first U.S. troops landing at Danang on March 8, 1965. The flyer has an image of four GIs crouching on

The above picture shows exactly what the brass want you to do in the Nam. The reason for printing this picture is not to put down G.I.'s but rather to illustrate the fact that the Army can really fuck over your mind it you let it.

It's up to you, you can put in your time just trying to make it back in one piece or you can become a psycho like the Lifer (E-6) in the picture who really digs this kind of shit. It's your choice.

After decapiting some guerillas, a GI enjoyed being photographed with their heads in his hands.

Figure 14. Page of "War Remnants in Vietnam" pamphlet, War Remnants Museum, Ho Chi Minh City, Vietnam.

the ground and smiling into the camera. In front of them are two decapitated bodies; the GI on the far left has his hand on the two severed heads. Underneath the photograph the following message addresses U.S. soldiers:

> The above picture shows exactly what the brass want you to do in the Nam. The reason for printing this picture is not to put down G.I.'s but rather to illustrate the fact that the Army can really fuck you over your mind it you let it.

> It's up to you, you can put in your time just trying to make it back in one piece or you can become a psycho like the Lifer (E-6) in the picture who really digs this kind of shit. It's your choice.

Figure 15. Cover of "War Remnants in Vietnam" pamphlet, War Remnants Museum, Ho Chi Minh City, Vietnam.

This message was clearly written to American soldiers, not only because of its direct second person address (what the brass want you to do, your mind, your time) but also because of its colloquial Nam language (brass, fuck you over, put in your time, psycho, digs this kind of shit) that surely implies it was written by someone with a reasonably intimate knowledge of American soldiers and slang during the war. The museum has provided its own explanation below the image: "After decapi[ta]ting some guerrillas, a GI enjoyed being photographed with their heads in his hands." The museum uses this propaganda to convey the atrocities committed by Americans but omits to explain how the group, whether the Viet Cong or the Northern Army, used it. Because the text accompanying the image goes unexplained, visitors to the museum and readers of the flyer will assume the museum shares the same perspective on the GIs as the group who wrote the text. The museum misses an opportunity to explain the purpose for which the flyer was originally used, but because explaining this purpose would not further the museum's agenda, it is ignored.

The front of the brochure depicts a grainy print of the arrival of U.S. ground troops into Danang (see Fig. 15). This photograph also is displayed in the room of "Historical Truths" as part of the chronology of U.S. involvement in the war. When I first saw this image when I visited the museum, I was struck by how it conveys the arrival of Americans from the Vietnamese perspective. In the forefront are three grim-faced GIs marching determinedly off the boat (this is easier to see in the larger reproduction on display in the museum). The soldier at the front left of the image is carrying a large American flag. Behind them a long line of soldiers stretches as far as the eye can see, conveying the feeling of Vietnam being overrun. The photograph captures a sense of movement both by the obvious fact of the soldiers walking but also by the way the soldier mass narrows and vanishes into the boat, creating perceptive distance. The photograph looks like so many AP images of American GIs in Vietnam that were dispatched across the world during the mid to late 1960s, but displayed in the War Remnants Museum in an exhibit on the historical truths of the war against the Vietnam, the image conveys the fear and surprise local Vietnamese must have felt as American soldiers poured onto the beach.

Considering the small part America played in the history of Vietnam at war as so many memorial sites in Vietnam attest, its presentation in the War Remnants Museum seems disproportionate. The museum's focus, however, reflects both the substantial impact of the American war on the Vietnamese landscape and the considerable resonance the war has had around the world. In addition, despite the fact that the museum presents its version of the historical truth of American involvement in a way that might be difficult for westerners to confront, its focus on this involvement ensures its appeal to western tourists. Thus, in ways similar to the Cu Chi tunnels, American tourists, drawn to the museum because it purports to focus on American involvement, instead are given an uncomfortable lesson about atrocities committed in their name.

Without *doi moi* and the subsequent commercialism of Vietnam, most veterans would never be able to return to Vietnam. But now they must negotiate their identities as veterans and tourists within the context of how Vietnam chooses to remember the war. If American veterans' memories were formed at what they perceive to be authentic sites in Vietnam, now that the American presence at those sites has been erased or minimized, their memories can no longer be tied to these specific places. As veterans shuttle from authentic places to organized and museum sites, they form new ideas about Vietnam that, in turn, complicate their previously formed memories about the country. Because these sites are important in different ways for both Vietnamese and American memorializing, new American memories about the war must be shaped dialogically with Vietnamese memories.

In contrast to the narrative conveyed at authentic sites, which suggests Vietnamese agrarian society can overcome American military might, the narratives at organized and museum sites convey Vietnam's politically motivated desire to rewrite its history into one of military victory and heroic martyrdom. This difference reveals a fundamental tension in Vietnamese society between agrarianism and tradition on the one hand and consumerism and development on the other. The developments in war-themed tourism in Vietnam reveal that the priorities of Vietnam's tourist industry lie not in maintaining the memory of American involvement but in supporting the development of the country's capitalist economy that is, both directly and indirectly, a result of the influence of U.S. imperialism during the war and capitalist investment after it. It is in this context that veterans return to Vietnam and in this context that they struggle to remember the war.

Afterword

In various memorializing practices, all of which can be described as physical and symbolic journeys away from the Wall, veterans use memorializing practices to revisit Vietnam in ways that are both symbolic and literal. By returning, veterans must confront how Vietnam—the country and its people—remembers the war in ways that must seem remarkably familiar: as with pervasive American narratives of the war, the Vietnamese versions erase the enemy's experiences and attitudes toward the war and the historical details that complicate the master narrative (in the Vietnamese case, this is a narrative of resistance against imperialist forces).

American veterans' practices in the United States and in Vietnam confirm John Gillis' argument that memorializing has become simultaneously more local and global. But if the return journey to Vietnam—whether real or imagined—suggests globalized memory, I would argue that for U.S. veterans, the imperative remains to find a particularly American memory of the war that is, nonetheless, increasingly informed by global memory practices; thus, veterans' memory practices may be better described as transnational rather than post-national. If American memorializing is defined by its individual, material, and ahistorical aspects, Vietnamese memorializing, in contrast, often is shamelessly revisionary. That revision challenges both the practices and the meanings of the war produced by American veterans, and it erases details of both countries' war history. And it is within this milieu of multiple and competing memory practices and war narratives that veterans continue to memorialize the war.

As I was making final revisions to this book in the fall of 2005, I attended an opening ceremony for The Moving Wall in the southern California valley community of Azusa. During one part of the ceremony, a group of approximately thirty Vietnam veterans was asked to gather at the area in front of the podium. About three quarters of them were wearing

Figure 16. Crowd at The Moving Wall, Azusa City Hall, Azusa, CA. Photograph by author.

biker clothing, including leather jackets with patches on the backs declaring their "Vietnam Vet" status or their objection to "Hanoi Jane [Fonda];" many were heavily tattooed and wore their hair and beards long. As these veterans stood in front of the crowd, we were told by the speaker that the veterans "didn't get the welcome home they deserved," but that "God will judge" those who treated them poorly on their return to the United States. Then the crowd of several hundred was asked to shout at once: "Welcome Home, Veterans."

The "welcome home" trope is a common one for Vietnam War ceremonies; one of its first uses was during a two-day ceremonial event in New York that culminated in a ticker tape parade on 7 May 1985. The previous evening, Mayor Ed Koch proclaimed that "we have opened the arms of this great city to Vietnam veterans from across America."[1] For these men in Azusa, veterans of the war as well as of war-related commemorations, the salutation will not be new to them. By replaying this welcome home scenario as part of a public commemoration of the war, the ceremony hints at the divisive response to the war at home. But more importantly, by suggesting that "God will judge" those who responded unfavorably to the returning veterans, the ceremony reclaims the war as religiously justifiable and its veterans as forgotten heroes.

This reclamation highlights the simultaneous process of remembering and forgetting that is a recurring dialogic in individual and cultural memory of the war. While the pool of veterans who attend ceremonies to commemorate the war inevitably decreases every year, those who do participate engage in an active, ongoing process of remembering and forgetting. The rhetoric used throughout the ceremony—of God's judgment, of honor and heroism, of fighting for freedom—demonstrates how these ceremonies are shaped more by the influence of the Christian Right and a cohesive conservative movement, and support for contemporaneous military actions than by individual, specific memories of the war. As the details of the Vietnam War that circulated in the media and in culture during the war fade from public and private memory, the Azusa ceremony is another indication of how the war is continually rewritten and reimagined through the lens of contemporary social and political ideologies.

But the fact that these versions of the war, presented at ceremonies such as the one outside Azusa City Hall on that hot October morning, are distorted by current thought does not necessarily mean that alternative memories of the war are forever forgotten or erased from cultural memory. Because public ceremonies, unlike private memory practices, must be planned through a long negotiation process with local veterans' organizations and other interested citizens, they must strive to satisfy as many participants as possible; ultimately, in this negotiation process patriotic celebration is likely deemed less controversial than commentary on war's divisiveness or futility. In addition, these public ceremonies—despite their long duration as they try to appeal to as many groups as possible (the Azusa ceremony lasted almost two hours)—must reduce the war's history to the simplest basics, which means, often, emphasizing the soldier and veteran as hero.

But perhaps most importantly, even though public ceremonies such as this one present a very subjective and limited version of the war, the Wall looms in the background—in this case, literally so—offering a silent alternative narrative to the noisy one of patriotism and honor with its accompanying rousing music and twenty-one gun salute. The Wall as it represents the war's divisiveness, therefore, haunts the proceedings, as Avery Gordon might suggest. "Haunting describes how that which appears to be not there is often a seething presence, acting on and often meddling with taken-for-granted realities," Gordon writes (8). "The ghost," she continues, "is just the sign . . . that tells you a haunting is taking place. The ghost is not simply a dead or missing person, but a social figure, and investigating it can lead to that dense site where history and subjectivity make social life" (8). When public ceremonies simplify the war's history, what is edited from the proceedings? At least, the following: The figure of the tormented soldier who felt, as John Kerry would put it, that he was going to die "for a mistake;" the belief that many incidents that occurred during the war were atrocities, with the My Lai Massacre being the most well known; the notion that the United States ultimately lost the war; and the bodies of the more than five million Vietnamese dead who haunt the Wall with their absent presence. Even if these details are erased from cultural memory of the war at ceremonies such as the one in Azusa, they indelibly altered everyone of that generation. Even if, in their memory practices, patriotic celebrants wish to forget details of the war, there will always be ghosts to remind them of the reluctant soldier, the atrocities, the loss, and the dead.

Notes

NOTES TO THE INTRODUCTION

1. Jane Perlez, "Hue Journal: Vietnam Slowly Restores Imperial City With a Grim Past," *New York Times*, 16 February 2004: 4.
2. Cited by Perlez as "Dispatches."
3. In *Witnessing the Past*, Scott Laderman shows how the myth of the Hue massacre perpetuates in contemporary travel guides of Vietnam. He discusses political scientist D. Gareth Porter's discrediting of the "bloodbath theory" put forward by Douglas Pike that was a concerted effort to discredit the Vietnamese "enemy" of the United States. In "The 1968 'Hue Massacre,'" Porter tries to correct inaccuracies about the massacre: "The official version of what happened in Hue has been that the National Liberation Front (NLF) and the North Vietnamese deliberately and systematically murdered not only responsible officials but religious figures, the educated elite and ordinary people, and that burial sites later found yielded some 3,000 bodies, the largest portion of the total of more than 4,700 victims of communist execution." However, Porter continues, "there is sufficient evidence to conclude that the story conveyed to the American public by the south Vietnamese and American propaganda agencies bore little resemblance to the truth, but was, on the contrary, the result of a political warfare campaign by the Saigon government, embellished by the U.S. government[,] and accepted uncritically by the U.S. press." D. Gareth Porter, "The 1968 'Hue Massacre,'" *Indochina Chronicle*, 24 June 1974, http://www.chss.montclair.edu/english/furr/porterhue1.html.
4. Because the war was never officially declared, the term "the war in Vietnam" is a more precise term for the conflict than "the Vietnam War." However, both terms can be problematic because they assume that only one war occurred in Vietnam whereas in fact the country was involved in several wars during the twentieth century—against France and Cambodia as well as America. The term also ethnocentrically assumes that *the* war—that is,

 the one America was involved in—is the most important one. For these reasons, the term Vietnamese-American War is more accurate. Nevertheless, because this book focuses on the subjectivity of American memories of and perspectives on the war, ultimately I chose the term most commonly used by Americans—that is, the Vietnam War.

5. Ronald Reagan, "The Unknown Soldier: Remarks at Memorial Day Ceremonies Honoring an Unknown Serviceman of the Vietnam Conflict," 28 May 1984, http://www.reaganfoundation.org/reagan/speeches/unknown.asp.

6. After Wilbur Zelinsky, I define patriotism as "an emotion experienced as love of, or loyalty toward, one's immediate environs, the personally perceived action-space an individual encounters in his or her everyday life." Zelinsky draws on the distinction in the French language between "*patrie* (one's whole nation or 'fatherland') and *pays* (one's immediate homeland)" to differentiate between nationalism and patriotism (4).

7. Dominick LaCapra, "Writing History, Writing Trauma," talk at University of Minnesota-Twin Cities, 3 March 2003.

8. In addition to Dominick LaCapra and Andreas Huyssen, discussed more fully in Chapter One, see Frederick Crews, "The Trauma Trap," *The New York Review of Books*, 11 March 2004, 37–40.

NOTES TO CHAPTER ONE

1. See Charles Cooper, "When Blogging Came of Age," *CNET News.com*, 21 September 2001, http://news.com.com/2010–1071–281560.html?legacy=cnet.

2. Pew Internet and American Life Project, "One Year Later: September 11 and the Internet," 5 September 2002, http://www.pewinternet.org/PPF/r/69/report_display.asp, 7.

3. See Chapter Two for a discussion of the "hearer's" role in recording the testimonies of survivors of trauma, as Dori Laub describes it.

4. See the essay collection *September 11 in History*, edited by Mary Dudziak, which questions the notion that the nation was transformed after 9/11, examining instead how the event ushered in a recapitulation of older political and social values and discourses.

5. "Stop That Monument," *National Review*, 18 September 1981, 1064.

6. I understand postmodernism to mean the philosophical and cultural movement that responds to perceived social conditions in postmodernity. In general terms, postmodernism rejects master narratives and the idea of a universal truth. Even more generally, postmodernity as a mode of society is often marked by, for examples, the end of the Cold War, the rise of a global economy, and the increase in availability of technologies. See Jean Baudrillard, *Simulacra and Simulation*; David Harvey, *The Condition of Postmodernity: An Enquiry into the Origins of Cultural Change*; Fredric Jameson,

Postmodernism or, The Cultural Logic of Late Capitalism; and Jean-François Lyotard, *The Postmodern Condition: A Report on Knowledge*.

NOTES TO CHAPTER TWO

1. An earlier version of the section in this chapter on Ron Kovic's *Born on the Fourth of July* was presented at the American Culture/ Pop Culture Association conference in Valley Forge, PA, November 1999, and an earlier version of the section on Bruce Weigl's *The Circle of Hanh* was presented at the Modern Language Association convention in New York, December 2002. The Winter Soldier Investigation was a series the hearings organized by Vietnam Veterans Against the War during January and February 1971 (Bibby 215).

2. After I formed the basic ideas in this chapter in 1999 and 2000, I read Mark Heberle's *A Trauma Artist* (2001), in which, in ways more eloquent than mine, he presents a similar argument: with relation to Tim O'Brien's short story "The Vietnam in Me," he discusses how traumatized veterans' writings are "not simply self-revelation but deliberately contrived trauma writing" (29). In revising, then, I have tried to draw connections between my ideas and Heberle's, here in my discussion of "How to Tell a True War Story" and, in Chapter Five, with "The Vietnam in Me."

3. Department of Psychology, Macalester College, "Phantom Limbs," undated, http://www.macalester.edu/psychology/whathap/UBNRP/Phantom/homepage.html.

4. Jacques Derrida's notion of iterability, which "includes the notion of alterity within that of repetition," and is used by Leslie Morris to descibe the stuttering motion of a gramophone, might also be usefully applied to the structural stuttering in veterans' memoirs (Derrida 1999: 65; Morris 372).

5. Bruce Weigl, interview with Krista Tippett, *Speaking of Faith*, American Public Media, 27 May 2005, http://speakingoffaith.publicradio.org/programs/2004/05/27_memorialday/particulars.shtml.

NOTES TO CHAPTER THREE

1. Michael Kimmelman, "Finding Comfort in the Safety of Names," *New York Times*, 31 August 2003, Sec 2, 1, 22.

2. Vietnam War Memorials made from black granite exist in Phoenix, Arizona; Little Rock, Arkansas; Sanger, California; West Hartford, Connecticut; Orlando, Florida; Mattoon, Springfield, and Streator, Illinois; Evansville, Indiana; Des Moines and Waterloo, Iowa; Greenville, South Carolina; Watertown, South Dakota; and Alleghany County, Virginia. For more information about Vietnam War memorials in the United States, see Jerry L. Strait and Sandra S. Strait, *Vietnam War Memorials: An Illustrated Reference to Veterans Tributes Throughout the United States* (Jefferson, North Carolina: McFarland,

1988). Since the book's publication, additional Vietnam War memorials have been erected throughout the country, some of which reference the Wall, including one at the State Capitol in St. Paul, Minnesota.

3. The First Federal Congress Project, 1999–2000, http://www.gwu.edu/~ffcp/exhibit/p12/p12.html.

4. Tom Carhart, "Insulting the Vietnam Vets," *New York Times*, 24 October 1981, 19.

5. "The Vietnam War in Memory Plaque Project," undated, http://members.aol.com/vietwarmem/plaque.htm (accesssed 15 December 2005). The plaque was dedicated on 11 November 2004. The website is no longer active and will eventually be archived at The Vietnam Project at Texas Tech University, http://www.vietnam.ttu.edu.

6. The Museum Management Program of the National Parks Services specifies 80,445 objects have been "abandoned" at the Wall, as of 15 October 2005. By 19 December 2005, an additional 1,200 items had been left, making a total of 81,645. Museum Management Program, undated, http://data2.itc.nps.gov/museum/mcollectiondetail.cfm?area=co&alphacode=vive, and Tyra Walker, email correspondence with author, 19 December 2005.

7. "History of the Last Firebase," undated, http://www.lastfirebase.com/lfb_story2.htm.

8. Ted Sampley, "Embattled Last Firebase POW/MIA Vigil Braces for another Assault," *U.S. Veteran Dispatch*, October 2000, http://www.usvetdsp.com/lfb_story.htm.

9. Petula Dvorak, "Antiwar Fervor Fills the Streets: Demonstration is Largest in Capital Since U.S. Military Invaded Iraq," *The Washington Post*, 25 September 2005, 1.

10. It remains to be seen how exactly the addition of the Vietnam Veterans Memorial Center will alter visitors' experiences at the Wall. The Fund articulates specific purposes for the Center: "to provide a profound and patriotic educational experience for interested visitors" and to "encourage and foster patriotism and an appreciation of those who have served and those who now serve in America's armed forces" (Vietnam Veterans Memorial Fund, Vietnam Veterans Memorial Center, 2003, http://www.vvmf.org/index.cfm?SectionID=51). The Center, to be built underground and close to the Wall, will offer a specific context, currently lacking, in which to appreciate the Wall. The Fund's purpose, as it is worded here, like the new military history exhibit at the Smithsonian's Museum of American History, "The Price of Freedom: Americans at War," seeks to present that context within the framework of contemporary understandings of patriotism that appear somewhat less complicated and contentious than those circulating during the war era.

11. People of Bremer Country, *Bremer County 150th Celebration, 1853–2003: 150 Years of Memories*, Volume II (Bremer County Board of Supervisors, 2003), 583.

12. Vietnam Veterans Memorial Fund, 2003, http://www.vvmf.org.

13. Jim Schueckler, "I Came to See My Son's Name," *The Moving Wall,* undated, www.themovingwall.org/docs/sonsname.htm.

14. Michael Oricchio, "Walls and Bridges," *San Jose Mercury News,* 16 July 1990, http://www.themovingwall.org/docs/sjmerc90.htm.

15. Karen Sandstrom, "Moving Wall Becomes Vet's Life Work," *The Plain Dealer,* 20 May 1990, http://www.themovingwall.org/docs/sandstro.htm.

16. A note on method: The Memorial Fund's Virtual Wall and The Vietnam Veterans Memorial Wall Page both use a searchable database of the official list of all those who died in Vietnam, while The Virtual Wall contains only the names from the official list of those for whom someone has posted a remembrance. Because The Virtual Wall does not contain all 58,235 names and knowing that I would find the same names on the other two complete lists, I used The Virtual Wall's list as a starting point to generate my own research sampling. From this site, I produced a list of fifty two names, two from each letter of the alphabet and using no other criteria for selection. Then I searched for every name at each of the three websites and recorded all the postings for the servicemen at the three sites. Because the Fund's Virtual Wall and The Vietnam Veterans Memorial Wall Page use the full database of all those who died, some searches turned up no postings for a particular name; conversely, the highest number of postings I found for one serviceman at one site was twelve. None of the eight women whose names are on the Wall showed up in my random sampling. Based on my survey of over 300 postings, I am able to draw some tentative conclusions. Many postings are written hesitantly or awkwardly, as if the visitors are somewhat unfamiliar with this format or find the process difficult. Many are poorly worded with grammar and typographical errors. For that reason, all postings referenced here are duplicated exactly as they appear online, misspellings included, with the exceptions of those postings that were edited in consultation with or at the request of the original poster. Men and women, friends, family members, and strangers post, but in my research I did not find a single posting from a parent of the deceased (although, of course, this does not mean this type of posting does not exist). While my survey was not sufficiently broad to draw definitive conclusions on this final point, postings appear to come from a range of ethnic and class backgrounds. I am indebted to Ed Martini's unpublished essay "Public Histories, Private Memories?: Cybermemorials and the Future of Public History," a revised version of which appears in his *Invisible Enemies: The American War on Vietnam, 1975–2000,* for its suggestion of a methodology for this section on virtual walls.

17. Lawrence L. Knutson, "Vietnam Memorial Names to be on Web," *Associated Press,* 10 November 1998.

18. Edwin Martini, "Public Histories, Private Memories?: Cybermemorials and the Future of Public History" (unpublished paper, University of Maryland), 30.

19. The Virtual Wall Vietnam Veterans Memorial, "About the Virtual Wall," 21 April 2005, http://www.virtualwall.org/about.htm.
20. Carol Becker, talk at Walker Art Center, Minneapolis, MN, 15 April 2003.

NOTES TO CHAPTER FOUR

1. National Vietnam War Museum, 6 June 2003, http://www.nvwm.org.
2. National Civil War Museum, 2002, http://www.nationalcivilwarmuseum.org.
3. Virginia War Museum, 2000, http://www.warmuseum.org.
4. Smithsonian's Museum of American History, "Collections," undated, http://americanhistory.si.edu/collections/index.cfm, and "Mission and History," undated, http://americanhistory.si.edu/about/mission.cfm.
5. For a discussion of the fetishization of the object, see Susan Stewart's "Objects of Desire" in *On Longing: Narratives of the Miniature, the Gigantic, the Souvenir, the Collection* (Durham, Duke University Press, 1993: 132–169).
6. Hooper-Greenhill follows Foucault in defining discipline "as a power/ technique [that] operates through hierarchical observation, normalising judgment, and examination" (169). She defines Foucault's use of episteme as "the unconscious, but positive and productive set of relations within which knowledge is produced and rationality defined" (12).
7. Smithsonian Institution Photographic Services, "Edward C. Ezell," undated, http://photo2.si.edu/vvm/ezell.html.
8. Smithsonian's Museum of American History, "Mission and History," undated, http://americanhistory.si.edu/about/mission.cfm, and "Director's Welcome," undated, http://americanhistory.si.edu/about/message.cfm.
9. The museum's vehement refusal to modify its collection to appease sponsors may be in jeopardy, however. The museum has undergone changes to its management structure, which now comprises curatorial committees, a professional gallery owner, Vietnam veteran board members, an organizer, and local business men—all designed to secure the museum's future, in part, by developing corporate sponsorship and promotional tie-ins with special exhibits. Staff member, on-site interview, August 2002.
10. Franklin argues that the "imperialism story" begins in 1945 "when America's economic and political leaders committed the nation to buttressing, maintaining, and becoming the dominant power within the 'Free World,' that is, a global Anglo-European-American imperial system that had controlled the planet's economy for about a century" (2000: 42). The "noble cause" story is attributed to Ronald Reagan, who referenced it repeatedly in speeches from 1980 on, including at a Vietnam Veterans Memorial Day celebration in 1984 (see introduction for excerpt from transcript).
11. Joe Fornelli, telephone conversation with author, 7 September 2005.

12. The Civil War was the first American war to be photographed, but photographic documentation of the Crimean War (1854–1856) occurred earlier. The British government's official Crimean War photographer Roger Fenton has become known as the first war photographer. However, Fenton's images avoid the horror of war itself: as Susan Sontag describes it in *Regarding the Pain of Others*, precluded from recording the dead or the maimed, "Fenton went about rendering the war as a dignified all-male group outing" (50).

13. See also Franklin's "Burning Illusions: The Napalm Campaign" (2000: 71–88) for a case study of how gratuitous images of napalm-burned Vietnamese were used to turn around attitudes towards the war in Redwood City, CA.

14. Staff member, conversation with author, August 2002.

15. C.E. Hanifan, "Etched in Memory," *Milwaukee Journal Sentinel*, 29 May 2000, Section E.

16. Lola Smallwood, "'It Sounds like Angels,'" *Chicago Tribune*, 31 May 2001, 5.

17. National Vietnam Veterans Art Museum, "Above and Beyond Memorial," undated, http://www.nvvam.org/aboveandbeyond/index.htm.

18. Visitor's book, noted by author, August 2002.

NOTES TO CHAPTER FIVE

1. Earlier versions of sections of this chapter have been presented at three conferences: Space-Place-Memory at the University of Minnesota, April 2001; American Geographers Association convention in Los Angeles, March 2002; and the Modern Language Association convention in New York, December 2004.

2. Tourism was identified as an "important branch of the strategy of economic development in the country" in "Government Resolution 45/CP, 22 June 1993," cited in "Master Plan of Vietnam Tourism Development period 1995–2010," *Vietnam National Administration of Tourism*, 24 April 1995, http://www.batin.vn/dbotweb/tourinfo/phan4b.htm (accessed 13 March 2001). Site no longer active; Vietnam National Administration of Tourism available at, http://www.vietnamtourism.com.

3. The White House, "Remarks by the President in Announcement of Lifting Trade Embargo on Vietnam," 3 February 1994, http://clinton6.nara.gov/1994/02/1994–02–03–presidents-remarks-on-lifting-vietnam-trade-embargo.html, and "U.S., Vietnam Sign Open Trade Agreement," *CNN.com*, 14 July 2000, http://archives.cnn.com/2000/ASIANOW/southeast/07/13/us.vietnam.03/.

4. Nine Dragons Travel and Tours, undated, http://www.nine-dragons.com/vietnam.htm, and MilSpec Tours, undated, http://www.gomilspec.com/asiantours.html.

5. Tours of Peace Personal Effects Program, 2003, http://www.topvietnamvet-erans.org/p-pe.html.

6. Sage Colleges, "Vietnam: Journeys of Learning and Reconciliation," 2004, http://www.sage.edu/rsc/programs/globcomm/division/activities/viettrip.html.

7. Jess DeVaney, President, Tours of Peace, email communication with the author, 31 January 2001, and written communication with the author, 9 August 2005: DeVaney details the work the group does in Vietnam:

    > Therapy in itself is not always enough. Not only do we go back to Vietnam and revisit old haunts, but we also have an Emotional Support Team that provides emotional support for participants. The group, in itself, supports each other. Emotional Support Representatives have thorough discussions with trip candidates prior to trip acceptance. Trip Emotional Support Representatives may "check-in" by phone or e-mail with trip members. In Vietnam, we conduct nightly group meetings at the end of each day. After each trip, the Emotional Support Team may address any residual issues with trip members. Furthermore, part of our healing and closure process includes not only providing support to other members of the group, but also helping the Vietnamese with our humanitarian projects there, in addition to retrieving personal effects left behind by American soldiers and reuniting them with surviving family members. The cumulative effect of going back to Vietnam and seeing it as it is today, being part of a group that supports each other, helping the Vietnamese with our humanitarian work, and reuniting personal effects of fallen comrades with surviving family members, all adds up to a positive and powerful healing experience for everyone who participates.

8. Richard Schonberger, director of Global Spectrum, quoted in "Visit the Vietcong's World: Americans Welcome," *The New York Times,* 7 July 1999; and Courteney Frobenius, Vietnam-Indochina Tours, 1999, bigjohn.bmi.net/vntours/new/Company.html (accessed 7 March 2001); website address since changed to, http://www.indochinatours.com.

9. L.P. Hartley, *The Go-Between* (London: H. Hamilton, 1953).

10. Edited by author for clarity.

11. Talking about a meal his tour group had, Downs describes how the white bread "tasted so good we ate a lot of it to off set the very Vietnamese flavor of the food" (67).

12. Tom Mintier, "'Hanoi Hilton' Now Only Holds Painful Memories," *CNN.com*, 27 April 2000, http://www.cnn.com/SPECIALS/views/y/2000/04/mintier.vietnam.apr27/.

13. Hoa Lo Prison, copied on site by author, 26 August 2003.

14. Brian Cogan, "Hilton in Hanoi: Irony or Apathy," *New York Post*, 21 March 1999, 57.

15. Delta Adventures tour to Cu Chi tunnels, personal observation of author, 18 August 2003.
16. "The Profit Hunters: Using Sites Made Famous By the Vietnam War as Tourist Attractions," *The Economist*, 11 June 1994, 31–32.
17. Peter Arnett, "Welcome to 'Cong World:' Vietnam War Sites are Tourist Attractions," *Newsweek*, 8 May 1995, 61; see also Seth Mydans, "Visit the Vietcong's World: Americans Welcome," *The New York Times*, 7 July 1999, A4.

NOTES TO THE AFTERWORD

1. Jane Gross, "New York Pays Homage to Vietnam Veterans," *New York Times*, 7 May 1985, late ed., A1.

Bibliography

Abrams M.H. *A Glossary of Literary Terms.* 6th Edition. Fort Worth, TX: Harcourt Brace College Publishers, 1993.

Anderson, Benedict. *Imagined Communities: Reflections on the Origins and Spread of Nationalism.* Revised Edition. New York: Verso, 1991.

Apocalypse Now. Dir. Francis Ford Coppola. Omni Zoetrope, 1979.

Bal, Meike. "Introduction." *Acts of Memory: Cultural Recall in the Present.* Eds. Mieke Bal, Jonathan Crewe, Leo Spitzer. Hanover and London: Dartmouth College, 1999: vii-xvi.

Balaban, John. *Remembering Heaven's Face: A Story of Rescue in Wartime Vietnam.* Athens, GA: University of Georgia Press, 2002. Originally published as *Remembering Heaven's Face: A Moral Witness in Vietnam.* New York: Poseidon Press, 1991.

Balogh, Brian. "From Metaphor to Quagmire: The Domestic Legacy of the Vietnam War." *After Vietnam: Legacies of a Lost War.* Ed. Charles Neu. Baltimore: Johns Hopkins University Press, 2000: 24–55.

Barthes, Roland. "The Photographic Message." 1961. *Image-Music-Text.* Trans. Stephen Heath. New York: Hill and Wang, 1978: 194–210.

Baudrillard, Jean. *Simulacra and Simulation.* Ann Arbor: University of Michigan Press, 1994.

Benjamin, Walter. "The Work of Art in the Age of Mechanical Reproduction." *Illuminations: Essays and Reflections.* New York: Schocken Books, 1968: 217–251.

Bennett, Tony. *The Birth of the Museum: History, Theory, Politics.* New York: Routledge, 1995.

Berger, James. "Trauma and Literary Theory." *Contemporary Literature* 38.3 (1997): 569–582.

Bibby, Michael. *Hearts and Minds: Bodies, Poetry, and Resistance in the Vietnam Era.* New Brunswick, NJ: Rutgers University Press, 1996.

Bodnar, John. *Remaking America: Public Memory, Commemoration, and Patriotism in the Twentieth Century.* Princeton, NJ: Princeton University Press, 1992.

Bolles, Edmund Blair. *Remembering and Forgetting: Inquiries into the Nature of Memory.* New York: Walker and Company, 1988.

Born on the Fourth of July. Dir. Oliver Stone. Universal Studios, 1989.

Brinkley, Alan. "The Problem of American Conservatism." *American Historical Review* 99.2 (1994): 409–429.

Brown, Roger and James Kulik. "Flashbulb Memories." *Memory Observed: Remembering in National Contexts*. Ed. Ulric Neisser. San Francisco: W.H. Freeman, 1982: 23–40.

Broyles, William Jr. "The Road to Hill 10: A Veteran's Return to Vietnam." *The Atlantic* April 1985: 90–116.

Calloway, Catherine. "'How to Tell a True War Story:' Metafiction in *The Things They Carried*." *Critique: Studies in Contemporary Fiction* 36.4 (Summer 1995): 249–257.

Caruth, Cathy. *Unclaimed Experience: Trauma, Narrative, and History*. Baltimore: Johns Hopkins University Press, 1996.

Connerton, Paul. *How Societies Remember*. New York: Cambridge University Press, 1989.

Crews, Frederick. "The Trauma Trap." *The New York Review of Books*. 11 March 2004: 37–40.

Culbertson, Roberta. "Embodied Memory, Transcendence, and Telling: Recounting Trauma, Re-establishing the Self." *New Literary History* 1.26 (1995): 169–195.

Davis, Natalie Zemon and Randolph Starn. "Introduction." *Memory and Countermemory*. Spec. issue of *Representations* 26 (1989): 1–6.

Del Vecchio, John. *The 13th Valley*. New York: Bantam, 1982.

Derrida, Jacques. *Archive Fever: A Freudian Impression*. Trans. Eric Prenowitz. Chicago: University of Chicago Press, 1995.

———. "Signature Event Context." *Glyph* I (1977): 172–76.

Downs, Frederick. *No Longer Enemies, Not Yet Friends: An American Soldier Returns to Vietnam*. New York: W. W. Horton, 1991.

DSM-IV. Washington, DC: American Psychological Association, 1994.

Dudziak, Mary L., ed. *September 11 in History: A Watershed Moment?* Durham: Duke University Press, 2003.

Edensor, Tim. *Industrial Ruins: Space, Aesthetics and Materiality*. New York: Berg, 2005.

Ehrhart, W.D. *Going Back: A Poet Who Was Once a Marine Returns to Vietnam*. Pendle Hill, PA: Pendle Hill Pamphlet 272, 1987.

Feifer, Maxine. *Going Places: The Ways of the Tourist from Imperial Rome to the Present Day*. London: MacMillan, 1985.

Felman, Shoshana and Dori Laub. *Testimony: Crises in Witnessing in Literature, Psychoanalysis, and History*. New York: Routledge, 1992.

Florence, Mason and Virginia Jealous. *Lonely Planet: Vietnam*. 7th Edition. Oakland, CA: Lonely Planet, 2003.

Franklin, H. Bruce. *M.I.A., or Mythmaking in America*. Brooklyn, NY: L. Hill Books, 1992.

———. *Vietnam, and Other American Fantasies*. Amherst, MA: University of Massachusetts Press, 2000.

Freud, Sigmund and Joseph Breuer. *Studies on Hysteria.* 1895. New York: Basic Books, 1957.

Freud, Sigmund. "Screen Memories." *Standard Edition* 3. London: The Hogarth Press, 1899: 301–322.

———. *The Interpretation of Dreams.* 1900. Trans. James Strachey. New York: Avon Books, 1965.

———. *Beyond the Pleasure Principle.* 1920. Trans. and Ed. James Strachey. New York: Norton, 1975.

Gillis, John, ed. *Commemorations: The Politics of National Identity.* Princeton, NY: Princeton University Press, 1994.

Gordon, Avery F. *Ghostly Matters: Haunting and the Sociological Imagination.* Minneapolis: University of Minnesota Press, 1997.

Goss, Jon. "The 'Magic of the Mall:'An Analysis of Form, Function, and Meaning in the Contemporary Retail Built Environment." *Annals of the Association of American Geographers* 83.1 (1993): 18–47.

Greenberg, Clement. "Avant-Garde and Kitsch." 1939. *The Collected Essays and Criticism Volume 1: Perceptions and Judgments, 1939–1944.* Ed. John O'Brian. Chicago: University of Chicago Press, 1986: 5–22.

Griswold, Charles. "The Vietnam Veterans Memorial and the Washington Mall: Philosophical Thoughts on Political Landscape." *Critical Inquiry* 12 (1986): 688–719.

Halberstam, David. *The Making of a Quagmire.* New York: Random House, 1965.

Halbwachs, Maurice. *On Collective Memory.* 1951. Chicago: University of Chicago Press, 1992.

Harvey, David. *The Condition of Postmodernity: An Enquiry into the Origins of Cultural Change.* New York, NY: Blackwell, 1989.

Hass, Kristin Ann. *Carried to the Wall: American Memory and the Vietnam Veterans Memorial.* Berkeley, CA: University of California Press, 1998.

Heberle, Mark A. *A Trauma Artist: Tim O'Brien and the Fiction of Vietnam.* Iowa City: University of Iowa Press, 2001.

Hendin, Herbert and Ann Pollinger Hass. *Wounds of War: The Psychological Aftermath of Combat in Vietnam.* New York: Basic Books, 1984.

Herman, Judith. *Trauma and Memory.* New York: Basic Books, 1992.

Hess, Elizabeth. "A Tale of Two Memorials." *Art in America* April 1983: 120–127.

Herr, Michael. *Dispatches.* New York: Vintage, 1977.

Hewison, Robert. *The Heritage Industry: Britain in a Climate of Decline.* London: Methuen, 1987.

Highmore, B. "Street Life in London: Towards a Rhythmanalysis of London in the Late Nineteenth Century." *New Formations* 47 (2000): 171–93.

Hirsch, Marianne. "Family Pictures: *Maus*, Mourning, and Post-Memory." *Discourse* 15 (1992–93): 3–29.

Hooper-Greenhill, Eilean. *Museums and the Shaping of Knowledge.* New York: Routledge, 1992.

Howells, Christina. *Derrida: Deconstruction from Phenomenology to Ethics*. Malden, MA: Polity Press, 1999.

Hunt, Andrew E. *The Turning: A History of Vietnam Veterans Against the War*. New York: New York University Press, 1999.

Huyssen, Andreas. "Monument and Memory in a Postmodern Age." *The Yale Journal of Criticism* 6.2 (1993): 249–261.

———. *Twilight Memories: Marking Time in a Culture of Amnesia*. New York: Routledge, 1995.

———. *Present Pasts: Urban Palimpsests and the Politics of Memory*. Stanford, CA: Stanford University Press, 2003.

James, William. *Principles of Psychology*. Vol. 1. New York: Holt, 1890.

Jameson, Fredric. *Postmodernism or, The Cultural Logic of Late Capitalism*. Durham: Duke University Press, 1991.

Janson, Anthony F. "Art as Experience: Works by Vietnam Veterans." *Vietnam: Reflexes and Reflections: The National Vietnam Veterans Art Museum*. Ed. Eve Sinaiko. New York: Harry N. Abrams, 1998. 199–208.

Jeffords, Susan. *The Remasculinization of America: Gender and the Vietnam War*. Bloomington: Indiana University Press, 1989.

Kammen, Michael. *Mystic Chords of Memory: The Transformation of Tradition in American Culture*. New York: Alfred A. Knopf, 1991.

Keating, Susan Katz. *Prisoners of Hope: Exploiting the POW/ MIA Myth in America*. New York: Random House, 1994.

Kermode, Frank. "Memory and Forgetting: Palaces of Memory." *Index on Censorship* 1 (2001): 87–96.

Kerry, John and Vietnam Veterans Against the War. *The New Soldier*. Eds. David Thorne and George Butler. New York: Macmillan, 1971.

Kirshenblatt-Gimblett, Barbara. *Destination Culture: Tourism, Museums, and Heritage*. Berkeley: University of California Press, 1998.

Kollock, Peter and Marc A. Smith, eds. *Communities in Cyberspace*. New York: Routledge, 1999.

Kovic, Ron. *Born on the Fourth of July*. London: Corgi, 1976.

Kristeva, Julia. *The Powers of Horror: An Essay in Abjection*. New York: Columbia University Press, 1982.

LaCapra, Dominick. *Representing the Holocaust: History, Theory, Trauma*. Ithaca, NY: Cornell University Press, 1994.

Laclau, Ernesto and Chantal Mouffe. "Post-Marxism Without Apologies." *New Left Review* I.166 (1987): 79–106

Laderman, Scott. *Witnessing the Past: History, Tourism, and Memory in Vietnam, 1930–2002*. Ph.D. diss., University of Minnesota, 2005. Minneapolis: UMI, 2005. ATT 3180001.

Laqueur, Thomas W. "Memory and Naming in the Great War." *Commemorations: The Politics of National Identity*. Ed. John Gillis. Princeton, NJ: Princeton University Press, 1994: 150–167.

Lifton, Robert Jay. *Home From the War: Vietnam Veterans, Neither Victims nor Executioners*. New York: Simon and Schuster, 1973.

Linenthal, Edward T. *The Unfinished Bombing: Oklahoma City in American Memory*. New York: Oxford University Press, 2001.

Lowenthal, David. *The Past is a Foreign Country*. New York: Cambridge University Press, 1985.

———. "Identity, Heritage, and History." *Commemorations: The Politics of National Identity*. Ed. John R. Gillis. Princeton, NJ: Princeton University Press, 1994: 41–60.

Lyotard, Jean-François. *The Postmodern Condition: A Report on Knowledge*. Minneapolis, MN: University of Minnesota Press, 1984.

MacCannell, Dean. *The Tourist: A New Theory of the Leisure Class*. 1976. Third Edition. Berkeley: University of California, 1999.

Martini, Edwin. *Invisible Enemies: The American War on Vietnam, 1975–2000*. Ph.D. diss. University of Maryland, 2004. College Park: UMI, 2004. AAT 3128874.

Mason, Bobbie Ann. *In Country*. London: Flamingo, 1987.

Mayo, James. *War Memorials as Political Landscape: The American Experience and Beyond*. New York: Praeger, 1988.

Massey, Doreen. "A Global Sense of Place." *Reading Human Geography*. Eds. T. Barnes and D. Gregory. London: Arnold, 1997: 315–323.

McLuhan, Marshall, Quentin Fiore, and Jerome Agel. *The Medium is the Massage*. New York: Random House, 1967.

Merck, Mandy, ed. *After Diana: Irreverent Elegies*. New York: Verso, 1998.

Michalowksi, Raymond and Jill Dubisch. *Run for the Wall: Remembering Vietnam on a Motorcycle Pilgrimage*. New Brunswick, NJ: Rutgers University Press, 2001.

Mills, Nicolaus. *Their Last Battle: The Fight for the National World War II Memorial*. New York: Basic Books, 2004.

Morgan, David H. J. "Theater of War: Combat, The Military, and Masculinities." *Theorizing Masculinities*. Eds. Harry Brod and Michael Kaufman. Thousand Oaks, CA: Sage Publications, 1994: 165–182.

Morris, Leslie. "The Sound of Memory." *The German Quarterly* 74.4 (2001): 368–378.

Mosse, George. *Fallen Soldiers: Reshaping the Memory of the World Wars*. New York: Oxford University Press, 1990.

Mueller, John E. *War, Presidents, and Public Opinion*. New York: John Wiley and Sons, Inc., 1973.

Nixon, Richard. *No More Vietnams*. New York: Ann Arbor, 1985

Nora, Pierre. "Between Memory and History: *Les Lieux de Mémoire*." *Representations* 26 (1989): 7–25.

O'Brien, Tim. *The Things They Carried*. Boston: Houghton Mifflin, 1990.

———. "The Vietnam in Me." *The New York Times Magazine* 2 October 1994: 48–57.

O'Nan, Stewart, ed. *The Vietnam Reader.* New York: Anchor Books, 1998.

Ozouf, Mona. *Festivals and the French Revolution.* Cambridge: Harvard University Press, 1988.

Palmer, Laura. *Shrapnel in the Heart: Letters and Remembrances from the Vietnam Memorial.* New York: Random House, 1987.

Parkin, Alan J. *Memory: Phenomena, Experiment, and Theory.* Cambridge, MA: Blackwell, 1993.

Podhoretz, Norman. *Why We Were in Vietnam.* New York: Simon and Schuster, 1993.

Preziosi, Donald. "In the Temple of Entelechy: The Museum as Evidentiary Artifact." *The Formation of National Collections of Art and Archeology.* Ed. Gwendolyn Wright. Washington, DC: National Gallery of Art, 1996: 65–171.

———. "Seeing Through Art History." *Knowledges: Historical and Critical Studies in Disciplinarity.* Eds. Ellen Messer-Davidow, David R. Shumway, and David J. Sylvan. Charlottesville: University Press of Virginia, 1993: 215–231.

———. "The Question of Art History." *Critical Inquiry* 18 (1992): 363–387.

Prown, Jules David and Kenneth Haltman, eds. *American Artifacts: Essays in Material Culture.* East Lansing, MI: Michigan State University, 2000.

Ritzer, George and Allan Liska. "'McDisneyization' and 'Post-tourism:' Complementary Perspectives of Contemporary Tourism." *Touring Cultures: Transformations of Travel and Theory.* Eds. Chris Rojek and John Urry. New York: Routledge, 1997: 96–109.

Rose, Gillian. *Visual Methodologies: An Introduction to the Interpretation of Visual Materials.* Thousand Oaks, CA: Sage Publications, 2001.

Rottmann, Larry, Jan Barry, and Basil T. Paquet, eds. *Winning Hearts and Minds: War Poems by Vietnam Veterans.* Brooklyn, NY: First Casualty Press, 1972.

Scarry, Elaine. *The Body in Pain: The Making and Unmaking of the World.* New York: Oxford University Press, 1985.

Schacter, Daniel L. *Searching for Memory: The Brain, the Mind, and the Past.* New York: Basic Books, 1996.

Schivelbusch, Wolfgang. *The Culture of Defeat: On National Trauma, Mourning, and Recovery.* New York: Metropolitan Books, 2003.

Schlereth, Thomas J. *Material Culture Studies in America.* Nashville,TN: American Association for State and Local History, 1982.

Schoenwald, Jonathan M. *A Time for Choosing: The Rise of Modern American Conservatism.* New York: Oxford University Press, 2001.

Scruggs, Jan and Joel Swerdlow. *To Heal a Nation: The Vietnam Veterans Memorial.* New York: Harper and Row, 1985.

Shanken, Andrew. "Planning Memory: Living Memorials in the United States during World War II." *The Art Bulletin* 84.1 (2002): 130–148.

Shay, Jonathan. *Achilles in Vietnam: Combat Trauma and the Undoing of Character.* New York: Touchstone, 1994.

Sinaiko, Eve, ed. *National Vietnam Veterans Art Museum: Vietnam: Reflexes and Reflections.* New York: Harry N. Abrams, 1998.

Sontag, Susan. *On Photography.* New York: Farrar, Straus, and Giroux, 1973.

———. *Regarding the Pain of Others.* New York: Picador, 2003.

Starn, Randolph. "Memory and Authenticity." *Studies in 20th Century Literature* 23.1 (1999): 191–200.

Stewart, Susan. *On Longing: Narratives of the Miniature, the Gigantic, the Souvenir, the Collection.* Durham: Duke University Press, 1993.

Stone, Albert E. *Autobiographical Occasions and Original Acts: Versions of American Identity from Henry Adams to Nate Shaw.* Philadelphia: University of Pennsylvania Press, 1982.

Strait, Jerry L. and Sandra S. Strait. *Vietnam War Memorials: An Illustrated Reference to Veterans Tributes Throughout the United States.* Jefferson, NC: McFarland, 1988.

Sturken, Marita. *Tangled Memories: The Vietnam War, The AIDS Epidemic, and the Politics of Remembering.* Berkeley: University of California Press, 1997.

———. "The Aesthetics of Absence: Rebuilding Ground Zero." *American Ethnologist* 31.3 (2004): 311–325.

Sullivan, Richard A. "The War in American Fiction, Poetry, and Drama." D. Michael Shafer, ed. *The Legacy: The Vietnam War in the American Imagination.* Boston: Beacon Press, 1990: 157–185.

Tagg, John. *The Burden of Representation: Essays on Photographs and Histories.* Minneapolis: University of Minnesota Press, 1993.

Tai, Hue-Tam Ho, ed. *The Country of Memory: Remaking the Past in Late Socialist Vietnam.* Berkeley, CA: University of California Press, 2001.

Tal, Kalí. *Worlds of Hurt: Reading the Literatures of Trauma.* New York, NY: Cambridge University Press, 1996.

Till, Karen. "Place and the Politics of Memory: A Geo-Ethnography of Museums and Memorials in Berlin." Ph.D. diss. University of Wisconsin-Madison, 1996. Madison: UMI, 1996.

———. "Places of Memory," *A Companion to Political Geography.* Eds. John Agnew, Katharyne Mitchell, and Gearóid Ó Tuathail. Malden, MA: Blackwell Publishers, 2003: 289–301.

———. *The New Berlin: Memory, Politics, Place.* Minneapolis, MN: University of Minnesota Press, 2005.

Tilley, Christopher, ed. *Reading Material Culture: Structuralism, Hermeneutics, and Post-Structuralism.* Oxford, Basil Blackwell, 1989.

Tomes, Robert R. *Apocalypse Then: American Intellectuals and the Vietnam War, 1954–1975.* New York: New York University Press, 1998.

Varco, Sondra. "Foreward." *Vietnam: Reflexes and Reflections: The National Vietnam Veterans Art Museum.* Ed. Eve Sinaiko. New York: Harry N. Abrams, 1998: 9–13.

Veale, Tony. "Metaphor, Memory and Meaning: Symbolic and Connectionist Issues in Metaphor Comprehension." Ph.D. diss. Trinity College Dublin, 1995.

Wagner-Pacifici, Robin and Barry Schwartz. "The Vietnam Veterans Memorial: Commemorating a Difficult Past." *American Journal of Sociology* 97 (1991): 376–420.

Weeks, Karissa Beth. "A Country, Not a War: Images of Vietnam in U.S. Travel Articles." MA Thesis. University of Oregon, 1997.

Weigl, Bruce. *The Circle of Hanh.* New York: Grove Press, 2000.

White, Geoffrey M. "National Subjects: September 11 and Pearl Harbor." *American Ethnologist* 31.3 (2004): 293–310.

White, Hayden. *The Content of the Form: Narrative Discourse and Historical Representation.* Baltimore: Johns Hopkins University Press, 1987.

Young, James. *The Texture of Memory: Holocaust Memorials and Meaning.* New Haven, CT: Yale University Press, 1993.

———. "The Holocaust as Vicarious Past: Art Spiegelman's *Maus* and the Afterimages of History." *Critical Inquiry* 24.3 (1998): 666–700.

Zelinsky, Wilbur. *Nation into State: The Shifting Symbolic Foundations of American Nationalism.* Chapel Hill, NC: North Carolina Press, 1988.

Zelizer, Barbie. "Reading the Past Against the Grain: The Shape of Memory Studies." *Critical Studies in Mass Communication* 12.2 (1995): 214–239.

———. *Remembering to Forget.* Chicago: University of Chicago Press, 1998.

SELECTED ELECTRONIC SOURCES

National Civil War Museum <http://www.nationalcivilwarmuseum.org>.

National Vietnam Veterans Art Museum <http://www.nvvam.org>.

National Vietnam War Museum <http://www.nvwm.org>.

Pew Internet and American Life Project <http://www.pewinternet.org>.

U.S. Veteran Dispatch <http://www.usvetdsp.com>.

Vietnam Combat Veterans, The Moving Wall <http://www.themovingwall.org>.

Vietnam Veterans Memorial Fund Wall, The Wall That Heals <http://www.vvmf.org/index.cfm?Section ID=3>.

Vietnam Veterans Memorial Fund <http://www.vvmf.org>.

Vietnam Veterans Memorial Fund, The Virtual Wall <http://www.vvmf.org/index.cfm?SectionID=2>.

Vietnam Veterans Memorial Wall Page, The <http://www.thewall-usa.com>.

Virginia War Museum <http://www.warmuseum.org>.

Virtual Wall Vietnam Veterans Memorial, The <http://www.virtualwall.org>.

Index